Cloud Computing Architected

Cloud Computing Architected

by John Rhoton and Risto Haukioja

RP

Recursive Press

Cloud Computing Architected

By John Rhoton and Risto Haukioja

Copyright © 2011 Recursive Limited. All rights reserved.

Recursive Press is an imprint of Recursive Limited.

The RP logo is a trademark of Recursive Limited.

Published simultaneously in the United States and the United Kingdom.

ISBN-10: 0-9563556-1-7

ISBN-13: 978-0-9563556-1-4

British Library Cataloguing-in-Publication Data

Application submitted.

Revision: 20110328112032

Contents

Preface

This book describes the essential components of a cloud-based application and presents the architectural options that are available to create large-scale, distributed applications spanning administrative domains.

The requirements of cloud computing have far-reaching implications for software engineering. Applications must be built to provide flexible and elastic services, and designed to consume functionality delivered remotely across of spectrum of reliable, and unreliable, sources.

As architects address these challenges, they need to consider the impact of scalability and multi-tenancy in a variety of areas:

- New tools allow developers to more efficiently develop, test and run cloud services.

- Internet-based delivery encourages the use of the browser, and other lean clients, as a presentation vehicle.

- Multi-tenancy and identity federation impose new authentication models.

- A fragmented landscape of disparate services and providers will not work together unless they are efficiently integrated.

- An exploding information volume, associated with a cloud scale, requires new storage mechanisms and data models.

- Availability and elasticity increasingly rely on redundancy that must be orchestrated efficiently and reliably.

- Utility-oriented services require new business models and monetization strategies to achieve profitability.

- Platform services provide efficiencies for the entire software development cycle, making it possible to accelerate deployment and incorporate changes more quickly.

- Increased automation facilitates a more efficient operational model that needs to reorient itself from infrastructure to services.

This text looks at these and other areas where the advent of cloud computing has the opportunity to influence the architecture of software applications.

Assumption

A bold assumption underpins the philosophy of the authors, namely that most, if not all, future applications should be designed to be cloud-ready. Granted, not all software will initially target opportunities where Internet scale and multi-tenancy are necessary. However, there is value in designing the solution so that it can grow to meet increasing needs and tap into potential revenue streams that may not have been originally planned.

The incentive for designing an application to be cloud-ready, even when the need is not immediately apparent, is based on three considerations:

- A solid design has intrinsic value.

- Elasticity is mandatory in a fast-changing business environment.

- Intellectual property is most valuable if it is flexible.

A solid design has intrinsic value. A service-oriented architecture allows a greater degree of flexibility over the lifetime of a service, so that it can cope with a changing set of requirements. If reliability, security and scalability are built into the software from the outset, it will be much more robust and will be able to handle unforeseen events, and new sets of demands, more easily.

Elasticity is mandatory in a fast-changing business environment. An increase in customers or sales is not the only reason you may need to scale up your service. A scalable architecture can cope with sudden spikes in demand through mergers and acquisitions. A flexible design will allow the application to be re-used for additional business purposes and user groups, such as partners and suppliers.

Intellectual property is most valuable if it is flexible. There is a compelling argument that even applications built for internal use should be architected for scalability and multi-tenancy. If the service replicates common functionality, then you should question why you need it in the first place and cannot obtain the same service from another provider. On the other hand, if it is unique in its offering and represents proprietary intellectual property, you should always keep the option open to license it, or package it as a service that you offer to create an additional revenue stream.

Scope

This book is not written as high-level overview of cloud computing and does not elaborate on the business benefits of the technology. There are numerous books on the market that cover these topics, including *Cloud Computing Explained* and others listed in the bibliography.

Nor do the authors provide any in-depth treatment of a particular platform or service. It is not realistic to expect to be able to engineer a cloud-based solution using only this book as a reference. However, the providers generally supply copious documentation on their own offerings and this book provides links to other excellent resources that give detailed advice on the techniques and technologies.

Instead, this book bridges the gap between these two perspectives, that of the executive and the programmer. It covers architectural options that may be relevant to cloud computing, but only in sufficient depth to assess their suitability for a design, not with the objective of detailing the implementation.

Audience

As implied above, this book caters primarily to consultants, architects, technologists and strategists who are involved with the planning an implementation of information technology at large enterprises or who are involved in designing a consumer-facing service that will need to scale to millions of users.

A secondary audience is those who are only peripherally involved in the above design. Almost everyone in IT, from administrators and programmers to high-level executives, will eventually have some contact with cloud computing. Those who wish to have a solid understanding of cloud software architecture will benefit from a conceptual description of the options and design trade-offs.

Feedback

A direct consequence of the print-on-demand model we have used for this book, and actually one of its primary benefits, is the flexibility it gives the author and publisher to incorporate incremental changes throughout the publication lifecycle. We would like to leverage that advantage by drawing on the collective experience and insights of our readers.

You may find errors and omissions. Or you may actually find some parts of the book very useful and interesting. Regardless of your feedback, if you have something to say then we'd love to hear from you. Please feel free to send us a message at:

john.rhoton@gmail.com or **risto.haukioja@gmail.com**

We can't guarantee that we will reply to every message but we will do our best to acknowledge your input!

Acknowledgements

This book is published and distributed through Lightning Source (Ingram Content Group), which runs a very efficient and agile production process that we appreciate. Furthermore, we have received considerable help from Gill Shaw, who provided excellent proofreading and copy editing assistance. We would also like to acknowledge Elisabeth Rinaldin, who contributed to the design of the cover and layout.

We are grateful to the reviewers who provided valuable technical input, including: John Bair, Jamieson Becker, Patrick Joubert, Kevin Laahs, Franz Novak and Vikram S. We applaud the many sources listed at the end of the book, which have helped us immensely as we have dived into the details of the topics we have presented. Last but not least, we would like to point out that there would be no content to describe without the vision and creative talent of engineers at Amazon, Google, Microsoft, Salesforce.com and other cloud service providers.

Model

This first section provides our perspectives on cloud computing and its implications for software developers and architects. It begins with a definition and overview of some of the main theoretical concepts associated with cloud-based delivery and cloud service architecture.

It then defines and illustrates a high-level reference architecture that serves as the structural basis for the remainder of this book.

Chapter 1

Cloud Definition

There has been a lot of buzz about cloud computing the last couple of years. By now, you probably have a good idea what the term means – and perhaps even how it works. But, if you are responsible for designing systems or applications, then a theoretical analysis of a new IT trend is only of limited use.

Instead, you need to understand how you can harness new options to build bigger, better and cheaper solutions. This book will look at how to harness new tools, implement elasticity, integrate disparate cloud services, model huge volumes of data, generate operational efficiency, and leverage new business models.

We have deliberately avoided spending much space on a foundational overview of cloud computing. If you are interested in a business-oriented perspective of the advantages and challenges to an enterprise implementation, then you may want to start with *Cloud Computing Explained* or one of the other introductory books listed in the bibliography. We will assume that you already have a good grasp of the basics and are ready to proceed to the next level.

That said, we did want to make sure that we are working on the same conceptual foundation. Your notion of cloud computing may be perfectly valid and yet significantly different from ours. To minimize any confusion and ensure a common framework and terminology, we will indulge in a brief characterization of what cloud computing means to us and describe the main services and delivery models that form cloud computing infrastructure and solutions.

Cloud Attributes

In the simplest sense, a cloud represents a network and, more specifically, the global Internet. Cloud computing, by inference, is the use of computational resources that are hosted remotely and delivered through the Internet. That is the basic idea underlying the term. It may be sufficient for your non-technical friends and colleagues, but shouldn't be adequate for anyone reading this book.

MODEL

If you have ever tried to isolate the core meaning of "Cloud Computing" by looking for an authoritative definition, you will have quickly discovered that the term entails many different notions. There is some disagreement among the experts as to what constitutes the essence of this fundamental shift in technology. Some are able to articulate their perspectives more elegantly than others, but that doesn't mean they are accepted any more universally.

The most commonly accepted definition in use today was articulated by NIST (2009):

> *Cloud computing is a model for enabling convenient, on-demand network access to a shared pool of configurable computing resources (e.g., networks, servers, storage, applications, and services) that can be rapidly provisioned and released with minimal management effort or service provider interaction.*

However, neither the NIST formulation, nor the interpretation of what it means, is universally accepted. A pragmatic approach to understanding common interpretations of the term is to examine the assortment of attributes of typical cloud solutions. This doesn't imply that every cloud attribute is essential to cloud computing, or that any combination qualifies a given approach as fitting the cloud paradigm. On their own, they are neither necessary nor sufficient prerequisites to the notion of cloud computing. However, the more of these attributes apply to a given implementation, the more likely others will accept it as a cloud solution.

An informal survey of blogs and tweets, as well as published literature, on the subject reveals some key components, including:

Off-premise: The service is hosted and delivered from a location that belongs to a service provider. This usually has two implications: The service is delivered over the public Internet, and the processing occurs outside the company firewall. In other words, the service must cross both physical and security boundaries.

Elasticity: One main benefit of cloud computing is the inherent scalability of the service provider, which is made available to the end-user. The model goes much further in providing an elastic provisioning mechanism so that resources can be scaled both up and down very rapidly as they are required. Since utility billing is also common, elasticity can equate to direct cost savings.

Flexible billing: Fine-grained metering of resource usage, combined with on-demand service provisioning, facilitate a number of options for charging customers. Fees can be levied on a subscription basis, or can be tied to actual consumption, or reservation, of resources. Monetization can take the form of placed advertising or can rely on simple credit card charges in addition to elaborate contracts and central billing.

Virtualization: Cloud services are usually offered through an abstracted infrastructure. They leverage various virtualization mechanisms and achieve cost optimization through multi-tenancy.

Service delivery: Cloud functionality is often available as a service of some form. While there is great variance in the nature of these services, typically the services offer programmatic interfaces in addition to user interfaces.

Universal access: Resource democratization means that pooled resources are available to anyone authorized to utilize them. At the same time, location independence and high levels of resilience allow for an always-connected user experience.

Simplified management: Administration is simplified through automatic provisioning to meet scalability requirements, user self-service to expedite business processes, and programmatically accessible resources that facilitate integration into enterprise management frameworks.

Affordable resources: The cost of resources is dramatically reduced for two reasons. There is no requirement for capital expenditures on fixed purchases. Also, the economy of scale of the service providers allows them to optimize their cost structure with commodity hardware and fine-tuned operational procedures that are not easily matched by most companies.

Multi-tenancy: The cloud is used by many organizations (tenants) and includes mechanisms to protect and isolate each tenant from all others. Pooling resources across customers is an important factor in achieving scalability and cost savings.

Service-level management: Cloud services typically offer a service-level definition that sets the expectation to the customer as to how robust that service will be. Some services may come with only minimal (or non-existent) commitments. They can still be considered cloud services, but typically will not be "trusted" for mission-critical applications to the extent that others (which are governed by more precise commitments) might.

Cloud Services

One salient aspect of cloud computing is a strong focus toward service orientation. It is quite common to hear expressions like "anything, or everything, as a service" (XaaS). In other words, the cloud is not a single offering but instead an often fragmented amalgamation of heterogeneous services.

Rather than offering only packaged solutions that are installed monolithically on desktops and servers, or investing in single-purpose appliances, you need to decompose all the functionality that users require into primitives, which can be assembled as needed.

Unfortunately, it is difficult to aggregate the functionality in an optimal manner unless you can get a clear picture of all the services that are available. This is a lot easier if you can provide some structure and a model that illustrates the inter-relationships between services.

The most common classification uses the so-called SPI (SaaS, PaaS, IaaS) model (NIST, 2009). Amazon Elastic Compute Cloud (EC2) is a classical example of IaaS (Infrastructure as a Service). Google App Engine is generally considered to be a PaaS (Platform as a Service). And Salesforce.com represents one of the best known examples of SaaS (Software as a Service).

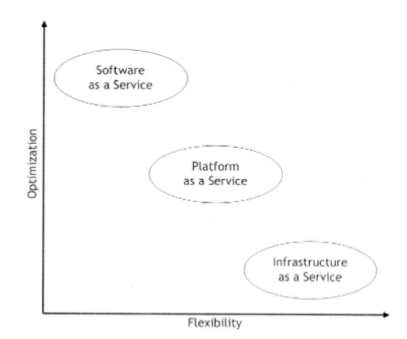

Figure 1-1: Software, Platform and Infrastructure Services

The three approaches differ in the extent of sharing that they provide to their consumers. Infrastructure services share the physical hardware. Platform servic-es also allow tenants to share the same operating system and application frame-works. Software services generally share the entire software stack. As shown in (Figure 1-1), these three approaches represent different tradeoffs in a balance between optimization, which leverages multi-tenancy and massive scalability, on the one hand, and flexibility to accommodate individual constraints and custom functionality, on the other hand.

The SPI model is a simple taxonomy that helps to present a first glimpse of the primary cloud-related services. However, as is often the case with classification systems, the lines are not nearly as clear in reality as they may appear on a diagram. There are many services that do not fit neatly into one category or the other. Over time, services may also drift between service types. For example, Amazon is constantly enhancing its AWS (Amazon Web Services) offering in an effort to increase differentiation and add value. As the product matures, some may begin to question if it wouldn't be more accurate to consider it a platform service.

Furthermore, in addition to the software and applications that run in the SPI model, and support a cloud application in its core functions, both the enterprise and service provider need to address core challenges, such as Implementation, Operation and Control, in order to successfully keep the solution going (Figure 1-2).

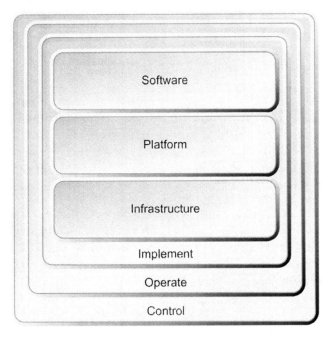

Figure 1-2: Implementation, Operation and Control

Implement: It is necessary to select and integrate all the components into a functioning solution. There are a large, and ever increasing, number of cloud-based services and solutions on the market. It is no simple task to categorize and compare them. And once that is done, it would be naïve to expect them all to work together seamlessly. The integration effort involves a careful selection of interfaces and configuration settings and may require additional connectors or custom software.

Operate: Once the solution has been brought online it is necessary to keep it running. This means that you need to monitor it, troubleshoot it and support it. Since the service is unlikely to be completely static, you need to also have processes in place to provision new users, decommission old users, plan for capacity changes, track incidents and implement changes in the service.

Control: The operation of a complex set of services can be a difficult challenge. Some of the challenge may be reduced by working with solution providers and outsourcing organizations who take over the operative responsibilities. However, this doesn't completely obviate the need for overseeing the task. It is still necessary to ensure that service expectations are well defined and that they are validated on a continuous basis.

As mentioned above, the SPI stack presents a simplified picture of how cloud services relate to each other. In reality, the lines are blurred, many services (such as Identity Management) span multiple categories, and a complete solution involves additional components. Nonetheless, it facilitates the discussion to have a common reference model.

Cloud Delivery Models

The previous section classified services according to the type of content that they offered. It can also be useful to examine the types of providers that are offering the services. In an ideal world, designed according to a service-oriented architecture, this distinction would not be meaningful. A service description should cover all relevant details of the service, so the consumer would be independent of the provider and therefore have no reason to prefer one over another.

Sadly, however, this is not the case. There are many implications in the choice of provider relating to security, governance, invoicing and settlement. It is therefore still very relevant to consider if the provider should be internal or external and the delivery should include an outsourcing partner, a community (such as the government) or a public cloud service.

In the earliest definitions of cloud computing, the term refers to solutions where resources are dynamically provisioned over the Internet from an off-site third-party provider who shares resources and bills on a fine-grained utility computing basis. This computing model carries many inherent advantages in terms of cost and flexibility, but it also has some drawback in the areas of governance and security.

Many enterprises have looked at ways that they can leverage at least some of the benefits of cloud computing while minimizing the drawbacks, by only making use of some aspects of cloud computing. These efforts have led to a restricted model of cloud computing, which is often designated as a Private Cloud. In contrast, the fuller model is often labeled the Public Cloud.

Private Cloud

The term Private Cloud is disputed in some circles as many would argue that anything less than a full cloud model is not cloud computing at all but rather a simple extension of the current enterprise data center. Nonetheless, the term has become widespread, and it is useful to also examine enterprise options that also fall into this category.

In simple theoretical terms, a private cloud is one that only leverages some of the aspects of cloud computing (Table 1-1). It is typically hosted on-premise, scales "only" into the hundreds or perhaps thousands of nodes, and is connected to the using organization through private network links. Since all applications and servers are shared within the corporation, the notion of multi-tenancy is minimized.

From a business perspective, you typically also find that the applications primarily support the business but do not directly drive additional revenue. So the solutions are financial cost centers rather than revenue or profit centers.

	Private	**Public**
Location	On-premise	Off-premise
Connection	Connected to private network	Internet-based delivery
Scale direction	Scale out (applications)	Scale up (users)
Maximum scale	100-1000 nodes	10 000 nodes
Sharing	Single tenant	Multi-tenant
Pricing	Capacity pricing	Utility pricing
Financial center	Cost center	Revenue/Profit center

Table 1-1: Private and Public Clouds

Common Essence

Given the disparity in descriptions between private and public clouds on topics that seem core to the notion of cloud computing, it is valid to question whether there is actually any commonality at all. The most obvious area of intersection is around virtualization.

Since virtualization enables higher degrees of automation and standardization, it is a pivotal technology for many cloud implementations. Enterprises can certainly leverage many of its benefits without necessarily outsourcing their entire infrastructure or running it over the Internet.

Depending on the size of the organization, as well as its internal structure and financial reporting, there may also be other aspects of cloud computing that become relevant even in a deployment that is confined to a single company. A central IT department can just as easily provide services on-demand and cross-charge businesses on a utility basis as could any external provider. The model would then be very similar to a public cloud with the business acting as the consumer and IT as the provider. At the same time, the security of the data may be easier to enforce and the controls would be internal.

Cloud Continuum

A black-and-white distinction between private and public cloud computing may therefore not be realistic in all cases. In addition to the ambiguity in sourcing options mentioned above, other criteria are not binary. For example, there can be many different levels of multi-tenancy, depending on the scope of shared resources and the security controls in place.

There are also many different options an enterprise can choose for security administration, channel marketing, integration, completion and billing. Some of these may share more similarity with conventional public cloud models while others may reflect a continuation of historic enterprise architectures.

What is important is that enterprises must select a combination that not only meets their current requirements in an optimal way but also offers a flexible path with the ability to tailor the options as their requirements and the underlying technologies change over time. In the short term, many corporations will want to adopt a course that minimizes their risk and only barely departs from an internal infrastructure. However, as cloud computing matures they will want the ability to leverage increasing benefits without redesigning their solutions.

Regardless of whether the cloud is hosted internally or externally, it needs to leverage a great deal more than virtualization in order to achieve maximum value. There are a host of other improvements related to cloud computing ranging from fine-grained metering for usage-based cost allocation to rigorous service management, service-oriented architecture and federated access controls. An organization that implements these systematically has the most flexibility in selecting from private and public offerings or combining them for their business processes.

Partner Clouds

The distinction between internal and external delivery of cloud computing is not always clear. Depending on whether these are described on the basis of physical location, asset ownership or operational control there may be three different perspectives on the source of a cloud service.

For the sake of completeness, it is also important to mention that there are more hosting options than internal/private versus external/public. It is not imperative that a private cloud be operated and hosted by the consuming organization itself. Other possibilities include co-location of servers in an external data center with, or without, managed hosting services.

Outsourcing introduces an additional dimension. Large IT providers, such as HP Enterprise Services or IBM Global Services, have been in the business of running data center operations for large customers for many years. They can manage these services in their own facilities, on customer premises or on the property of a third party.

In some ways, you can consider these "partner" clouds as another point on the continuum between private and public clouds. Large outsourcers are able to pass on some of their benefits of economy of scale, standardization, specialization and their point in the experience curve. And yet they offer a degree of protection and data isolation that is not common in public clouds.

Community Clouds

One last delivery model that is likely to receive increased attention in the future is a community cloud. It caters to a group of organizations with a common set of requirements or objectives. The most prominent examples are government clouds that are open to federal and municipal agencies. Similarly, major industries may have an incentive to work together to leverage common resources.

MODEL

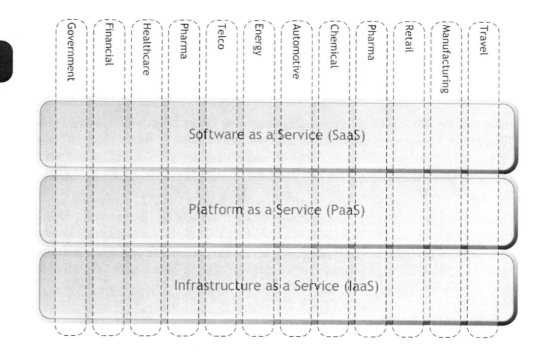

Figure 1-3: Community Clouds

The value proposition of a vertically-optimized cloud is initially based on the similarity of their requirements. Companies operating in the same industry are generally subject to the same regulations and very often share customers and suppliers who may impose additional standards and interfaces. A provider that caters to these specific demands can offer platforms and infrastructure with default service levels that meet all participants' obligations at a reasonable price.

However, the real benefits begin to accrue when a critical mass of industry players build a co-located ecosystem. When providers and consumers of software and information services are protected behind common security boundaries, and are connected with low-latency network links, the potential to share resources and data is greatly improved. The synergy that develops in this kind of cloud can spawn a virtuous cycle that breeds both additional functionality and efficiencies, and thereby allows the industry to advance in concert.

Hybrid or Multi-sourced Delivery

The categorization of cloud providers in the previous section into private, partner and public is a great simplification. Not only is there no clear boundary between the three delivery models but it is very likely that customers will not confine themselves to any given approach. Instead, you can expect to see a wide variety of inter-cloud constellations (Figure 1-4).

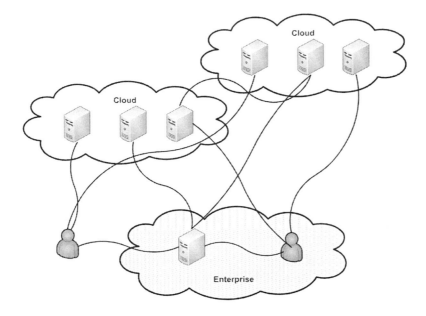

Figure 1-4 : Hybrid Delivery Model

Hybrid models can implement sourcing on the basis of at least four criteria.

Organizational: The simplest distinction would be that some business units use one source and other parts of the organization use another. This might be the case after a merger or acquisition, for instance.

Application: Another point of segregation would be the application. CRM, Email, ERP and Accounting may run from different delivery points for all applicable users in the organization.

Service: It is also possible that some services, such as Identity Management or a monitoring tool, are not immediately visible to the users but are transparently sourced from disparate cloud providers.

Resource: Virtual private clouds offer a means of extending the perimeter of the organization's internal network into the cloud to take advantage of resources with more elastic capacity than the internal systems. This extension is also invisible to end users.

Multi-sourced delivery models are inherently complex and therefore require careful planning. A framework such as eSCM (eSourcing Capability Model), developed by ITSqc, can be useful to ensure the design is systematic. It defines a set of sourcing life-cycle phases, practices, capability areas and capability levels as well as their interrelationships and suggests best practices both for the service providers and the customers who consume the services.

Cloud Maturity

While a hybrid model is the most likely end-point for many enterprises, a realistic look at the industry today reveals that we still have a way to go before we achieve it. It is not uncommon to find small startups today that are fully committed to cloud computing for all their service requirements. Large organizations, on the other hand, have been very cautious, even if they recognize the value that cloud computing can bring to them.

Corporate reluctance comes as no surprise to anyone who has followed the adoption path of emerging technologies over the past few years. Legacy applications, infrastructural investment, regulatory concerns and rigid business processes represent tremendous obstacles to change. Even if there are obvious early opportunities, the transition is likely to take time.

However, this doesn't mean that enterprises are completely stationary. In their own way, most of them began the journey to a private cloud years ago and they are gradually evolving in the direction of a public cloud. We can break down this path by identifying three steps, which are each associated with an increasing level of efficiency.

Resource efficiencies are usually the first objective of a private cloud implementation. Standardization of components sets the scene for data-center consolidation and optimization. Each level of resource abstraction, from server virtualization to full multi-tenancy, increases the opportunity to share physical capacity, and thereby reduces the overall infrastructural needs.

Operational efficiencies target human labor, one of the highest cost factors related to information technology. Ideally, all systems are self-healing and self-managing. This implies a high degree of automation and end-user self service. In addition to a reduction of administration costs, these optimizations also enable rapid deployment of new services and functionality.

Sourcing efficiencies are the final step and represent the flexibility to provision services, and allocate resources, from multiple internal and external providers without modifying the enterprise architecture. This agility can only be attained if all systems adhere to rigorous principles of service-orientation and service management. They must also include fine-grained metering for cost control and a granular role-based authorization scheme that can guarantee confidentiality and integrity of data. On the plus side, the benefit of reaching this level of efficiency is that applications can enjoy near infinite elasticity of resources, and costs can be reduced to the minimum that the market has to offer.

Once the businesses have full sourcing independence, they are flexible in terms of where they procure their services. They can continue to obtain them from IT or they may switch to an external provider that is more efficient and reliable. However, this independence can work in both directions (Figure 1-5).

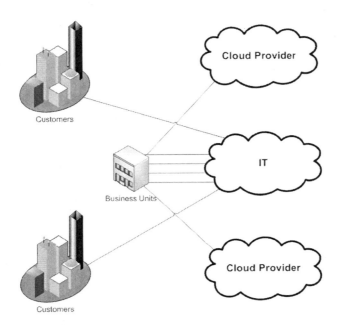

Figure 1-5 : Multi-source and Multi-target Services

If IT develops its services in a generic and modular form, then the organization also has the flexibility to offer parts of the functionality on the external market, and therefore monetize the investment in ways that were not possible before.

Impact on Application Development

This book examines cloud computing from the perspective of the application developer or system architect. The potential impact on an application is both broad and profound; however it is up to the individual designers how deeply they are to immerse themselves into the cloud and which aspects to leverage.

There are certain parallels to the enterprise maturity model, described above, in the area of software engineering.

Resource optimization: Applications must provide the option of a high degree of resource efficiency. Decoupling the software from any constraints of the environment, such as hardware or platform features, facilitate virtualization. However, they can also go further in supporting multi-tenancy by providing systematic instrumentation and enforcing fine-grained authorization and accounting.

Operational optimization: Software needs to minimize required human intervention. This implies a high degree of internal resilience and automatic scaling. At the same time, end-user self service and fulfillment workflows should minimize administrative involvement.

Target optimization: While flexibility in sourcing resources and services can help to drive down costs, the ultimate objective of an IT system is to create value. A well-designed package can be repurposed for many objectives and user groups. However, this means that the architecture must be decomposed along the lines of SOA and that instrumentation, authorization and accounting must be bulletproof, in order to support external multi-tenancy.

Put another way, minimalists could continue as before, coding on the desktop with the same tools and interface, and then deploy the compiled modules to an IaaS system. They could call the result a cloud solution. However, such an approach wouldn't take advantage of any benefits of cloud computing (such as auto-scaling) and may expose the service to more significant risks in some areas (e.g. privacy, reliability) than they would encounter in a private environment.

On the other hand, a fully cloud-oriented approach involves re-planning the design to consider several key aspects:

New Services: The cloud opens a vast assortment of new programmable web services, ranging from storage and computation to identity management and complex data analysis.

New Platforms: A new set of platforms have emerged that provide a scalable and secure foundation for cloud-oriented applications.

New Development Environments: A change in execution platform may have a significant impact on the environment the developer requires for coding, testing and deployment.

New Architectures: Developing an application for exponential scalability and reactive elasticity may require different data models and parallelization techniques.

New Partners: As new cloud offerings storm onto the scene, it is obvious that an ecosystem has the potential for faster functional growth than any single provider can offer. In order to accelerate the adoption of innovative capabilities, there is a need to expose and consume a large number of integration points.

New Opportunities: The cloud computing landscape is largely based around the SPI model and a set of implementation, operational and governance services. However, few of these fully meet the needs of a given customer. There are a number of niches where there is tremendous potential for new applications and services.

New Challenges: A service-oriented architecture that relies on the public Internet and an external provider using multitenant delivery generates significant new risks that the customer must consider. If the application can help to address these concerns (for instance, through reduced sensitivity to failures, latency and intermittent connectivity), the chances of successful adoption will increase.

MODEL

Chapter 2

Reference Architecture

The design of a solution that leverages every aspect of cloud computing is no small feat. In addition to far-reaching implications of virtualization, multi-tenancy and public service delivery, there are many other important technological developments that closely accompany the new breed of platforms and applications.

While these trends are interrelated, they are largely independent of each other and are not necessarily planned as a cohesive unit. In order to add some structure to the chaos, we have devised a simple reference architecture. It is not the only way that you could decompose an Internet application; but it serves our purpose of reducing the design to a set of manageable elements.

MODEL

Cloud Component Model

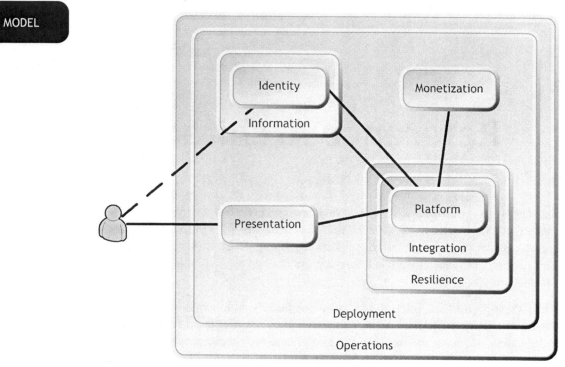

Figure 2-1: Cloud Component Model

As shown in Figure 2-1, we have broken down the structure of a given cloud solution into components in order to describe several key aspects/components in more detail.

Platform: Environment and set of tools aimed to assist application developers in engineering, integrating and delivering the application

Presentation: Interface through which content is exposed to the user

Identity: Information about the primary consumers of the application that is used to optimize and customize their experience

Integration: Framework that simplifies federated data transfer and task processing

Information: External repositories providing highly scalable storage of structured and unstructured, static and volatile data

Resilience: Reliability of applications and infrastructure, as well as long-term capacity planning to ensure scalability

Monetization: Fine-grained instrumentation coupled with billing and payment settlement

Deployment: Application release process that includes development, testing, staging and eventually deployment into production

Operation: Monitoring and support for applications that have been moved into production

These also form the basic structure of the rest of the book. We will briefly go over each component so that you understand the roadmap for the subsequent sections and can follow the individual topics more easily.

Platform

At the center of the model is the platform, an environment and set of tools aimed at application developers to assist them in engineering, integrating and delivering the required functionality.

As you might expect, the choice of platform is fundamental to the architecture since it will imply a set of basic services that are available and also entails limitations that need to be overcome. Platform services such as Google App Engine and Microsoft Azure lend themselves well to development of cloud-based services. However, there is no absolute need to leverage a cloud platform in order to build a cloud-scale solution. You can also build your own platform on an infrastructure service or even on a traditional hosting site.

In making the selection, you will want to consider general criteria like costs, performance and scalability. But ultimately you will be dependent on your team to implement and support any solutions that you design. It is therefore important to determine the programming languages and application frameworks that you currently use and make sure that your future evolution is compatible with your current skills and preferences.

Presentation

The functionality delivered by the platform is exposed to the user through a presentation layer. This interface consists both of input provided by the user and content delivered to the user.

The typical cloud interaction model is browser-based. HTTP is the most common application protocol and HTML is optimal for providing a consistent presentation layer across all client platforms. However, these base protocols do not guarantee an optimal user experience. So, other browser-oriented techniques have been developed to improve the performance and responsiveness of the applications and also support rich media and an engaging user interaction, especially in light of real-time social content that is increasing in importance.

Even so, there are often reasons to resort to non-browser protocols and connectivity options. Mobile devices, in particular, have unique constraints and features that differentiate them from the desktop and from each other. Since mobility represents a usage model that is closely aligned with cloud computing, it is important not to neglect this large population of users with special requirements.

Cloud computing also complicates the optimization process because it is tightly associated with a federated service-oriented architecture that consumes granular services from a variety of sources. These function calls are often opaque to the user and may rely on many additional network requests. When the program logic is sequential, the risk of additive latency being exposed to the user is quite real. At the same time, the lack of transparency makes it difficult to identify the root causes. You therefore need to look at the architecture very carefully.

Identity

Most applications have a need to distinguish between users in order to optimize the experience with customized, highly relevant content and enforce any access controls on sensitive and personal data. Typically, the data related to individuals is stored in a directory, which needs to scale to very large sizes in order to accommodate multi-tenant enterprise applications and global consumer-oriented services.

Scalability is not the only challenge. There is also a requirement to simplify the user experience with minimal manual re-authentication between services, which is difficult in a distributed multi-vendor architecture and leads to a need for federated identity management for which there are new standards that have yet to converge. Due to the dispersed nature of cloud services, a high level of security is mandatory in order to protect credentials and any personal information.

In addition to security there is also the potential to leverage user-based preferences, context and history to maximize accessibility; improve the efficiency, clarity and aesthetics of the experience; and generate custom content that is tailored to the user's geographical location and social networking environment.

Integration

Cloud computing features a high level of scalability, such that processing cannot always take place on a single machine. A high degree of service decomposition for a granular service-oriented architecture also allows providers to achieve maximum efficiency and flexibility. Since the core functionality of the application is not completely self-contained, there is a need for an integration framework that simplifies federated data transfer and task processing.

In order to leverage widely distributed applications, systems and services, you need to achieve network connectivity across physical links and security boundaries and to optimize these connections for performance. A second step is to ensure compatibility of the application end-points and include suitable synchronous and asynchronous mechanisms to integrate with legacy applications. At a higher level, the application decomposition may need to be revisited to impose loose coupling and avoid single points of failure or performance bottlenecks.

Information

The Internet, and therefore by implication also the cloud, are becoming increasingly data-centric. Applications usually consume or provide data to data stores external to their native platform, whereby the specific solutions may vary in using structured, unstructured, static, and volatile data with or without transactional restrictions. The biggest challenge again is size. Large datasets frequently require partitioning, which leads to a trade-off between availability and transactional integrity.

While SQL still governs the interaction of the majority of transactions, there is an increasing need for other data architectures. Graph and tree structures lend themselves for some applications, such as social networking. Furthermore, there are many initiatives to abandon SQL for large tabular data due to its scalability constraints. Unfortunately, the alternatives imply a loss of many rich and useful features and a lack of compatibility with legacy code. However, in some cases they appear to be the only viable options.

While scalable information presents a challenge for cloud-based applications, there are also many advantages to a service-based model. For example, the developing area of storage services helps to address elasticity challenges while at the same time abstracting both the physical and logical implementation and often exposing new data architectures.

Resilience

Outsourced services can complicate availability guarantees. They require new techniques for monitoring; and recovery usually involves a high degree of redundancy. In order to ensure the availability of the application, it is necessary to look at short-term uptime including reliability of applications and infrastructure. However, it is also important to plan capacity for the long term and ensure that the application is scalable.

Elasticity and reliability may sound like independent objectives but they are related in two ways. Both attempt to address the availability of the service. Reliability relates to the short-term performance of all the components, whereas elasticity ensures that sufficient resources are always accessible whether they are needed suddenly or gradually. The two are also related in their implementation. For both purposes, a common strategy is to decompose the system into modular components that can be scaled up through increased parallelism. They can also serve as redundant failover and hot-standby systems to cover outages and system errors in addition to service growth.

Monetization

A key requirement for most applications is for them to deliver value that justifies their costs. Externally facing applications need a mechanism for charging usage and collecting payment. Even internal applications require instrumentation to establish usage and allocate costs effectively. These demands are not necessarily unique to cloud. They are mandatory for all profitable applications. However, the cloud presents new services and is usually associated with flexible and ad hoc payments that are difficult to achieve with traditional payment systems.

After building it, the business task for a successful application is to ensure the application is recognized and used. Marketing techniques may include paid placement or active optimization of appearance on the most visible related pages. In the cloud, this usually means increased appearance on search engines and social media.

The payment involves a few steps. The first is to decide on what basis to charge for usage. Services vary according to whether they are subscription-based or consumption-based. In the case of the former, users pay a fixed fee, while for the latter they are billed according to the number of users, volume of data, transactions, etc, and there is an implied requirement to measure these indicators and allocate charges correctly.

Next comes the challenge of settling the transaction. Credit card payments are the easiest place to start for consumer and small businesses. Larger organizations may require centralized billing, which could also be handled with a credit card; however, it is more common for corporations to prefer to use the banking system to make their payments. In this case, a separate invoicing and collection system may be necessary, which can, of course, also be consumed as a service.

Deployment

Applications typically run through a lifecycle that includes development, testing, staging and eventually deployment into production. The initial stages of this process constitute a great opportunity for cloud platforms since each project requires temporary resources with volatile loads. Development usually begins with very limited infrastructural demands that gradually increase through unit testing to high volume beta testing and then terminate abruptly when the service is launched in production.

The cost savings through utility pricing of resources and lower fixed costs are quite intuitive. Beyond these, there is also potential for cloud computing to impact the process itself. By minimizing the associated costs, you can afford to engage in more frequent and higher load testing. You can also consider the possibility of multiple simultaneous deployments since it is easier and faster to switch between instances.

Even though there are many benefits in shortening the release cycle and introducing more experimental innovation into your services, you also need to examine some of the challenges of the new model. If alternate instances rely on their own data then it may not be trivial to reconcile changes. On the other hand, if they share the same storage facilities the opportunity to update the data structures is limited. Furthermore, you need to make provisions for rolling back versions when a deployment doesn't work as expected. This can be difficult as it may impact the user experience and requires an accurate change log and testing process to ensure application integrity.

Operation

After an application has been launched, the challenge becomes operational: it is necessary to configure, administer, monitor and support it. As more providers enter into the mix, the administration has the potential to become excessively complex. To minimize confusion, there is a clear need to integrate processes with well-defined policy-based service management. At the same time, there is also the opportunity to avail of cloud-based services for monitoring, service desk, and other management tasks.

All of these facilities need to be planned at the design stage in order to reach the highest level of automation. While standardization and abstraction of components will facilitate this process, constructive collaboration between development and operations is necessary to ensure that the requirements of both groups are fully addressed.

Chapter 3

Use Cases

The last chapter introduced a reference architecture that we have adopted to classify some of the primary elements of a cloud-based solution. Behind this relatively simple model are a wide range of implementation options that may be easier to visualize if we illustrate them more practically. Most components can be hosted in a private data center or built on public infrastructure. Solutions can integrate almost any combination of infrastructure, platform and software services.

In fact, it may be necessary to leverage a range of services to fulfill all the requirements of a single architectural building block. For example, you may want to break down services such as computation and storage into smaller units, which are provided by different sources.

Typically, there is a tradeoff between the simplicity of using a single provider for all services and the potential cost and functionality benefits of using best-in-class services for each component. The choice of how to decompose the solution will consider factors such as latency, integration points, data transfer (bandwidth), provider pricing structure and troubleshooting implications.

You may also want to favor platforms and tools that your developers have already mastered. And typically there will be requirements for interoperability with legacy applications as well as connectivity with suppliers, partners and customers.

The theoretical number of platform and service combinations is virtually infinite; so it isn't feasible, or even useful, to enumerate each of them. However, we have chosen a few that we feel are indicative of some of the most common scenarios and also representative of the set of options you are likely to consider.

- Hosted server with IaaS storage

- Dedicated IaaS

- Private application with IaaS extensions

MODEL

- PaaS only

- PaaS application with IaaS extensions

Let's look at these more closely.

Hosted Server with IaaS storage

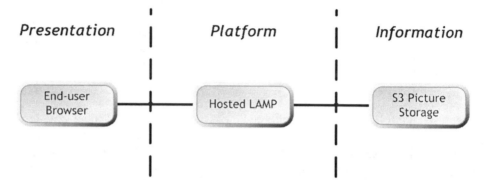

Figure 3-1: Hosted Server with IaaS Storage

One simple way to begin using cloud computing is to leverage the elastic storage of an infrastructure provider. In this scenario, the actual application platform including all the architectural components could be running on a dedicated server at any hosting provider (e.g. GoDaddy or 1and1). Hosting sites often offer a variety of frameworks and tools that range from FrontPage and .NET ASP to ColdFusion, PHP and Perl.

They typically include a limited amount of local storage, often accompanied by a MySQL database, which may be sufficient for small sites. However, when applications rely on high levels of scalability as well as other specific requirements such as versioning or backup service levels, then a cloud-based storage service, such as Amazon S3, may be more appropriate. Since most storage services are accessible through SOAP and RESTful APIs, they can be easily integrated into almost any hosted application.

Dedicated IaaS

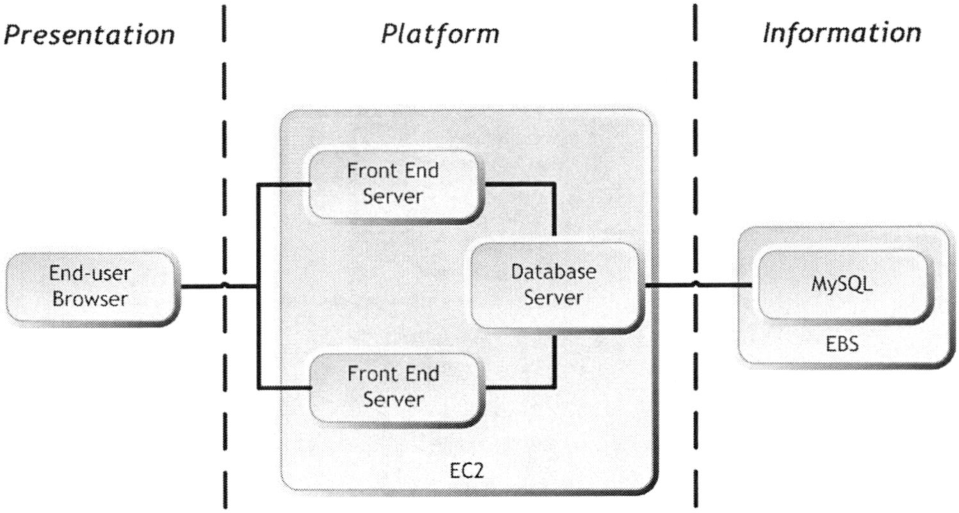

Figure 3-2: Dedicated IaaS

Another easy entry into cloud computing is to leverage IaaS with a traditional LAMP or .NET stack. This approach involves taking the data and code from an existing three-tier application and migrating them onto an infrastructure service, such as Amazon Web Services (AWS), Rackspace Cloud or GoGrid.

A typical scenario could include a pair of EC2 Servers serving as web front-end servers, supported by a large EC2 instance acting as a database server that resides on Amazon's Elastic Block Storage (EBS) (Figure 3-2). EBS or S3 may also be used to backup the database and store snapshots.

The solution benefits from its similarity to a traditional database model and also the familiarity of developers and engineers with both the operating systems and software applications that are involved. It also facilitates front-end elasticity and opens the way for an alternate database tier if higher levels of scalability are needed. Over time, the solution could leverage some additional cloud-based capabilities, but there is no immediate need for overhauling the existing application simply to transition to the cloud.

Private Application with IaaS Extension

MODEL

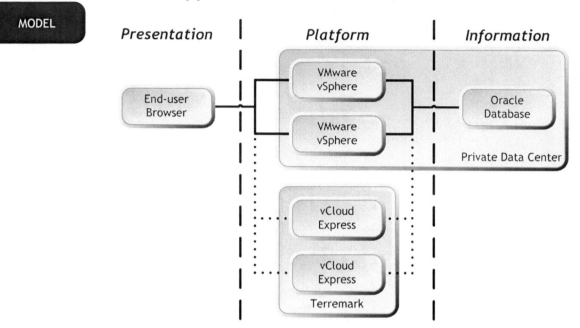

Figure 3-3: Private Application with IaaS Extension

Enterprises may be able to satisfy some of their needs on premise, but still be interested in tapping into the cloud to handle peak loads for internal applications. This approach, often called 'cloudbursting' (Perry, 2008), involves extending an existing enterprise application, written on a private platform, to be able to leverage external services once internal capacity has been exhausted.

For example (Figure 3-3), an organization may use VMware vSphere to build an internal virtualization infrastructure with Oracle as a back-end database. VMware partners, such as Terremark, provide a compatible public offering, which customers can lean on for additional resources, improved redundancy, or disaster recovery.

The approach involves some obvious challenges in managing multiple providers and ensuring privacy of all sensitive data. However, if these issues can be addressed effectively, then the model offers a financially attractive means of exploiting all internal fixed resources and yet facilitating a high level of scalability when it is required.

PaaS only

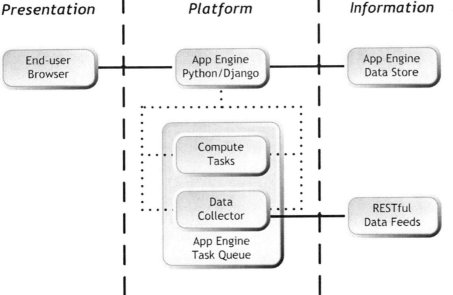

Figure 3-4: PaaS-only Platform

A solution based on a cloud-based platform is able to leverage the advantages of elasticity and efficiency most effectively. In Figure 3-4, all data resides on a PaaS platform (e.g. Google App Engine) and all computation is performed on that platform. The applications and workloads are modeled according to the capabilities of the provider.

A major advantage of this approach includes the ease of implementation. The front end is simple to create and administer since most PaaS providers offer SDKs and tools to monitor and measure traffic. The application can also take advantage of any auto-scaling capabilities inherent in the platform.

On the downside, the application usually needs to be re-written from the ground up to cater to the specific limitations and capabilities of the platform. In some cases, compute-intensive tasks need to be broken into smaller pieces. For example, App Engine imposes a 30 second runtime limitation so it is necessary to break larger workloads into tasks and manage them with the Task Queue API.

The code also needs to take into account any outages that a PaaS service will have. Using App Engine for illustration again, Google provides specific API calls for detecting scheduled outages. The application can leverage these to make failover provisions, or at least inform the user of the expected downtime.

Highly scalable data modeling is also no small chore. While BigTable and other noSQL stores are capable of holding huge data sets, a simple key-value store lacks sophisticated querying and indexing capabilities that the application may require. It is not trivial, and yet very important, to balance the needs of the program logic with the business's speed and scale requirements.

PaaS Application with IaaS Storage and Computation

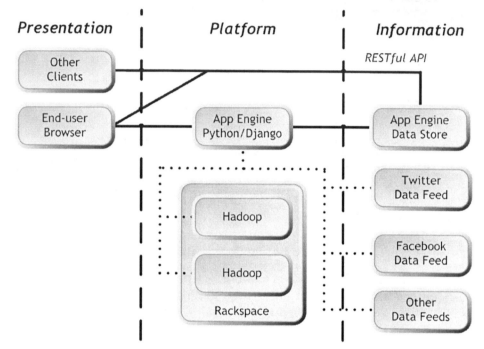

Figure 3-5: PaaS Application with IaaS Storage and Computation

This last model is the most ambitious (Figure 3-5). It aims to harness the best of both PaaS (e.g. Google App Engine) and IaaS (e.g. Amazon Web Services) in a combined architecture. The idea is for the PaaS components to handle the front-end scaling and availability, whereby the owners can allocate quotas to limit the traffic to their budget. The storage and computation intensive work involves Hadoop instances running on IaaS that can be scaled up and down on a per-instance basis.

For example, the web application could be written in Python and run on App Engine using the local datastore for end-user related data. A part of the service (implemented at Amazon) is collecting data from third party data providers and storing them in a Hadoop File System running on AWS.

Separately from the collectors, a Hadoop cluster runs proprietary map/reduce algorithms to perform analytics. (While this example highlights Hadoop, the external compute job could be anything that is not optimized on PaaS.) After the map/reduce jobs have completed, the summary is served via a RESTful web interface to the end-user application at App Engine.

Practical Considerations

We hope these examples help to illustrate some of the options that you can consider in architecting your cloud-based applications.

Some of the main factors to consider as you make your choice are:

How much code do you already have in place?

If you have an application that you want to enable for the cloud, then you may want to look into repositioning it on an infrastructure service, and/or simply enhancing it by replacing existing functions and storage with cloud-based equivalents. On the other hand, if you are starting from scratch, or have a need to overhaul your application anyhow, then it is worthwhile considering a cloud-based platform, such as Microsoft Azure or Google App Engine, so that you can benefit from the inherent elasticity that they provide.

What application and infrastructure dependencies do you have?

If you need to connect to other applications, or interact with physical infrastructure, then you may be forced to look at internal options for at least some of your components. This doesn't mean cloud computing is out of the question. One option is to cluster together several components and migrate them externally. Running off-the-shelf software off-premise can be challenging, but is a definite possibility with an appropriate infrastructure service.

How sensitive is your data?

In the case of highly confidential data, a public cloud may not be the best option. You may still want to look at hybrid combinations that leverage external offerings for non-sensitive components. Or you may consume cloud-based storage services, taking care to ensure that all information is securely encrypted. If the data is only minimally sensitive, you might feel comfortable entrusting it to a public service but only after you have carefully scrutinized the specific offerings.

How high should your application scale?

A platform service lends itself well for moderate scalability needs since it automatically provides a degree of auto-scaling and load-balancing out-of-the-box. However, if you need to accommodate extremely large data sets, or track huge numbers of users, then an infrastructure, or hybrid, service may fit your needs

MODEL

better. Likewise, if your workload involves complex, computation-intensive tasks, then you may be more effective distributing and coordinating them through a farm of infrastructure services.

What do your developers prefer?

The choice of platforms and services carries significant implications in terms of available programming languages and tools. If you have a team of seasoned Java programmers, it might not be most effective to choose a platform that is based on Ruby, Python or C#. Many developers appreciate the chance to try something new, but it is important to consider the time and cost of their learning curve.

What availability requirements do you have?

You may want to differentiate between scheduled outages, where you have some leeway in mitigating the damages, and unplanned downtime, which is unpredictable in timing, duration and scope.

If you have stringent needs, then you can choose premium SLAs from the service provider or else implement redundancy and failover yourself. However, these both have costs associated with them, so it is imperative to understand the business justification for higher availability. There is less than a tenth of a percent difference in uptime between three nines and ten nines; so before you invest, it is worth looking at the business case considering not only the opportunity cost of lost transactions but also the impact on reputation, customer satisfaction, third-party liability, etc.

Platform

At the center of the model is the platform, an environment and set of tools aimed at application developers to assist them in engineering, integrating and delivering the required functionality.

As you might expect, the choice of platform is fundamental to the architecture since it will imply a set of basic services that are available and also entails limitations that need to be overcome. Platform services such as Google App Engine and Microsoft Azure lend themselves well to development of cloud-based services. However, there is no absolute need to leverage a cloud platform in order to build a cloud-scale solution. You can also build your own platform on an infrastructure service or even on a traditional hosting site.

In making the selection, you will want to consider general criteria like costs, performance and scalability. But ultimately you will be dependent on your team to implement and support any solutions that you design. It is therefore important to determine the programming languages and application frameworks that you currently use and make sure that your future evolution is compatible with your current skills and preferences.

Chapter 4

Platform Definition

What is a platform? Depending on the context, the word can carry very diverse meanings. For our purposes, it is the set of tools and resources that a programmer uses to develop an application. Every web-application is designed, built and deployed in some environment and is therefore based on a platform.

Some of the features of a platform might include an integrated development environment, a set of programming languages and compilers, a software development kit, run-time libraries and application programming interfaces. The developer may also make use of tools to test, debug and deploy the application. All of these help a programmer and therefore constitute his or her platform.

To illustrate the point, let's consider the alternative. There may be some appliance-based web application that runs hand-coded machine instructions to process HTTP requests. We apologize if our generalizations above don't accommodate these cases, which may well be feats of technical genius.

In our experience, most readers will choose to pursue an easier path. We must emphasize that this doesn't automatically mean using a platform service. Platform as a Service (PaaS) is merely one approach to building cloud-based applications, but virtually everyone uses a platform since it is generally more effective and efficient to leverage existing tools and services than to reinvent the wheel.

Components

By automating routine tasks and providing a generic infrastructure and set of reusable components, a platform allows the developer to abstract many repetitive tasks and focus on designing added value. In other words, they become more productive.

Chapter 4: Platform Definition

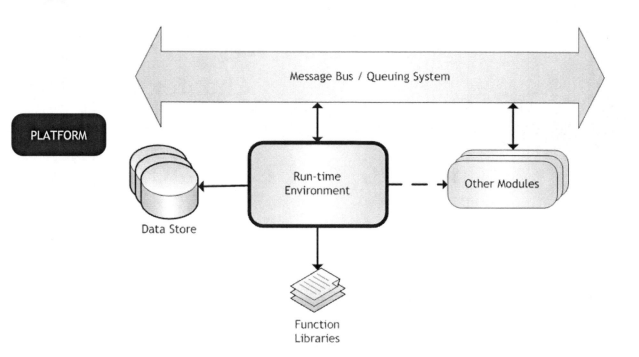

Figure 4-1: Platform Components

Many reusable components will be hosted separately (Figure 4-1). There could be storage facilities that offer highly available and scalable means to persist data and applications. Function libraries may offer computation and other services so that the applications can concentrate on their unique value and take advantage of capabilities that have already been optimized by others. There may also be queuing systems, and other integration infrastructure, that allows the application to easily scale out while working on common tasks in a coordinated fashion.

Platforms may also offer further functions to support the developers, for example:

Integrated Development Environment to develop, test, host and maintain applications

Integration services for marshalling, database integration, security, storage persistence and state management

Scalability services for concurrency management and failover

Instrumentation to track activity and value to the customer

Workflow facilities for application design, development, testing, deployment and hosting

User Interface support for HTML, JavaScript, Flex, Flash, AIR

Visualization tools that show patterns of end-user interactions

Collaboration services to support distributed development and facilitate developer community

Source code services for version control, dynamic multiple-user testing, rollback, auditing and change-tracking

Run-time Environment

One primary feature of the platform is the run-time environment. For a web-based application, this means a server that is on the public Internet and accepts requests, which it processes and passes on to the application. While a simple web site only needs to serve HTML over HTTP, it is very cumbersome to build complex and dynamic web sites that do not utilize some level of server-side business logic and information storage.

In order to facilitate the necessary functionality, a number of application frameworks have developed that alleviate the overhead of authentication, authorization, database access, page templating, server-side caching and session management.

These are often classified according the programming languages that they support:

*Visual Basic, C#:*ASP.NET is based on Microsoft's Active Server Pages (ASP) technology, revised to leverage the Common Language Runtime (CLR), which is compatible with all Microsoft .NET languages such as Visual Basic and C#. It leverages .NET pages, which consist of HTML as well as dynamic code that is pre-processed when the page is rendered. In addition to in-line mark-up, it is possible to separate the .NET code into a separate file that is only referenced in the .NET page.

While ASP.NET is a component of Microsoft Internet Information Server (IIS), and is closely connected with Microsoft Visual Studio, it is also possible to extend it with other frameworks, such as DotNetNuke, Castle Monorail or Spring.NET.

Ruby: Ruby on Rails is an open-source framework that supports Ruby, a dynamic and reflective object-oriented programming language that is based on Perl, Smalltalk, Eiffel, Ada and Lisp. Ruby on Rails received considerable attention as the original basis for Twitter. However, it suffered when Twitter switched to Scala for a significant portion of their infrastructure needs.

Java: Java requires little introduction as it is a de facto standard for open-source software. However, not all Java environments are identical. There are several Java application frameworks. The best-known include Apache Struts and Spring Framework.

Perl: Perl is a general-purpose programming language that was originally developed for manipulating text, but is now used for a variety of applications including system administration and web development. It is used in a variety of popular frameworks including Catalyst, Jifty and WebGUI.

PHP: PHP was originally developed for building dynamic web content, typically acting as a filter that processes input data and renders HTML. Application frameworks such as Drupal and Joomla have spawned popular ecosystems, which have delivered thousands of modules that enable developers to build extensive content management systems without any custom coding.

Python: Python is characterized by its support of multiple programming paradigms including object-oriented, structured, functional and aspect-oriented programming. One of its most popular application frameworks is Django, which is tailored toward complex, database-driven websites with multiple smaller applications forming the complete web experience. Since Google App Engine was initially only released with Python support, Python (in conjunction with Django) is very popular for Google applications.

Hosting

In addition to the languages and flavors of the run-time environment, we will look at four hosting options.

- On-premise

- IaaS

- Web Hosting

- PaaS

On premise

If an organization already owns extensive infrastructure, then there will be a tendency to try to leverage existing hardware and software as much as possible, enhancing these to take advantage of some of the benefits of cloud-based resources.

Both internal (development and employee-facing) and external (customer-facing) servers as well as software licenses, tools and processes represent a significant past investment and therefore potential future value at little incremental cost. Rather than replacing these, it makes sense to utilize them to the extent that they are suitable and economically attractive.

In addition to financial benefits, it may be easier to create connectivity, ensure privacy and maintain control over the applications if these are retained in a private data center. This doesn't mean that no cloud benefits would accrue to the services. It may be possible to deliver some aspects of cloud-based computing in-house through virtualization, better instrumentation, automation and self service. However, only very few private organizations would have the capacity to scale like a public cloud provider. There would, therefore, be a tighter limitation on resources consumption.

PLATFORM

IaaS

A relatively easy transition from private to public cloud hosting is to use Infrastructure as a Service. In this case you can retain existing software and many development processes but you would host these on external hardware operated by the service provider.

You wouldn't necessarily need to move a full application suite, or even the entire application lifecycle, outside the organization. A first step is to focus on certain tasks, such as development, testing, debugging, production and support. These activities derive tangible benefits from cloud computing as we shall see in our Deployment section.

Any combination of internal and external systems is possible, at least theoretically. However, the choice and combination will directly affect connectivity, privacy and control. Also, the more complex the picture becomes, the more difficult it will be to manage the entire system.

IaaS replicates the platform for every virtual instance, so it doesn't achieve maximal resource sharing. It is therefore less efficient than PaaS or SaaS. However, it does offer an easy path to begin leveraging some benefits of cloud computing. It offers elasticity for variable needs and also taps into the inherent benefits of virtualization (consolidation, standardization, automation) through the provider's specialization and economy of scale. It does this while still offering a high degree of application flexibility and backward compatibility.

Web Hosting

Web hosting sites presents an alternate approach that specializes in platform simplicity and standardization. GeoCities and others offered services as early as the mid-90s, whereby users could upload HTML pages to a server in order to establish an Internet presence. Simple hosting services still only allow HTML and, at most, client-side scripting capabilities, such as VBscript or JavaScript. Providing server interfaces, such as the Common Gateway Interface (CGI), is more complex to implement and exposes the provider to significantly more security threats.

PLATFORM

Nonetheless, there has been a marked increase in the number of web hosting services that support a variety of active server-side components ranging from Microsoft ASP.NET and Java to scripts such as PHP, Python and Ruby on Rails. Compared to infrastructure services, these platforms reduce the storage requirements of each application and simplify deployment. Rather than moving virtual machines with entire operating systems, the application only requires the code written by the developer. An additional benefit is the increased ease for the service provider to sandbox each application by only providing functions that cannot disrupt other tenants on the same system and network.

PaaS

Platform as a Service has evolved as a hybrid that combines the efficiency of web hosting with the pricing model of infrastructure services. It represents a design that tries to take the best of both while also addressing some of their respective limitations.

Infrastructure-as-a-Service offers many benefits to customers who wish to extend or shift their applications into a cloud-based environment. However, infrastructure services tend to run on platforms that were designed for desktops and traditional client-server environments. They may now be virtualized, but they have not been optimized for the cloud.

To better address the specific needs and advantages of cloud delivery models, some vendors have crafted new platforms that enable faster time-to-market, a common user experience, and an easier development environment. You might see them as an evolution of conventional integrated development environments to support on-line collaboration and a cloud target platform. Ideally, these platforms enable the creation of a new ecosystem that benefits both users and vendors.

Cloud platforms act as run-time environments, which support a set of (compiled or interpreted) programming languages. They may offer additional services such as reusable components and libraries that are available as objects and application programming interfaces. Ideally, the platform will offer plug-ins into common development environments, like Eclipse, to facilitate development, testing and deployment.

From the provider perspective, PaaS is a mechanism for vendors to apply a specific set of constraints to achieve goals that they feel represent the value proposition for their end-users (developers directly, but indirectly also the enterprise IT organization). Those goals tie to the core attributes of cloud computing as follows:

- Elasticity
- Multi-tenancy

- Rapid provisioning and deployment

- Leverage of web technologies and open source

- Integrated monitoring, management and billing facilities

To achieve the above goals the platform vendors usually must apply a set of constraints preventing functionality that might interfere with the required elasticity and security:

PLATFORM

- Only specific languages and run-times are provided.

- Not all language/library features are enabled.

- Generic APIs typically replace some of the features or capabilities of traditional stacks.

- There may be size constraints on individual requests.

- Statelessness is encouraged to minimize the overhead of state management.

- Applications need to be written to support scalability following the PaaS vendors' specific requirements

While these constraints are meant to allow the vendor to achieve the cloud computing goals, vendors usually also add additional value to sweeten the incentive of targeting applications to their platform:

- IDE plug-ins, SDKs and a local emulation environment

- Frameworks that provide the scaffolding and hooks to the platform

- Free developer accounts to accelerate or eliminate provisioning time

- APIs to ease the use of popular services and specifications (e.g. OpenID, Jabber IM)

In summary, the value proposition for PaaS is that it shows some benefits over traditional web platforms in terms of geographically distributed collaboration, facilitation of web service aggregation through centralization of code, reduced costs of infrastructure through the pay-as-you-go model and cost reduction through higher-level programming abstractions. At the same time, PaaS is also simpler to manage than IaaS, represents a smaller platform to distribute, and can leverage more functionality and services from the provider.

Selection Criteria

Is it better to use a platform service or to build your own platform that you either host on premise or deliver through IaaS? There is no simple answer, but a starting point is to ask whether any platform service exists that meets your requirements. If so, then it will typically be simpler to use PaaS – but not always. If you have a need to integrate legacy code or envisage tight integration with system level components (dedicated processes), PaaS may not be your best choice.

The rest of this chapter, we will examine the distinctions you can expect to find between competitive offerings. We listed some of the optional services above that are not universally included in every service and that depend on the layered services and object libraries included. Some other key areas of differentiation in platforms include the programming languages (e.g. Python, Java, C#) supported and development environments (e.g. Eclipse, Visual Studio) for which there are plug-ins available.

Programming Languages

Infrastructure services are largely language agnostic. A virtual machine can host any application that is compiled to a processor architecture supported by the machine. Platform services are a little different. They typically host run-time engines that are specific to a limited set of languages.

Consequently a set choice of programming languages may limit, or dictate, the set of platform services that can run the application. For example, .NET languages (C#, Visual Basic) lend themselves well to Microsoft Azure. Some hosting services may also support .NET but it is by no means a given and it is rather difficult to find current PaaS offerings that accommodate .NET. At the same time, .NET lends itself well to integration with Microsoft products, which are ubiquitous in the enterprise, so there may be an additional incentive to consider it even when other languages would be an easier choice.

Java has historically been the counterweight to .NET for the open source community. It has been the language of choice for a number of software vendors. Since it comes with a very rich set of tools and is widely adopted across the industry it is also a logical option for cloud-based development.

But neither Java nor .NET is unchallenged. In the past few years, we have seen a boost in popularity for both Python and Ruby. While they both tend to run slower than Java, they require less extraneous scaffolding and therefore lead to cleaner code. In contrast to Java, these are both interpreted (rather than compiled) and use dynamic (rather than static) typing. Their proponents feel that these lead to significant developer productivity gains.

Development Environment

An Integrated Development Environment (IDE) assists the programmer with development and deployment. Often a language-sensitive editor will provide method/class help and code completion. It may also perform syntax checking and assist in debugging with breakpoints and variable inspection. Some tools include compute and storage emulators for off-line testing. When it comes time to deploy the code, the IDE may have tools to package and upload the software.

PLATFORM

Clearly, the development environment is closely linked to the programming language. Not all IDEs support all programming languages. However, even where there is an IDE available, there is usually no absolute requirement to use it. Eclipse plug-ins are available for some languages and cloud services (e.g. Force.com or App Engine), but some developers find it heavy and slow to use. Depending on your needs, there may be occasions where a simple text editor and an FTP upload tool work just as well.

The choice is up to you – as long as you ensure the platform supports the programming languages and development environment you plan to use.

Developer Preferences

Working backwards, perhaps your main driver in deciding on languages and development tools will be the experience and expertise of your current programming staff. For example, in spite of its limitations, Java programmers are currently easier to find than Python/Ruby experts.

There are, however, limits on how far it is wise to indulge in accommodating past preferences. For example, some may consider that the Java run-time of Google App Engine has opened up the possibility of using Scala, Clojure, Jython and other languages that can be compiled to Java bytecode. On the surface, it seems like it would give the benefits of a larger selection of Java resource libraries but retain the productivity gains of more dynamic and compact languages. However, until these are officially supported by the vendor (in this case Google), they are more suitable as technology prototypes than realistic choices for production.

Other Factors

In summary, factors that may influence the platform selection decision include:

Skills of developers: For example, experience with .NET will lead to favoring Azure, strength in Java/Python may bias the choice toward Google, while PHP and other development and run-time environments may encourage adoption of IaaS.

Data types and structures: Highly data driven applications, such as CRM, may be well aligned with Force.Com. On the other hand, if you need to analyze huge datasets then Pig on a Hadoop cluster (for example on an Infrastructure service) may be a good candidate.

Resource requirements: Expected end user behavior will drive consumption of computation, storage and network. The platform must offer these resources with good performance at low cost. In some cases, there may also be a need for specific capabilities such as load-balancing and failover.

Application integration model: The requirement to integrate modules and interface with other applications may mandate queuing, SOAP/REST support as well as the ability to host and consume other data feeds/sources. In particular, dependencies to legacy systems and potential data migrations need to be explored.

Update cycle: The expected lifetime and refresh-rate of the application will have implications on staging and deployment.

Hybrid Combinations

If the selection process above isn't challenging enough for you, then consider that it is also possible to design hybrid combinations with multiple cloud services. While an expansion in the number of service providers will invariably lead to higher complexity, the increase in choice and specialization can also facilitate a higher degree of optimization.

If you pursue this approach, the platform may be partitioned according to two primary dimensions:

- Function: specific services carried out on different platforms

- Pooled: same services run in multiple environments in order to address issues of:

    o Scale: by increasing the pool of elastic resources

    o Redundancy: reducing the threat of lock-in or provider-based unavailability

Depending on your applications and requirements, the resulting architecture can take many shapes. In most cases, the critical challenges will lie in integrating all of the components securely, efficiently and reliably.

Chapter 5

Google App Engine

Google App Engine is one of the best known platform services. In addition to a basic run-time environment, it eliminates many of the system administration and development challenges involved in building applications that can scale to millions of users. It includes facilities to deploy code to a cluster as well as monitoring, failover, automatic scaling and load balancing.

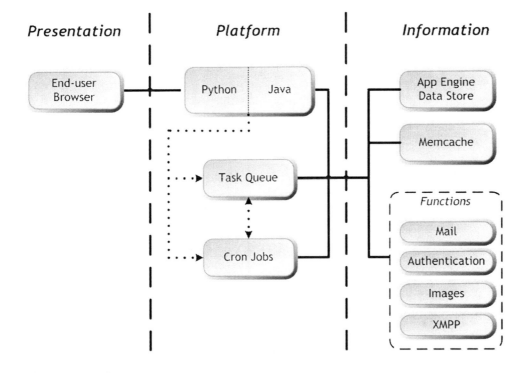

Figure 5-1: Google App Engine Architecture

Figure 5-1 offers a simple view of the Google App Engine Architecture. Users access the application through a browser, which connects to a hosted application written either in Python or Java. In addition to the run-time environment, batch jobs may run in the background either through a task queue or as scheduled "cron" jobs. The compute instances can access a persistent data store as well as a high-speed distributed cache. They can all take advantage of a number of library functions. This chapter will look at the components of the application in a little more detail.

PLATFORM

Programming Languages

App Engine originally supported runtime environments based only on Python. It has since added support for Java Virtual Machines (JVMs) thereby enabling applications written not only in Java but also other JVM languages such as Groovy, JRuby, Jython, Scala, or Clojure. The SDK includes a full local development environment that simulates Google App Engine on the developer's desktop.

There are some limitations to the programming languages. For example, Python modules must be pure-Python since C and Pyrex modules are not supported. Likewise, Java applications may only use a subset (The JRE Class White List) of the classes from the JRE standard edition, and they are prevented from creating new threads.

```
from google.appengine.ext import webapp
from google.appengine.ext.webapp.util import run_wsgi_app
class MainPage(webapp.RequestHandler):
  def get(self):
    self.response.headers['Content-Type'] = 'text/plain'
    self.response.out.write('Hello, World!')
application = webapp.WSGIApplication(
                                    [('/', MainPage)])
def main():
  run_wsgi_app(application)
if __name__ == "__main__":
  main()
```

Listing 5-1 : Google App Engine "Hello World"

The actual code required will obviously vary according to the application. As shown with a Python example inListing 5-1, the instructions can be very simple if there is little application logic. It is necessary to import a couple of modules that are included in the SDK and then define a request handler called MainPage, which processes all HTTP GET requests to the root URL. The method can write the HTTP response using the self.response object. The function run_wsgi_app() takes a WSGIApplication instance and runs it in App Engine's CGI environment. That's all there is to it when your needs are modest.

Unfortunately, even though the supported languages are quite standard, it isn't typically possible to take existing code and launch it by simply copying it to the

Google AppSpot hosting environment. Nor is it always easy to port Google code to another web host running the same application framework.

There are two obstacles that tend to interfere. Most existing web applications use a relational database to store data. They may also leverage some of the rich functionality of their original platform. For instance, they may write to the local file system, interface with other installed software, or make a variety of network connections. The first challenge is that Google provides a non-relational datastore as the default option. And the second is its use of a sandbox approach to isolate instances in its multi-tenant environments. Let's look at these in more detail.

Datastore

The App Engine datastore supports queries, sorting and transactions using optimistic concurrency control. It is a strongly consistent distributed database built on top of the lower-level BigTable with some added functionality. Unfortunately for legacy code, the App Engine datastore is not like a traditional relational database. In particular, the datastore entities are schemaless. Two entities of the same kind are not required to possess the same properties, nor do they need to use the same value types if they do share properties. Instead, the application is responsible for ensuring that entities conform to any schema required by the business logic. To assist, the Python SDK includes a data modeling library that helps enforce consistency.

Google App Engine's query language (called GQL) is similar to SQL in its SELECT statements, however, with some significant limitations. GQL intentionally does not support the JOIN statement and can therefore only accommodate single table queries. The rationale behind the restriction is the inefficiency that queries spanning more than one machine might introduce.

Google does provide a workaround in the form of a ReferenceProperty class that can indicate one-to-many and many-to-many relationships. Unfortunately, for high data volume apps the use of ReferenceProperty can become a performance bottleneck and should not be used to directly mimic an SQL-like relationship. A preferred way to optimize high volume queries is to 'mark' data with qualities that are common in searches and try to return all the results via possible equality filters.

Sandbox

The second issue for legacy applications is the sandbox, which isolates programs from other instances and tenants that may be running on the same web server. In order to limit the attack surface, the application can only make outbound connections to other computers on the Internet through the URL-fetch and email services provided. It can only receive inbound connections through HTTP and HTTPS on the standard ports. Also, a significant performance-related restriction of HTTP is that an outbound request is limited to 10 seconds.

In order to protect from malware, an application cannot write to the file system. It can read files, but only those files that have been uploaded with the application code. In order to persist data between requests, the application must use the App Engine datastore, Memcached or other services.

The only events that can trigger an application are a web request or a scheduled ("cron") job. Furthermore, a request handler cannot spawn a sub-process or execute code after the response has been sent.

Although the environment comes with some limitations, it also provides a rich set of APIs. We saw the datastore functionality above, but there are additional library functions:

Authentication: Applications can interface with Google Accounts for user authentication. It can direct the user to sign in with a Google account and then access the email address and display name once the user has authenticated.

URL Fetch: Applications can request resources on the Internet, such as web pages, services or other data with the URL fetch service. It leverages the same page retrieval mechanism that Google uses for its own services.

Mail: Applications can send electronic messages using App Engine's mail service. The service uses Google mail transport system to send email messages.

Memcached: The Memcached service offers applications an in-memory key-value cache that is accessible by multiple instances of the application. It is useful for temporary data that does not need persistence and transactional features, such as a local cache of the datastore for high speed access.

Image Manipulation: The image manipulation allows the application to resize, crop, rotate and flip images in JPEG and PNG formats.

Scheduled Tasks: The cron service allows the user to schedule tasks that run at regular (e.g. daily or hourly) intervals. The application can even execute tasks that it added to a queue itself. For example, it might submit a background task while handling a request.

Task Queues: While cron jobs are good for periodic tasks they are not always reliable and do not perform well for high-volume, high-frequency workloads. Task queues (currently only released as an experimental feature for the Python runtime environment) on the other hand are very scalable, low-latency, reliable services processed on a first-in-first-out (FIFO) basis.

Blobstore*:* GQL Data Store items are limited to a maximum of 1MB. However, the Google Blobstore provides an effective alternative for serving larger chunks of data, such as images, audio, video or executable files. Blobstore values, or blobs, can hold a maximum of 2GB. The store provides details about the object including its content type and upload time. Given the lack of structure, there is no facility to edit a blob. However, it is possible to delete and re-create it.

XMPP API: The Extensible Messaging and Presence Protocol (XMPP) is a standardized instant-messaging (IM) protocol based on Jabber. It provides instant messaging, presence information, and contact list maintenance and has also been extended for use in VoIP (Voice over Internet Protocol) and file transfer signaling. App Engine supports the API, which can be useful as an alternative to email for time-sensitive communications, such as alerts. In this scenario, the recipient must actively use an XMPP client, like Google Talk or Jabber, and must add the application to their buddy list.

OpenID Authentication: OpenID is a standard for federated authentication. OpenID users can create an identity (username and password or other credentials including one-time passwords and biometrics) at any OpenID provider and use that same identity to authenticate to an App Engine Appliation if the developers have chosen to support OpenID as an authentication mechanism.

MapReduce: Although Google has been a pioneer in developing the MapReduce processing model, the App Engine implementation is currently only experimental and not complete. Nonetheless, the mapper provides a fast and efficient way to iterate over datastore entities and blob files.

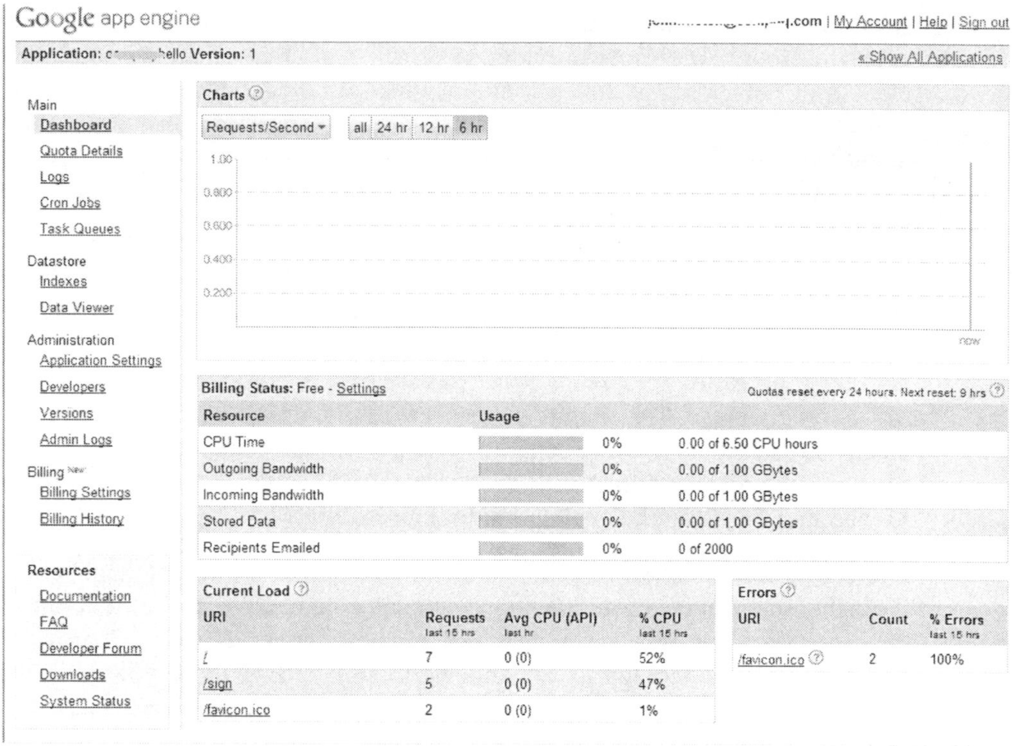

Figure 5-2: Google App Engine Console

Once development is complete and has been tested locally, the user can upload the file using tools from the SDK or the Google App Engine Launcher. The Administration Console (Figure 5-2) is a web-based interface that can then be used to create new applications, configure domain names, switch version of the application to be live, examine access and error logs, and browse an application's datastore.

Development Environment

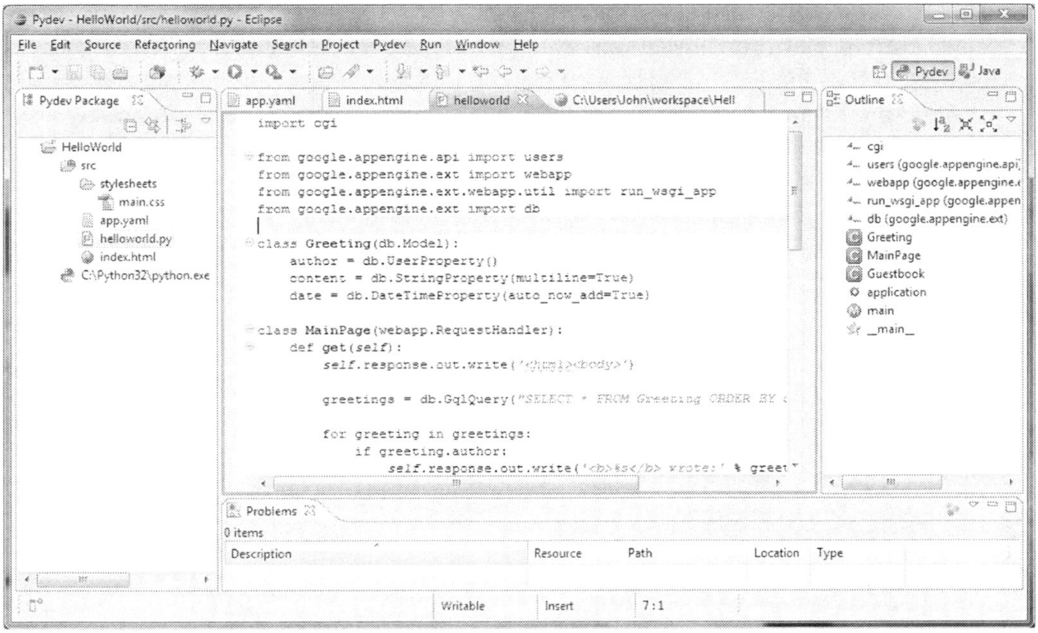

Figure 5-3: Pydev Plug-in for Eclipse

The Google App Engine SDK includes all the functionality needed to run applications locally with limited performance and data volumes. To maintain a simplified development environment, Google supports Eclipse for Java developers. There is no equivalent for Python. However, they do document how to install and configure the Pydev plug-in for the same results (Figure 5-3).

Practical Considerations

One of the key points of attraction of Google App Engine is that it is very easy to get started (for free) with simple applications. Google takes care of the entire system administration so the developer can focus on the end-user functionality. The SDK does include good management and performance profiling tools (appstats and admin console) if they are needed. Furthermore, as usage increases Google can scale the application seamlessly since App Engine is optimized for large numbers of users.

On the negative side, complicated workflows and processes may stretch the App Engine platform beyond its limits (which implies a steep learning curve for the developer). The data model needs to be designed to use the key/value store (DataStore), which is usually quite a transition for people who are used to relational databases. This can result in a front heavy development effort (especially for those coming from an SQL background) with a lot of work spent in data modeling before the usage of the real application can even be tried out.

Some current platform limitations also include the selection of languages and tools as well as the lack of integrated backup and archiving. The processing environment is unable to keep connections open to other services and the process lifetime is limited to 30 seconds. Moreover, the service has regular scheduled outages, where it goes to read only mode during business hours. It is possible to work around any of these restrictions, but it is additional work that must be factored into the design and selection decision.

Chapter 6

PLATFORM

Microsoft Windows Azure

Windows Azure is Microsoft's Platform-as-a-Service. Similar in concept to Google App Engine, it allows applications based on Microsoft technologies to be hosted and run from Microsoft data centers. Its fabric controller automatically manages resources, balances load, replicates for resilience and manages the application lifecycle.

Development Environment

To access the platform you typically use Visual Studio. Microsoft has made additional SDKs for Java and Ruby available to improve interoperability so there is no strict limitation to the .NET Framework. Eventually there should be some level of support for Java, Python, Ruby, PHP, OpenID and Eclipse. Nonetheless, you will have much more information and community support available if you keep to a native Microsoft implementation, at least to get started.

What this means is that a Visual Studio[1] developer must download and install both:

- The Windows Azure Software Development Kit
- Windows Azure Tools for Microsoft Visual Studio

---

[1] Supported on Visual Studio 2008 or higher

PLATFORM

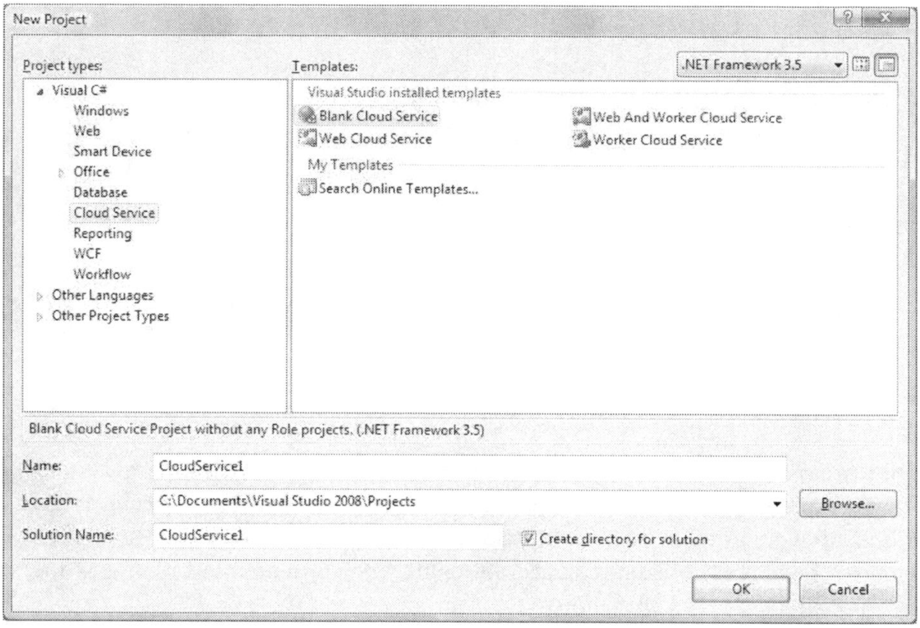

Figure 6-1: Visual Studio Cloud Service

After installing these components, a new set of solution templates appears in Visual Studio, called Cloud Service (Figure 6-1). These are similar to the Visual Studio Web project types but are tailored to Azure.

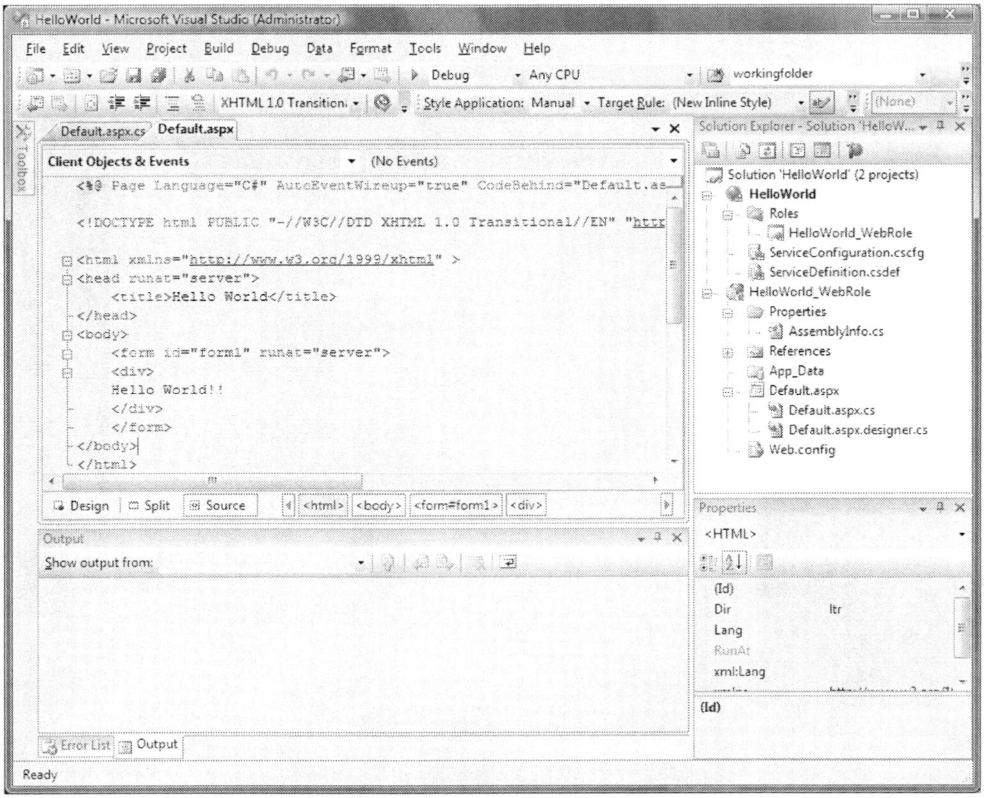

PLATFORM

Figure 6-2: Visual Studio Azure Page

As shown in Figure 6-2, the simplest applications consist of a few lines of an .ASPX page along with a class structure in a .NET language such as C#.

The developer can test applications locally (on port 81) until they are ready and then publish the solution to Azure. To support the testing phase, the SDK simulates the cloud offering with a development fabric and storage, called Dev Fabric and Dev Storage. While these are both essential for any local debugging, it should be clear that they lack the full infrastructure for exhaustive testing.

In particular, it is impossible to perform load or performance testing of the application. Similarly, any interfaces to the local environment or machine may behave differently on the Azure platform and will need to be retested in the cloud.

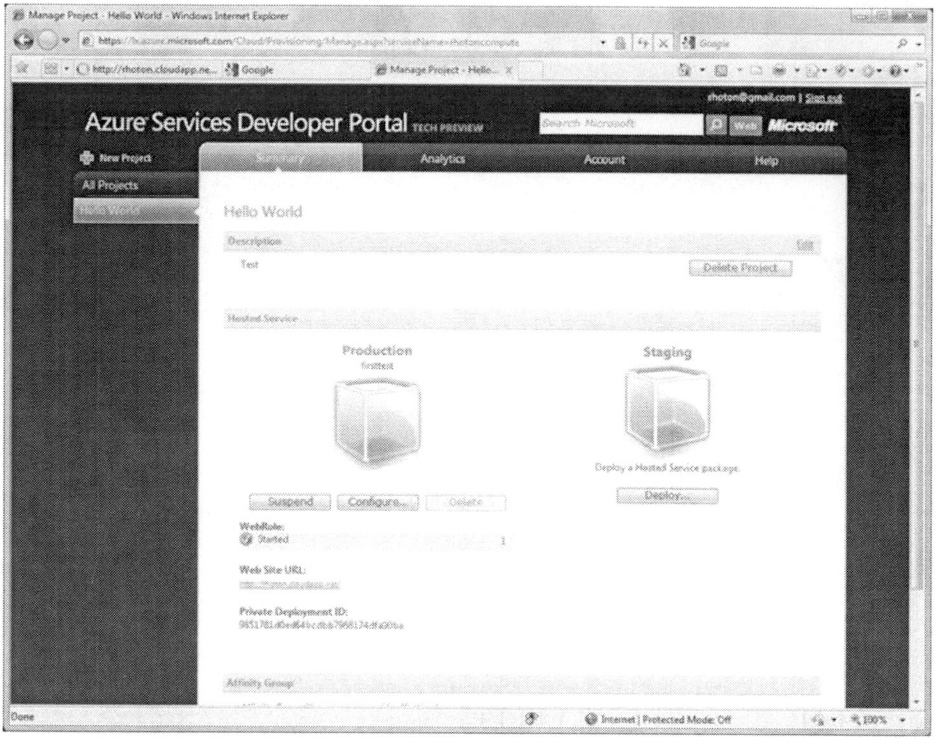

PLATFORM

Figure 6-3: Azure Services Developer Portal

Once the application has been tested locally, it can be uploaded to Azure through Visual Studio and then managed through the Azure Services Developer Portal (Figure 6-3). It offers facilities to stage the application before deploying it publicly. Users can also suspend instances when they are not needed and restart them at a later time.

Azure Platform

The Windows Azure platform is built as a distributed service hosted in Microsoft data centers and built on a special-purpose operating system called Windows Azure. It is implemented as three components: Compute, Storage and a Fabric to manage the platform.

The *Compute* instances are exposed to the customer as role types that specify tailored configurations for typical purposes. The Web Role instances generally interact with the end user. They may host web sites and other front-end code. On the other hand, Worker Role instances cater to background tasks similar to Google App Engine cron jobs.

While Web and Worker role types are the most popular, Windows Azure provides additional templates for specific needs. For example, the CGI web role supports the FastCGI protocol and thereby enables other programming languages including PHP, Ruby, Python and Java. The WCF (Windows Communications Foundation) service is a web role that facilitates support of WCF services. Azure now also provides an infrastructure service, in the form of a VM Role, which accepts the upload of a Windows Server 2008 R2 Virtual Machine Image.

For each service role, the developer can specify static configuration settings such as the end-point (URL), the number of instances and the size (indicated in number of cores and amount of memory and disk space). Load balancers will automatically distribute the incoming traffic to the full set of running instances. It is also possible to inspect and update the configuration using the Service Runtime and Service Management APIs, for example to implement auto-scaling based on computational load.

Azure *Storage* provides services that host three kinds of data:

- Blobs
- Tables
- Queue

A blob is simply a stream of unstructured (or at least opaque) data. It can be a picture, a file or anything else the application needs. There is a four-level hierarchy of blob storage. At the highest level is a storage account, which is the root of the namespace for the blobs. Each account can hold multiple containers, which provide groupings (e.g. similar permissions or metadata). Within a container can be many blobs. Each can be uniquely identified and may hold up to 50GB. In order to optimize uploads and downloads (especially for very large files) it is possible to break a blob into blocks. Each transfer request therefore refers to a smaller portion of data (e.g. 4MB) making the transaction less vulnerable to transient network errors.

Tables are used for structured data. As you might expect from the name, they typically hold a set of homogenous rows (called entities) that are defined by a set of columns (called properties). Each property is defined by a name and type (e.g. String, Binary, Int). Despite the conceptual similarity there are important distinctions to make between Windows Azure storage tables and relational tables. Azure does not enforce a schema nor does it support SQL as a query language. While this may lead to portability challenges for many legacy applications, Microsoft's strategy is similar to that of Google and reflects the importance of ensuring the new technology is optimized for the scalability requirements of cloud-based services.

Queues provide a mechanism for applications to communicate and coordinate asynchronously. This is an important requirement when applications are geographically distributed over high-latency links. Synchronous communication can severely degrade performance and introduces stability risks that must be mini-mized. Like Blobs and Tables, Queues are associated with a Storage Account. They hold a linear set of XML messages. There is no limit to the number of messages per queue but they typically will be removed from the queue if they are not processed within seven days (or earlier if requested).

PLATFORM

Similar to Amazon S3, it is possible to specify a region for any storage require-ments in order to ensure compliance with local data privacy laws and minimize latency between applications and users. If performance is critical, the Azure CDN (Content Delivery Network) also provides distributed delivery of static content from Azure Storage from Microsoft's worldwide network of data cen-ters.

The *Fabric*, in Azure terminology, refers to a set of machines running the Azure operating system that are collectively managed and generally co-located in the same region. The Fabric Controller is the layer of code that provisions all the user instances (web and worker roles) and performs any necessary upgrades. It also monitors the applications, re-provisioning and reallocating resources as needed to ensure that all services remain healthy.

Azure Services

Azure also provides a set of services that can be consumed both from the Inter-net (including the Azure platform itself) and on-premise applications.

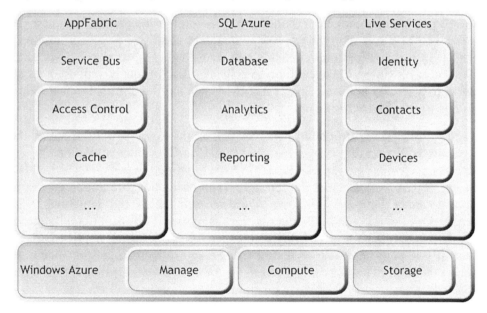

Figure 6-4: Azure Services

As shown in Figure 6-4, the main Azure services can be loosely categorized as:

- AppFabric

- SQL Azure

- Live Services

Azure applications can also access a set of Microsoft SharePoint and Microsoft Dynamics CRM services.

AppFabric provides a cloud-oriented service framework that is available through REST, SOAP, Atom/AtomPub and WS-*

- Microsoft .NET Service Bus

- Microsoft .NET Access Control Service

- Windows Azure AppFabric Cache

The purpose of the Service Bus is to relay connectivity between systems. When two applications share a Local Area Network, they can usually communicate directly. However, in a cloud environment physical adjacency cannot be guaranteed. Firewalls, NAT, Mobile IP, Dynamic DNS, and other advanced network components can make it difficult to maintain connectivity or even addressability. The Service Bus provides proxy connections where direct connectivity is difficult or impossible.

The Access Control Service authenticates and authorizes users, relying on Windows Live ID and other user account stores such as corporate Active Directories or federated identity management systems. An administration portal allows service owners to define the rules that grant access and authorization rights.

The AppFabric Cache delivers a distributed, in-memory, cache service for Windows Azure and SQL Azure applications. Similar to Memcached, it improves performance and scalability. It is also possible to enable a high availability option that ensures all data is replicated to multiple servers.

SQL Azure is relational storage that should not be confused with Azure Storage described above. It is essentially SQL Server offered as a cloud service. As such, it lacks the massive scalability potential of Azure Storage. (It can handle up to 10GB per database). However, it provides all the benefits of SQL including transactional integrity and powerful multi-table analysis. SQL Azure Reporting also extends the capabilities of SQL Server Reporting Services to SQL Azure with facilities to create reports with charts, maps, gauges and sparklines. But perhaps the most compelling argument in its favor is that it is easy to integrate with legacy (SQL) code.

Live Services provide a set of building blocks that can be used to handle user data and application resources including Identity and Contacts. These include Windows Live Messenger, Live Search and Maps.

At the foundation of the services is the Live Framework, or LiveMesh, which offers data synchronization across multiple devices using FeedSync (RSS extensions). They offer several benefits in terms of extending the reach of client devices accessible from the cloud and creating an integrated, comprehensive and consistent view of user data.

PLATFORM

Practical Considerations

Microsoft is a clear leader in both the consumer and enterprise software space. They also have a very complete cloud offering that includes all layers of the infrastructure, platform and software stack. This combination makes them a solid proposition that entails little risk of failure.

The community that will be most attracted to the Azure platform is the set of developers who have invested heavily in .NET technologies and would like to take this expertise into the cloud. Likewise services that can benefit from hooks into other Microsoft products, such as Windows or Office, are likely to find better support from Azure than elsewhere.

By the same token, software that is geared toward open-source and industry-dominant languages, such as Java, Python or Ruby, may prefer to build on other platforms. That is not to say that they cannot reside on Azure – and there may be good reason to include a few non-Microsoft modules in an Azure solution. However, an application that is built from the ground up on another technology will not be able to leverage Microsoft's advantages and may find better support in another environment.

Chapter 7

Amazon Web Services

The de facto standard for infrastructure services is Amazon. They are not unique in their offerings yet virtually all IaaS services are either complements to Amazon Web Services (AWS) or else considered competitors to them. AWS includes a rich set of cloud services. In fact, the set is so complete that some people like to consider AWS a platform service. Amazon's announcement of the Elastic Beanstalk further strengthens this perspective.

We don't want to split hairs on terminology, but the main distinction between AWS and a more typical platform service is that Amazon doesn't establish a particular run-time environment. You can use one of their pre-build machine images but you are not limited to those and can run almost any platform in their environment. A corollary to this observation is that while Amazon provides means of managing and distributing virtual machines they do not directly provide specific capability to manage applications.

Figure 7-1 gives an overview of some of the main services that are available from AWS. As you can see, the offering is very broad. There are many options for computation, storage, integration and scalability, not to mention functions for management and billing that are not even represented on the diagram.

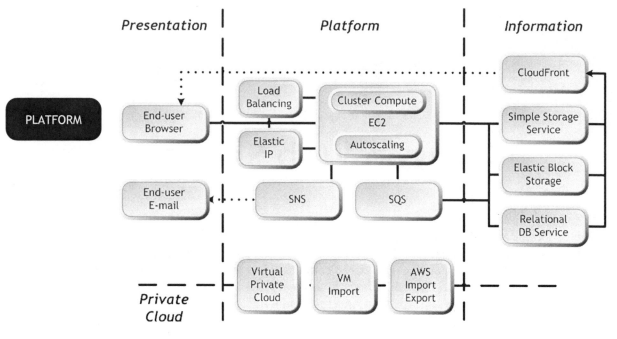

Figure 7-1: AWS Architecture

To help Amazon Web Services novices, we have tried to assemble the elements into one conceptual framework. However, although they are portrayed here in unified form, keep in mind that it is possible to consume almost every Amazon service independently of the others.

Computation

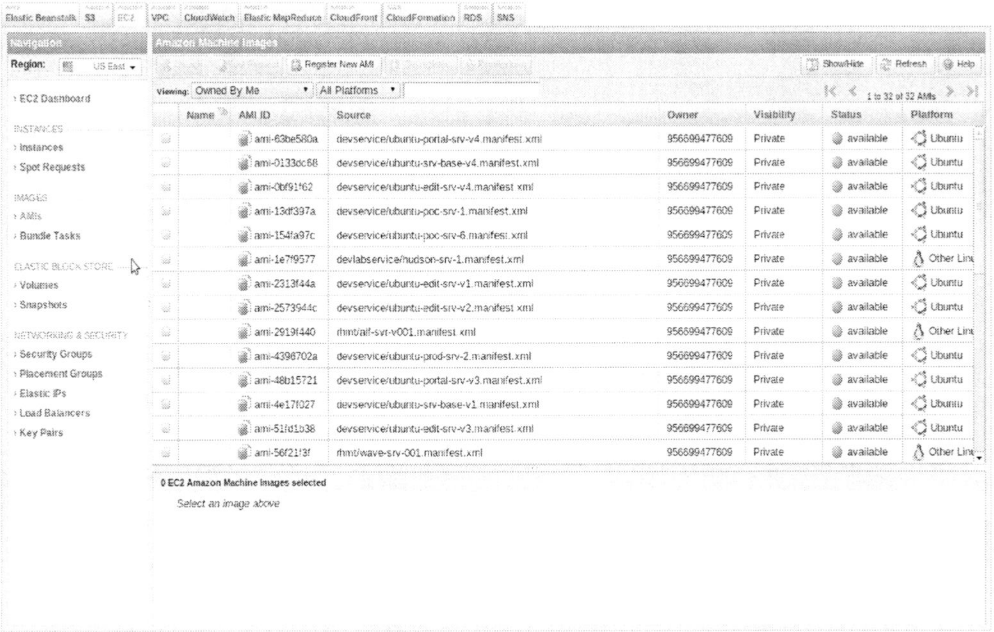

Figure 7-2: Amazon EC2

The core component of AWS is the Elastic Compute Cloud (EC2) and its supplementary storage services. EC2 offers the user a choice of virtual machine templates that can be instantiated in a shared and virtualized environment (Figure 7-2). Each virtual machine is called an Amazon Machine Image (AMI). The customer can use pre-packaged AMIs from Amazon and 3rd parties, or they can build their own. Images vary in resources (RAM, compute units, local disk size), operating systems (Several Windows versions and many Linux distributions) and the application frameworks that are installed on them (e.g. JBoss, MySQL, Oracle).

The Amazon AMIs do not have any persistent storage but they can be used for logs, results and interim data while the instance is active. Since the locally mounted disks of AMIs are lost between instantiations, Amazon also offers two persistent storage capabilities: The Simple Storage Service (S3) and Elastic Block Storage (EBS).

Storage

Simple Storage Service

S3 is an opaque storage service accessible through both REST and SOAP APIs. It offers distributed, redundant buckets that are replicated with Amazon's

CloudFront content delivery network across Europe, Asia and the United States. S3 can accommodate data sizes from a single byte to 5TB and provides permissions for controlling access based on Amazon Web Services authentication.

Elastic Block Storage

PLATFORM

The Elastic Block Storage is intended as a high-performance virtual hard disk. It can be formatted as a file system and then mounted on any EC2 instance. The size can range from 1GB to 1TB. Amazon also provides a mechanism to store an EBS snapshot in S3 for long-term durability.

Simple DB

The Amazon Simple DB (SDB) is available for more structured data. It does not use a schema but instead defines "domains" with items that consist of up to 256 attributes and values. The values can contain anywhere from one byte to one kilobyte. It also supports simple operators such as: =, !=, <, >, <=, >=, STARTS-WITH, AND, OR, NOT, INTERSECTION, UNION. So, most common queries are possible as long as they are confined to a single domain.

Relational Database Service

Amazon Relational Database Service (Amazon RDS) is a web service with functions to set up, operate, and scale a relational database in the cloud. It provides resizable capacity while managing database administration tasks.

Amazon RDS gives the capabilities of a MySQL database with future support of Oracle announced. This means the code, applications, and tools used with existing MySQL databases work seamlessly with Amazon RDS. Amazon RDS automatically patches the database software and backs up the database, storing the backups for a user-defined retention period and enabling point-in-time recovery. Customers can scale the computational resources or storage capacity associated with a relational database instance via an API call. In addition, Amazon RDS facilitates replication to enhance availability and reliability for production databases and to enable horizontal scale out.

CloudFront

Amazon CloudFront is a web service for content delivery. It delivers static and streaming content using a global network of edge locations. Requests for objects are automatically routed to the nearest edge location, so content is delivered with the lowest latency. Amazon CloudFront is optimized to work with other Amazon Web Services, like S3 and EC2, but also works with origin server hosted by other providers.

In Amazon CloudFront, objects are organized into distributions. A distribution specifies the location of the original version of the objects. It can carry a unique

CloudFront.net domain name (e.g. abc123.cloudfront.net) or map a proprietary domain (e.g. images.example.com).

Distributions can be defined that either download definitive content from the origin server using the HTTP or HTTPS protocols, or stream the content using the RTMP protocol. After registering the distribution with CloudFront (either through the console or an API call) all end-user requests for objects using this domain name are automatically routed to the nearest edge location for high performance delivery of the content.

PLATFORM

Integration

One key differentiator of AWS, compared with many infrastructure and hosting providers, is its rich set of integration services that enable network and application connectivity and support the application lifecycle.

Elastic IP Addresses

Elastic IP addresses are static IP addresses designed for dynamic cloud computing. An Elastic IP address is associated with an account rather than a particular instance. Unlike traditional static IP addresses, Elastic IP addresses can mask instance failures by programmatically remapping public IP addresses to any instance in an account, which takes effect immediately in contrast to a DNS update that needs to propagate to all the end users.

Simple Queue Service

The Simple Queue Service (SQS) provides an unlimited number of queues and messages with message sizes up to 8 KB. The customer can create queues and send messages. Any authorized applications can then receive and/or delete the messages. Since the messages remain in the system for up to four days, they provide a good mechanism for asynchronous communications between applications.

Simple Notification Service

Applications that require publish/subscribe messaging functionality can use Simple Notification Service (SNS). SNS is a distributed and redundant service that enables applications, end-users, and devices to send and receive notifications from the cloud. The service works on specified topics, which are Universal Resource Identifiers (URIs) that specify communication channels based on content or event types. Any web server, email address or SQS queue can subscribe to notification messages associated with a particular topic. Similarly, authorized publishers can post messages to the channel and they will automatically be delivered to all subscribers.

Virtual Private Cloud

Recently, Amazon has begun to target corporate customers with more sophisticated offerings. The Virtual Private Cloud initially provides a means for enterprises to extend their private data center offerings into Amazon's cloud in a secure and reliable fashion. In simple terms, it is a virtual private network permitting secure transparent network connectivity between systems on a corporate Intranet and EC2.

VM Import

VM Import is a facility for customers to import virtual machine images from their existing environment into Amazon EC2. In addition to migrating or extending applications into the public cloud this option is also used as a mechanism for Disaster Recovery.

Customers can use the Amazon EC2 API tools to point to a virtual machine (VM) image and specify which Availability Zone and instance type to run in Amazon EC2. VM Import will then automatically transfer the image file, migrate the image and create the instance.

Although the service is currently limited to VMware VMDK images for Windows Server 2008 SP2, Amazon appears to be planning additional support in the near future.

AWS Import/Export

AWS Import/Export accelerates moving large amounts of data into and out of AWS by bypassing the Internet with portable storage devices for transport. This service may be of interest for data migration, content distribution, offsite backup and disaster recovery.

To import data, the customer simply prepares a portable disk, securely identifies the device with a signature file and ships it to the Amazon facility. Similarly, Amazon can store a snapshot of any AWS data on physical media and ship it to the customer upon request.

Scalability

In addition to integration services, Amazon also caters to enterprise needs for elastic computing with capabilities to scale both vertically and horizontally.

High Performance Computing

The Amazon EC2 Cluster Compute and Cluster GPU instance types are specifically designed to combine high compute and networking performance for HPC applications that utilize protocols like Message Passing Interface (MPI) for tightly coupled inter-node communication. These instances can be configured as clusters with up to 128 nodes with low latency and 10 Gbps bandwidth between them. Cluster sizes up through and above 128 instances are supported.

Customers can also specify the processor architecture so that developers can tune and compile their applications for the specific processor and thereby further optimize performance.

Elastic Load Balancing

Elastic Load Balancing distributes incoming traffic for a given service across multiple Amazon EC2 instances in order to spread the load and maximize the efficiency of each system. Load balancing also leads to greater fault tolerance, since it detects unhealthy instances within a pool and reroutes traffic to healthy instances until the unhealthy instances have been restored.

Customers can enable Elastic Load Balancing within a single Availability Zone or across multiple zones for improved worldwide performance. They can configure any load balancing groups and health checks through APIs, a Command Line or the console.

The service supports sticky sessions, SSL termination and a variety of application protocols including HTTP and HTTPS. It integrates with other Amazon web services such as CloudWatch by providing metrics including request count and latency and also scales its request handling capacity in response to incoming application traffic.

Auto Scaling

Amazon Auto Scaling is particularly well suited for applications that experience hourly, daily, or weekly variability in usage. It ensures that the number of EC2 instances increases seamlessly during demand spikes to maintain performance, and decreases automatically during demand lulls to minimize costs.

Amazon provides tools to define triggers (for example, based on CPU utilization) for adding and removing EC2 instances. It is not dependent on the Elastic Load Balancing service but can be effectively combined with it to ensure a given number of healthy instances for a particular service.

Elastic MapReduce

Amazon Elastic MapReduce is a web service that enables businesses and researchers to process very large amounts of data. It is based on a hosted Hadoop framework running on the Amazon Elastic Compute Cloud (Amazon EC2) and Amazon Simple Storage Service (Amazon S3).

As we shall see later in this book, Hadoop initially divides the dataset into smaller chunks that are processed in parallel (the "map" function) and then combines the intermediate data into the final solution (the "reduce" function). Amazon S3 serves as both the source for the input data being analyzed and as the output destination for the end results.

Amazon Elastic MapReduce supports SQL-like tools, such as Hive and Pig as well as many programming languages including C++, Cascading, Java, Perl, PHP, Python, R, or Ruby.

PLATFORM

Management

The primary interface for managing AWS applications is the AWS Management Console. However, it is also possible to connect directly to the instances, for example through SSH or HTTP and interact directly with them. In addition, the console service management can be configured programmatically through APIs and command-line tools that run inside, or outside, the Amazon cloud.

The console is certainly the first place to start since it provides convenient management of your compute, storage and other cloud resources. You can enable Multi-Factor Authentication if security is a significant concern. Typically the first function of the console is to subscribe to all relevant services and then deploy the application by creating machine instances, allocating storage and defining connectivity. There are also screens to configure settings for most of the AWS offerings and options to monitor instances, take storage snapshots, manage job and view real-time metrics.

CloudFormation

AWS CloudFormation gives customers the option to collect related AWS resources in a so-called stack and provision them in an orderly and predictable fashion. A stack includes Amazon services such EC2 instances, security groups, SQS queues, RDS instances, load balancers and auto-scaling groups.

There are default templates for content management, collaboration, project management, code review and other common applications. These can be configured and customized with sizing and connectivity parameters. It is also possible to create and use completely new sets of templates to describe the resources, along with any associated dependencies or runtime parameters, required to run the application.

CloudWatch

Amazon CloudWatch is a web service that provides monitoring for AWS cloud resources. The AWS Management Console displays the real-time information in graph format, but data is also accessible through CloudWatch Command Line Tools and APIs.

The service gives visibility into EC2 resource utilization and performance through metrics such as CPU utilization, disk reads and writes, and network traffic. These numbers can be aggregated by Auto Scaling Group and Elastic Load Balancer. There is reporting for other entities, such as request count and latency of Load Balancers, read/write latency for EBS volumes and freeable memory of RDS DB instances.

AWS Ecosystem

Finally, it is worth noting that Amazon's services are not necessarily self-sufficient. AWS has spawned a whole ecosystem of products that fill in any gaps that Amazon may have left open. Specifically, there are several services that help to manage established infrastructure providers. Elastra, RightScale and enStratus, for example, offer front ends to managing Amazon EC2 as well as other IaaS offerings.

Billing

One last area of EC2 differentiation is its support for monetization. Amazon has long fostered a strong ecosystem in its marketplace and exposes some of those financial services to its developers.

Flexible Payments Service

Amazon Flexible Payments Service (FPS) is a service that Amazon has created for developers, which leverages Amazon's sophisticated retail billing system. The customers can use the same identities, shipping details and payment information as they would for ordering directly with Amazon.

DevPay

Amazon DevPay is an online billing and account management service supporting applications that are built on Amazon Web Services. It utilizes Amazon's authentication and settlement framework to manage customer subscriptions and billing for Amazon EC2 Machine Images (AMIs) or applications that use Amazon S3.

DevPay automatically tracks end-customers' usage of AWS services, calculates their bills based on the prices the developer has set, and ensures only paying customers have access to the application. The service owner can charge customers one-time or recurring monthly fees, or instead meter the usage and calculate charges on a utility basis.

Elastic Beanstalk

Building your own platform on Amazon Web Services can be an attractive option if you require a maximum of flexibility and control. It is possible to select system parameters such as server size, operating system and memory allocation for greatest efficiency. You can choose any programming languages or run-time environments and complement them with commercial software and middleware.

Amazon Web Services is also much further along the experience curve than most other cloud providers so customers can benefit from the robustness and maturity of the offering. For those that need additional reliability or isolation the Amazon VPC provides a premium service that can satisfy many enterprise requirements.

The main challenges of AWS directly relate to its benefits. Full flexibility and control imply a lack of standardization and automation. The onus is on the customer to develop and support the run-time environment and to keep it current with all the necessary application updates. It is also up to the application to set load thresholds and initiate new instances as they are needed.

At the time of writing, it appears that Amazon also has intentions that target the more typical platform-as-a-service market. Elastic Beanstalk is still undergoing beta testing. As such, it is premature to try to gauge its success and impact on Amazon's cloud offerings. However, it is certainly worth considering and tracking.

The first release of Elastic Beanstalk targets Java developers and is built on the Apache Tomcat software stack. The customer can upload any standard Java Web Application Archive (WAR file) to the Elastic Beanstalk using the AWS Management Console, the AWS Toolkit for Eclipse, the web service APIs or the Command Line Tools.

Elastic Beanstalk is really just a package of AWS resources. In fact, Amazon only bills for the resources and doesn't charge for the Elastic Beanstalk itself. You could therefore accomplish the same objectives with your own EC2 images running Tomcat. However, the Elastic Beanstalk facilitates the process and also handles the provisioning, load balancing and scaling of its applications. It automates a simple default configuration, which developers can fine-tune to handle advanced requirements.

Practical Considerations

Amazon is the undisputed market leader in infrastructure services, which was their initial focus and continues to be their source of strength. Over the past few years, they have gradually worked their way into the platform layer with a very broad set of services. Even though their intention has been clear for some time, it was with the announcement of the Elastic Beanstalk that it became unambiguous.

AWS is most interesting for organizations and solutions that have similar requirements. If you have a need for a strong suite of infrastructure services where you can install your own platforms but also require a solid platform service, then Amazon can fit the bill. They have attained a level of reliability that is admirable and offer premium service levels that are attractive to critical services.

PLATFORM

At the same time, Amazon may be overkill for very small solutions that can find more cost-effective services elsewhere. Similarly, services that have very specific platform demands, relating to languages, tools and configurations, may find that another provider offers a better match.

Chapter 8

Other Platform Options

A large number of cloud applications are based on the services of Google, Microsoft and Amazon. As illustrated in Figure 8-1, they each have a rich set of offerings that span the spectrum from Infrastructure to Platform services.

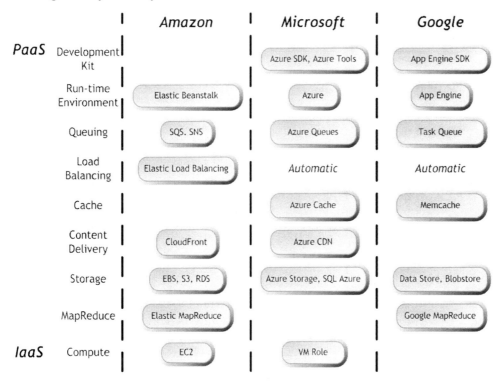

Figure 8-1: Amazon, Microsoft, Google - Compared

However, these three are not the only platform providers. The landscape is very dynamic with vendors constantly redefining their offerings so that an extensive analysis, or even an exhaustive list, of the options would be pointless. To help give you a clearer picture and stimulate your imagination, we briefly characterized a few vendors and delivery mechanisms.

Some of the choices include:

PLATFORM

- Private Cloud

- Partner Cloud

- Rackspace

- Engine Yard

- Intuit

- Facebook

We hope that they, in addition to Google, Microsoft and Amazon, are somewhat representative of your choices and will help you as you assess the platform options that might make sense for your needs.

Private Cloud

The choice to host your applications in a private data center gives you the most control and flexibility. After you install Apache or Microsoft IIS on the hardware of your choice with any web frameworks you need, you can upload applications developed in your own environment.

You can choose your programming language and have complete freedom to implement any interfaces that may be necessary to connect to legacy or partner systems. It is only a matter of installing PHP, Python/Django, Ruby/Rails or a complete set of Java tools.

The biggest drawback is that you don't automatically gain any benefits related to cloud computing. You can replicate many of the advantages internally, but it requires significant effort as well as a level of investment that may only be realistic for large enterprises.

For those that do decide to implement a private cloud, there are tools, product and services that can be instrumental to attaining benefits in performance, utilization and automation. We will briefly cover a few of them.

VMware

VMware's cloud-oriented activity comes largely under the umbrella of its vCloud initiative. It represents a set of enabling technologies including vSphere, the vCloud API and the vCloud service provider ecosystem.

The *vSphere* platform, VMware's flagship product, is a virtualization framework that is capable of managing large pools of infrastructure, including software and hardware both from internal and external networks.

The *vCloud API* is a RESTful interface for providing and consuming virtual resources in the cloud. It enables deployment and management of virtualized workloads in private, public and hybrid clouds. The API enables the upload, download, instantiation, deployment and operation of virtual appliances (vApps), networks and "virtual datacenters". The two major components in vCloud API are the User API, focused on vApp provisioning, and the Admin API, focused on platform/tenant administration.

PLATFORM

The *vCloud service provider ecosystem* is a common set of cloud computing services for businesses and service providers – with support for any application or OS and the ability to choose where applications live, on or off premise. It is delivered by service providers, such as Terremark and Hosting.com, and includes a set of applications available as virtual Appliances.

Beyond these infrastructure-oriented offerings, VMware vFabric offers a viable private platform service. It combines the Spring Java development framework with a set of integrated services including an application server, data management, cloud-ready messaging, load balancing and performance management.

Joyent

Joyent offers infrastructure services for both public and private cloud deployments as wells as their own web application development platform. For their infrastructure services, they use the term 'Accelerators' to refer to their persistent virtual machines. They run OpenSolaris with Apache, Nginx, MySQL, PHP, Ruby on Rails and Java pre-installed and the ability to add other packages. A feature called "automatic CPU bursting" provides reactive elasticity.

Joyent also offers a private version of their framework called CloudControl for enterprise data centers. Cloud Control is software that runs on top of your existing hardware, or on new dedicated machines. Cloud Control manages physical networking equipment and virtualized compute instances that are hosted within traditional physical servers and storage servers.

Nirvanix

Nirvanix CloudNAS is a storage service that enterprises can implement internally to achieve cloud benefits in the areas of compliance, performance and availability. The service is exposed as a virtual mount point for Linux and Windows. In addition to a high level of scalability, it ensures dual/triple replication and allows zone specification (e.g. data should reside in the EU only).

Eucalyptus

Eucalyptus ("Elastic Utility Computing Architecture for Linking Your Programs To Useful Systems") is an open-source equivalent to Amazon Web Services that offers roughly compatible interfaces. It is developed and supported by a company that is also called Eucalyptus. They make the software available as a source package, RPM, and a Rocks disk image. It is also shipped with Ubuntu 9.04 and higher as the default cloud computing tool.

Eucalyptus might be interesting for customers who either need to replicate the functionality of AWS internally or simply want to avoid being locked in to Amazon. By combining an internal Eucalyptus infrastructure with AWS, it is possible to create a hybrid environment where workloads can be shifted internally and externally depending on resource utilization and business requirements.

Flexiscale

Flexiscale is an infrastructure service provider comparable to Amazon EC2 or Rackspace Cloud (discussed later). Similar to its competition, it supports Linux and Windows operating systems and facilitates self-provisioning of Cloud servers via the Control Panel or API. Customers can start, stop and delete instances and change memory, CPU, Storage and Network addresses of cloud servers.

They offer extensive firewall rules based on IP addresses and protocols, and each customer has their own dedicated VLAN. Unlike some IaaS providers, their virtual machines offer persistent storage, which is based on a virtualized high-end Storage Area Network.

In addition to Flexiscale, Flexiant also offers a licensed virtualized platform, called Extility, for customers to build their own cloud or sell cloud services under their own brand. A control panel portal is available, as well as an API, to allow end users to provision, stop, start and delete virtual dedicated servers, as well as to resize their memory and storage.

Partner Cloud

A similar solution to a private cloud might be to enlist the services of an outsourcing partner, such as IBM, HP, or UNISYS. Since outsourcing is primarily an enterprise offering, the solutions provide a high degree of isolation and privacy. They also accommodate stringent service levels and an allowance for customization that is typically not available in the public cloud.

They will typically use some of the software and services of a private cloud. In addition, they often leverage a broad set of management tools and considerable experience in consolidation, standardization and automation. Their differentiation in these areas, along with a significant economy of scale, allow them to create a compelling value proposition to enterprises. They may be much more expensive than public cloud offerings due to the enhanced service levels and customization options they offer. Nonetheless, they represent significant potential for costs savings for many enterprises.

The implications of using an outsourcing partner for developing a cloud architecture need not be great. The same products and technical infrastructure could underpin a private or partner implementation. However, it is very important to ensure the contracts and service agreements are compatible with the preferred choice of development tools and run-time services. If the partner excludes these tools, for example in an effort to maximize standardization, then they are no longer viable. On the other hand, it is quite possible that a large outsourcing partner would be able to support a larger array of platform option than many customers could provide on their own.

Rackspace Cloud

The Rackspace Cloud was formerly called Mosso, which is a label still frequently seen in the press to reference its services. It is an infrastructure and platform provider with three primary offerings: Cloud Servers, Cloud Files and Cloud Sites.

The Rackspace Cloud is perhaps best known through its Cloud Servers as an IaaS provider with many managed hosting options in addition to virtual servers offerings covering a number of Linux distributions (such as Ubuntu, Fedora, Centos and RedHat Enterprise Linux) as well as Windows Server 2008. It has a large pool of dedicated IP addresses and offers persistent storage on all instances.

The servers run on quad-core CPUs with RAID-10 disk storage and are managed with a custom control panel that provides server statistics as well as management of DNS and snapshots. The Cloud Servers API allows programmatic access to create, configure, and control Cloud Servers from within customer applications. The interface uses a REST-based format supporting both XML and JSON data types.

Cloud Files is similar to Amazon S3 with access through a REST API. It provides containers for static content which can be replicated via the Limelight content delivery network to over 50 edge data centers. Cloud Files is optimized for:

- Backups/archives
- Serving images/videos (streaming data to the user's browser)
- Secondary/tertiary, web-accessible storage
- Scenarios where amount of storage is difficult to predict

Cloud Sites represent fully managed platforms that can host Windows .NET or a complete LAMP (Linux, Apache, MySQL, Perl/Python/PHP) stack and would typically qualify as a PaaS offering. Access to the platform is supported through File Transfer Protocol (FTP) and Secure File Transfer Protocol (SFTP).

GoGrid

PLATFORM

GoGrid is an infrastructure service provider that offers preinstalled images of Windows and Linux with Apache, IIS, MySQL and several other applications. Although GoGrid's services are not as broad a Amazon's there is still some opportunity to use them as a cloud-based platform. MyGSI is a semi-automated process for creating, editing, saving, and deploying a GoGrid Server Image (GSI). A GSI is a Golden Image and contains pre-configured and customized applications, as well as the server operating system.

GoGrid Cloud Storage is a file-level backup service for Windows and Linux cloud servers running in the GoGrid cloud. Windows and Linux cloud servers mount the storage using a secure private network and common transfer protocols to move data to and from the Cloud Storage device.

GoGrid Cloud Storage supports other interface mechanisms such as Secure Copy (SCP), FTP, Samba and rsync. For large data sets GoGrid will perform a manual transfer of a physical hard drive into GoGrid's Cloud Storage – in other words, the customer can transfer data to an external hard drive and mail it to GoGrid.

GoGrid API provides programmatic communication for controlling GoGrid's control panel functionality. Typical API use cases include auto-scaling cloud server networks, listing assigned public and private IP addresses, deleting cloud servers and listing billing details.

F5 Load balancing can spread internet traffic across two or more servers. In the event a server crashes, the load balancer will redirect all traffic to the remaining online servers preventing application downtime. If a web application sees a drastic increase in internet traffic adding additional servers to the load balancer ensures the servers will not crash due to an overload of incoming HTTP requests.

The following load balancing algorithms and persistence settings are supported:

- Round Robin
- Sticky Session
- SSL Least Connect
- Source address

GoGrid Dedicated Servers is a virtual private cloud offering that allows users to connect GoGrid cloud infrastructure with a separate dedicated infrastructure, within a private network.

Engine Yard

Engine Yard Cloud provides a Ruby on Rails technology stack, including web, application and database servers, monitoring and process management. The Linux distribution is optimized for Rails and includes in-memory cache.

PLATFORM

Security Updates: All components are monitored for security issues and updated as vulnerabilities are discovered and patched.

Monitoring & Alerting: Engine Yard Cloud tracks resource utilization for the application and alerts users when they need additional capacity, or the application is performing poorly. Storage, CPU and memory utilization levels are tracked for conformance to pre-configured thresholds, and email alerts provide warnings. Engine Yard Cloud also monitors essential services, including configurable application URLs, and sends alerts when there is any unexpected downtime.

Application Cloning: It is relatively easy to clone (or shut down) a full production environment even if it is running across many different instances with multiple volumes and databases. Cloning is a particular benefit in the application development lifecycle since there is no need to maintain a persistent staging environment.

Auto Deploy-From-Source: Engine Yard integrates with source code management. Special comments in the source code check-in can trigger deployment to a staging or test environment.

Application Capacity Management: Capacity management is application aware. Additional system instances automatically deploy with the correct application configuration and join a selected load-balanced group.

Application Templates: Application templates encapsulate source code, Ruby gems, Linux packages and other configuration information.

Extensible Configurations: Engine Yard supports recipes that extend the configuration management system. A configuration recipe is a Ruby-based domain specific language that indicates installation and configuration steps for any package.

Replicated Database Tier: Engine Yard Cloud provides a means to scale out by adding database read replicas, which can be used to perform complex analytics, backups and maintain high availability without sacrificing application performance.

Utility Tier: If web applications require specialized components outside of the application and database tier, the customer can create a utility instance tier and associate configuration recipes with it. For example, they can add new servers to do repeatable deployments of custom applications or to off-load complex processing to dedicated servers.

Salesforce.com

Heroku is another cloud application platform for Ruby. It is a managed multi-tenant platform and hosting environment. Following an acquisition in 2010 it is now owned by Salesforce.com.

Each service consists of one or more dynos, or web processes running code and responding to HTTP requests. Additionally, background processes called workers process jobs from a queue, similar to Google's Task Queue. On the storage side, customers can choose between a relatively low-cost shared database (typically used for testing and staging) and a series of dedicated databases scaling up to 68GB of RAM and 26 compute units.

An ecosystem of partners also provide add-ons such as interfaces for Twitter and Facebook or database options based on Memcached, Amazon RDS, CouchDB, MongoDB and Solr. There are facilities for billing, release management, email as well as video encoding.

Although Heroku has significant potential for Ruby applications, we will focus this section on Salesforce.com's primary platform service, which is called Force.com. Like both Google's and Microsoft's offerings in this space, it offers hosting services based on its technology with the usual features of redundancy, security and scalability. However, Force.com is much more data-oriented than code-oriented and this difference in focus leads to a very different approach and target set of applications.

External Programmatic Access

Force.com exposes all customer specific configurations (forms, reports, workflows, user privileges, customizations, business logic) as metadata which is programmatically accessible. A Web Services API (SOAP) allows access to all Force.com application data from any environment. The platform also provides developer toolkits for .NET, Java, Facebook, Google and Amazon Web Services as well as pre-packaged connectors from:

- ERP: SAP R/3 and Oracle Financials

- Desktop software: Microsoft Office, Lotus Notes

- Middleware: Tibco, Pervasive, Cast Iron

In addition to conventional database access, Force.com also employs an external search engine that provides full-indexing and allows searching for unstructured data.

Apex

Force.Com applications are built using Visualforce, a framework for creating graphical user interfaces, and Apex, a proprietary programming language that uses a Java-like syntax but acts much more like database stored procedures, (Listing 8-1).

```
// This class updates the Hello field on account records
that are
// passed to it.
public class MyHelloWorld {
   public static void addHelloWorld(Account[] accs){
      for (Account a:accs){
        if (a.Hello__c != 'World') {
            a.Hello__c = 'World';
        }
      }
   }
}
```

Listing 8-1: Apex Account Update

Force.com distinguishes between three kinds of program logic:

- Declarative logic: audit logging, workflow, approvals

- Formula-based logic: data validation, workflow rules

- Procedural logic: Apex triggers and classes

```
trigger helloWorldAccountTrigger on Account (before insert)
{
   Account[] accs = Trigger.new;
   MyHelloWorld.addHelloWorld(accs);
}
```

Listing 8-2: Apex Trigger

Apex can run as a stand-alone script on demand or as a trigger on a data event (Listing 8-2). The language allows developers to add business logic to events, such as (user) button clicks or (data) record updates and Visualforce pages.

The workflow logic can also trigger tasks and it can send electronic messages, update the database or interface with external applications through outbound SOAP messaging to any Internet destination.

Chapter 8: Other Platform Options

There are three options for developing and creating the Apex code.

- The Salesforce.com user interface allows the user to include Apex code.

- Any text editor such as Notepad can be used to enter code which can subsequently be uploaded to the server.

- The preferred and most powerful mechanism is the Force.com IDE, which is a plug-in for Eclipse.

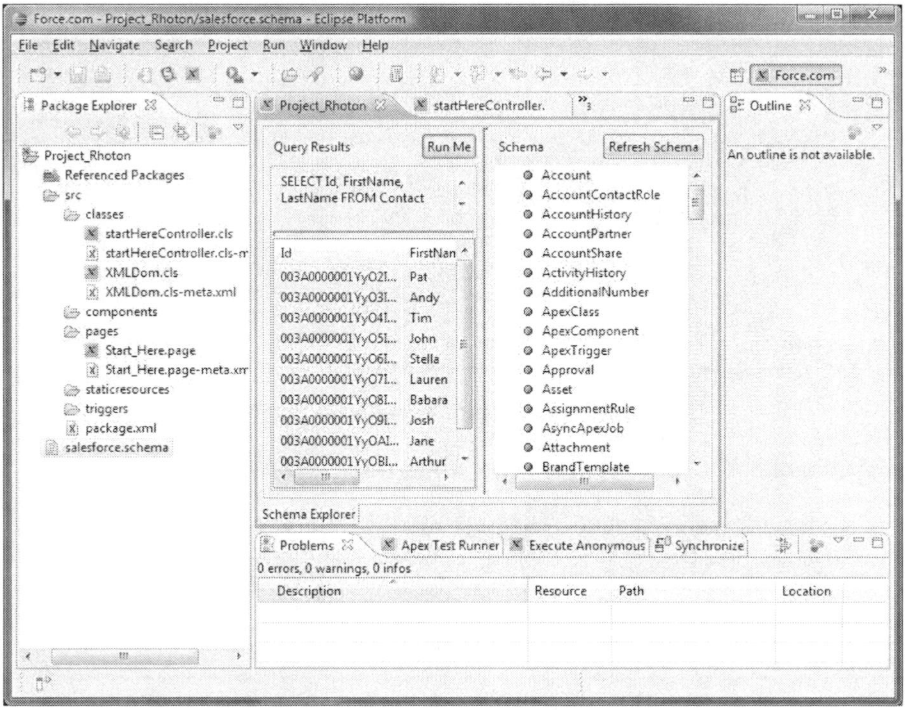

Figure 8-2: Force.com IDE

The Force.com Integrated Development Environment (IDE) is simply a plug-in to the Eclipse platform which connects directly to the Force.com services in the cloud and acts on the test environment (Figure 8-2). It includes an embedded schema explorer for a live view of the application data base schema. The browser can also view and edit any metadata components.

Since Apex code is automatically sent to server when saved, the developer is always working with server-based data in staging mode. In order to deploy the application into production, it must first pass a minimum threshold of unit tests.

Even though it is very convenient, there is no technical requirement to use the Force.com IDE. The full set of web services to deploy, compile and test the application are exposed and documented so it is possible to call them directly and, indeed, even to develop another IDE that uses them.

User Interface

Two tools are available for building the user interface for on-demand applications: UI builder and VisualForce.

The *UI Builder* is the simpler approach. It generates a default user interface based on the data properties of the application. This includes data structures, internal composition and inter-relations. For example, the defined data types will influence input display components and options. The UI can be modified to change the layout and appearance or to add search functionality. However, it becomes difficult to make changes that involve business logic.

VisualForce is much more powerful and can be used to create almost any user interface. It implements the MVC (Model: Data, View: User Interface, Controller: Business Logic) paradigm to enforce strict separation of logic from presentation and storage. The user interface can include callouts (e.g. to create mashups) and leverage dynamic client-side display functionality such as CSS, DHTML AJAX or Adobe Flex, in addition to ordinary HTML.

Facebook

A key differentiator of Facebook applications is that they revolve around a "social graph", which connects people with other people and their interests. One way to conceptualize the potential of the Facebook Platform is by thinking of it in terms of a three-tier model: Presentation, Application Logic and Data.

Presentation

The Facebook user experience is driven by the personal home page of any subscriber. The first integration task is therefore to ensure the application is loaded onto the canvas of the target user. Many older applications accomplished this with FBML (Facebook Markup Language), an HTML-like language for specifying the user interface. However, Facebook now recommends that applications run within an iframe, using the JavaScript SDK and social plugins for client-side integration with Facebook services.

Application Logic

If the application requires only simple internal logic then it may be possible to code these in JavaScript and perform all processing on the user's client. However, for complex applications that require server-side processing, it will be necessary to find a place to host the code.

In this case, you can use any platform you like as long as it is accessible from the client-side JavaScript. You might choose to host the business logic on Amazon EC2, GoGrid or EngineYard using any of the available frameworks.

Data

PLATFORM

Regardless of where you run your code, there is a good chance you will want to tap into some of the Facebook data. The Facebook Platform is the set of APIs and tools that enable you to integrate with the social graph to drive registration, personalization, and traffic — whether through applications on Facebook.com or external websites and devices.

Graph API: The Graph API provides a consistent view of the social graph, uniformly representing objects (like people, photos, events, and pages) and the connections between them (like friendships, likes, and photo tags).

Authentication: Facebook authentication lets applications interact with the Graph API on behalf of Facebook users, and provides a single sign-on mechanism across Web, mobile, and desktop apps.

Social plugins: Social plugins enable applications to provide social experiences to users with minimal HTML. Because the plugins are served by Facebook, the content is personalized to the viewer.

Open Graph protocol: The Open Graph protocol facilitates integration of custom pages into the social graph. These pages gain the functionality of other graph objects including profile links and stream updates for connected users.

Facebook Query Language: Facebook Query Language, or FQL, is a SQL-style interface to query the data exposed by the Graph API. It provides for some advanced features not available in the Graph API, including batching multiple queries into a single call.

Intuit

Intuit offers a platform service, called the Intuit Partner Platform (IPP), which focuses on the development, sale and distribution of multitenant SaaS applications. Initially it consisted of an Adobe Flex-based development environment with functions to target the large installed base of QuickBooks users.

It has since expanded into a set of APIs that can be leveraged from any platform, notably including Microsoft Azure, a strong partner of Intuit. Some key external integration points include:

Data: Federated Applications must program against APIs provided by Intuit to enable data synchronization.

Login: A Federated Identity Web API facilitates single sign-on by authenticating Intuit Workplace login credentials for access to Federated Applications within Intuit Workplace.

User management and permissions: Intuit provides developers with a Web API to handle processes such as inviting additional users to the application.

Navigation: The Intuit Workplace provides sign-in/sign-out links in its toolbar to provide users a seamless experience between applications.

PLATFORM

The developer sets up a QuickBase database and then uses Adobe Flex Builder 3.0 with the IPP SDK to develop the SaaS application.

The Intuit Workplace can accommodate isolated development environments for testing and staging. It is also where customers subscribe to applications. A synchronization agent facilitates the integration of subscribers' QuickBooks data so that changes to data in the SaaS application are reflected within the subscriber's QuickBooks product and vice-versa.

Another advantage of the IPP is its marketplace. With Federated Applications on the IPP, existing SaaS applications built with any programming language, database or cloud computing resource can be published to the Intuit Workplace and marketed to the entire QuickBooks customer and user base. When uploading the application, the developer determines the pricing plan and Intuit takes care of billing (subscription fee collection) and making developer payments.

Infrastructure-based Platforms

Some of the most important infrastructure services, Amazon, Rackspace and GoGrid, were mentioned above with their platform offerings. However, as we discussed in Chapter 3, there is no absolute need to use a platform service in order to build a cloud-based solution. One service that has gained appeal for a number of startup companies is SoftLayer.

SoftLayer offers a set of traditional hosting services that range from dedicated servers with a variety of hardware options to virtual servers running XenServer, Hyper-V, VMware or Virtuozzo. They also provide cloud-based infrastructure services including compute instances, storage and a content delivery network

This combination may be of interest to organizations that need to combine multiple delivery models for a hybrid solution. The same customer are also likely to need local and global load balancing, fine-grained bandwidth options, disaster recovery provisions, all of which are available as part of the solution.

Practical Considerations

Amazon, Google and Microsoft offer very complete cloud portfolios that are able to meet most demands. However, this doesn't mean they are always the best fit in terms of functionality or price:

- Data-driven applications may be easier to implement on Force.com.
- Services built around Intuit and Facebook are likely to use their platforms.
- Ruby-oriented developers should consider Heroku or Engine Yard.
- Other infrastructure providers are also an option, either with their platform services or else with custom platforms installed on their infrastructure.
- Enterprises often prefer private or partner cloud platforms built on VMware, Hyper-V or XenServer.

Presentation

The functionality delivered by the platform is exposed to the user through a presentation layer. This interface consists both of input provided by the user and content delivered to the user.

The typical cloud interaction model is browser-based. HTTP is the most common application protocol and HTML is optimal for providing a consistent presentation layer across all client platforms. However, the base protocols do not guarantee an optimal user experience. So, other browser-oriented techniques have been developed to improve the performance and responsiveness of the applications and also support rich media and an engaging user interaction, especially in light of real-time social content that is increasing in importance.

Even so, there are often reasons to resort to non-browser protocols and connectivity options. Mobile devices, in particular, have unique constraints and features that differentiate them from the desktop and from each other. Since mobility represents a usage model that is closely aligned with cloud computing, it is important not to neglect this large population of users with special requirements.

Cloud computing also complicates the optimization process because it is tightly associated with a federated service-oriented architecture that consumes granular services from a variety of sources. These function calls are often opaque to the user and may rely on many additional network requests. When the program logic is sequential, the risk of additive latency being exposed to the user is quite real. At the same time, the lack of transparency makes it difficult to identify the root causes. You therefore need to look at the architecture very carefully

Chapter 9

Browser Interface

PRESENTATION

The presentation layer of a cloud computing application is not fundamentally different from that of any other modern web application. There is an implicit assumption that it uses a network, but there is no particular reason that it has to adopt any specific protocol or technology.

There are some instances where a native client may be necessary or more practical than an Internet-based application. In the past, desktop applications were able to take advantage of richer graphic capabilities than HTML could offer and use functions, resources and capabilities of the operating system that the browser couldn't easily replicate. With the recent rise in portable devices, which has a more diverse set of interfaces than desktops, we have seen a surge in mobile applications that are tailored to the local characteristics of the devices.

Nonetheless, in most cases a browser application is simpler to deploy than a native client and will reach more devices. As the development of web standards, most significantly HTML5, and browser technologies move forward, bringing features like off-line access, rich client computation and tighter integration, the barrier is continuously pushed toward the browser and away from native clients.

Advantages	Disadvantages
No installation required	Limited capabilities
Easy to update	Security limitations
Standards-based	
Operating System agnostic	

Table 9-1: Browser interface advantages and disadvantages

As shown in Table 9-1, a browser interface has several advantages:

Installation: There is no need to install any software on the user's device since browsers come pre-installed or are distributed by the browser authors.

Even a plug-in, if necessary, is less intrusive than an application installation. If it is a common plug-in, then many users will already have installed it, or can download it from an external site without any significant involvement from the application. In the worst case, the application can provide the plug-in through HTTP with minimal encumbrance on the user.

Update: It is similarly easy to update the application. Since there is no local installation, the provider only needs to migrate server-side code and data. This approach is not dependent on any user configuration or activity and is not visible to the user.

PRESENTATION

Standards: Browsers interpret the IETF and W3C standards for HTTP, HTML and related protocols and formats. As a result, there should be a high degree of interoperability between browsers and web-sites. Any pages and code that are written to conform to these specifications should be accessible to the most common browsers. As we shall see below, there is still room for improvement in this area, but even considering all the issues of non-standard browser behavior, there is no comparison to a purely proprietary protocol that interlocks client and server.

Portability: One last advantage of the browser is its portable run-time environment that is independent of the underlying operating system. As such, it acts as a common platform to further extend interoperability to a wide range of devices and systems.

The primary disadvantages of the browser derive almost directly from its homogenous nature. Browser applications cannot leverage the platform in the same way that native clients can. As a result, both performance and processing capability tend to be limited. There may also be significant security limitations since the browser can only use the security components made available by the browser vendor.

From the perspective of the application owner, the browser presents new business models that are not necessarily a disadvantage, but require new perspectives on how to market the service. The Internet is replete with applications offered for different business purposes, which is creating a niche for marketplaces. The Google App Market Place, for example, is already trying to establish itself as a single point where people can come to and find web applications for their business needs.

However, there is still some work to be done. Unlike the mobile application space, where the Apple App Store and comparable competitive offerings have established themselves as unique points of contact for finding relevant applications, there is no single portal listing the majority of browser tools.

Browser Support

If you decide to pursue a browser based solution, then your first task will be to determine which browsers, versions and plug-ins you will support. The simplest approach is to restrict access to the most common browsers. In addition to making your job easier, in terms of conditional coding and testing, you can take advantage of leading edge technologies, such as HTML5. On the other hand, any limitation of the clients you support automatically excludes potential users from your application and alienates others.

Source	Internet Explorer	Firefox	Chrome	Safari	Opera	Mobile browser	Unknown
Net Applications	56.00%	22.75%	10.70%	6.30%	2.28%	3.79%	
StatCounter	46.00%	30.68%	15.68%	5.09%	2.00%	4.30%	
StatOwl	61.28%	19.57%	8.80%	9.40%	0.39%		
W3Counter	40.00%	31.10%	14.20%	5.90%	2.00%		6.80%
Wikimedia	41.56%	28.71%	11.75%	9.26%	4.25%	6.90%	
Median	46.00%	28.71%	11.75%	6.30%	2.00%	4.30%	6.80%

Table 9-2: Usage Share of Browsers for January 2011[1]

The table from Wikipedia (Table 9-2) presents a composite picture of the browser market as reported by a number of sources. The actual numbers will vary from site to site but there is a degree of consistency across the statistics. It also worth noting that the Internet Explorer share has been gradually decreasing from a near-monopoly a few years ago, while all others have been increasing.

	IE 9	IE 8	IE 7	IE 6	IE Total
January 2011	0.5%	16.60%	5.70%	3.80%	26.60%

Table 9-3: Internet Explorer Version Statistics[2]

Of course, it isn't the general market that you are interested in as much as the users who might visit your application. And while the browser vendor is a critical element it is actually a specific version that you will need to accommodate. If your application is targeted to leading edge early adopters, it may be probably sufficient to support only the latest browsers (currently Internet Explorer 8,

---

[1] Retrieved February 2011 from: en.wikipedia.org/wiki/Usage_share_of_web_browsers

[2] Retrieved February 2011 from: www.w3schools.com/browsers/browsers_explorer.asp. W3schools statistics are based on a population that leans towards newer technologies and therefore all the more revealing.

Chapter 9: Browser Interface

FireFox 3.x and Safari 5, Google Chrome 9). On the other hand, in enterprises, many users are stuck with the preferred browser version supported by their company. Even today, that's often IE 7 or IE 6, which is notorious for its non standard behavior (Table 9-3).

Another option is to provide a conditional presentation contingent on the browser. Outlook Web Access has long offered two different flavors of its user interface, one with a richer set of features and the other targeted at the broad set of less capable browsers. The advantage of this approach is that the primary user base can benefit from an elegant and efficient experience, but other users can still access all the functionality. The disadvantage is that it requires server-side coding and conditional processing depending on the HTTP User Agent. The additional complexity also implies further testing and more challenging support.

PRESENTATION

Browser Interface Types

The simplest web sites present static content on the server, which is interpreted passively by the client. At the other end of the spectrum are dynamic sites that update server-side data and regularly refresh and optimize client-side presentation.

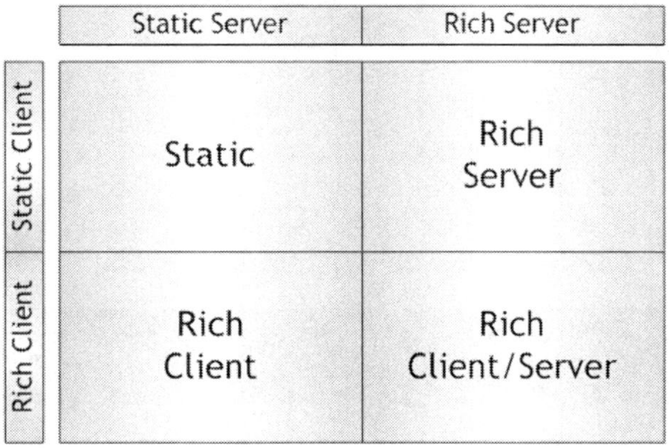

	Static Server	Rich Server
Static Client	Static	Rich Server
Rich Client	Rich Client	Rich Client/Server

Figure 9-1: Browser Interface Types

As shown in Figure 9-1, typical browser applications can be divided into four categories, depending on the volatility of the content and the location of processing. We will look at each category individually.

Static Websites

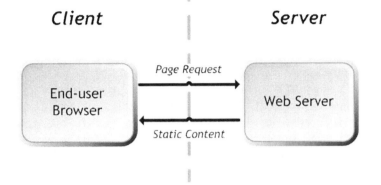

Figure 9-2: Static Website

The content of static web sites does not typically change much. It is mostly a one-way representation of information that is updated irregularly. In this scenario (Figure 9-2), the Client/Browser requests the static information from the server and renders the page based on the exact content received.

On a small scale, a static web site is probably still best served by a traditional hosted website provider. In a cloud computing environment, a typical implementation could be an EC2 instance running Apache. Serving this type of content to a large user base and scaling up web sites is relatively easy. Since the requests are typically stateless, the server-side content can be cached and served by multiple web servers.

Rich Server-side Interface

If there is a need for dynamic content, one approach is to use a server side technology, such as PHP, Python (Django), Ruby on Rails or ASP.NET.

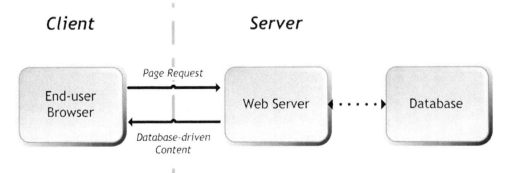

Figure 9-3: Dynamic Server Content

As illustrated in Figure 9-3, the dynamic content of the application is prepared on the server and sent to the client (browser) in its final shape. From a user's perspective the content on these sites gives the appearance of being static. For example, there is no evidence of the server-side processing in the HTML source that the user can view from the browser.

The content on the pages can change based on client requests or updates in the underlying information - but the changes typically require a complete page re-fresh to become visible to the user. Nonetheless, the presentation and content of websites are still more dynamic than true static sites, which never change.

PRESENTATION

A typical cloud installation for this approach could be dedicated web servers and dedicated database servers running a LAMP stack on Amazon EC2. However, when building this type of a web stack on Infrastructure as a Service, the infra-structure needs to handle scaling for both the Web Servers and database servers. This is where PaaS offerings, such as Google App Engine, excel since they promise infinite scalability without any application interaction.

Server-side processing has the advantage of being able to integrate and display information from a variety of sources without impacting the user. Sensitive con-tent can more easily be secured if it is stored and processed centrally. And this approach relieves both the network and user device from potentially extensive data traffic and computation. However, the user experience suffers since the browser must refresh for every change in data. These operations can be slow and visually distracting.

Rich Client

The Rich Client type is often referred to as an RIA (Rich Internet Application). To improve the user interaction it is necessary to utilize some client-side tech-nologies that are integrated into the browser.

JavaScript: The most common means of client-side processing is through Ja-vaScript. It is the only functional language that is supported by the majority of browsers. It does not automatically provide the rich visual interface of Flash or Silverlight but it has other strengths, notably the ability to perform almost any type of processing. Since it is so pervasive there are many tools and resources available that facilitate its use.

jQuery is currently the most popular JavaScript Library. It is actively pro-moted by its developer community and is attractive to newcomers since it is relatively easy to learn and use. The library provides a number of functions to simplify traversal of the HTML Document Object Model (DOM), handle events, animate graphics, and fetch server content through AJAX.

There are also a number of JavaScript frameworks, such as YUI, Dojo, MooTools and Prototype/Scriptaculous that target advanced developers. In contrast to a library, which passively provides a set of functions to the calling application, a framework typically involves a more active integration. To achieve this, some of the frameworks, such as MooTools and Prototype, focus on augmenting native prototypes such as Function, String, Array, Number and Element. By extending the essence of the language, they enable powerful cross-browser code.

HTML5: At this stage, probably one of the most important distinctions between browsers is support for HTML5. The newest version of HTML brings many of the capabilities common to traditional native applications right into browser, such as (Pilgrim, 2010):

- Drag and drop files from the desktop into the browser

- Modify large files (pictures, documents etc.) while offline

- Support vector and native rich graphical content (canvas element in HTML5)

Adobe Flash: Another option for rich content applications is to use Flash. Flash has gained sizeable market share mostly because of the development tools that Adobe provided and the ease of developing rich web applications with Flash. With the arrival of HTML5, perhaps Flash's days are numbered. Before we jump to any conclusions, however, it's worth noting that while HTML5 offers native video, many developers still find Flash superior for richer interaction. HTML5 also lacks Digital Rights Management (DRM) control for sharing protected content (e.g. video with commercials).

Microsoft Silverlight: We should also take care not to neglect Microsoft Silverlight in this discussion. Silverlight builds on the Windows Presentation Foundation to provide a user experience that is portable both inside and outside the browser, comparable in that sense to a combination of Adobe Flash and Adobe Flex. In contrast to Adobe, which uses an opaque library to aggregate elements, Silverlight exposes the elements through its eXtensible Application Markup Language (XAML). As a result the objects can be manipulated in a variety of programming languages and can be indexed more easily by search engines. Nonetheless, as powerful as Microsoft may be in many other areas, Adobe is clearly the incumbent with regard to rich graphic applications.

Rich Client / Server Interface

Client-side and server-side technologies are not mutually exclusive. In fact, most applications considered to be Web 2.0 combine the two. In this case, the server side is built with PHP, Ruby, Python or one of the other server side scripting technologies. The client functionality and browser view is typically modified with JavaScript running in the browser. JavaScript modifies the visual components within the browser and users can experience a variety of different features without requiring the browser to refresh a complete page.

The rich client/server interface has the advantage of combining a data-driven back-end with a very responsive and user-friendly front-end. It also facilitates additional models of interaction as we shall see when we return to the real-time web in Chapter 12.

Practical Recommendations

PRESENTATION

As you develop browser-based applications for cloud delivery, consider some suggestions:

- Tailor the user interface to new browsers, especially those supporting HTML5!
- However, don't ignore or exclude other common versions!
- Make the browser experience as dynamic as possible, both on the client and server!

Chapter 10

Native Clients

Browser-based applications have a distinct advantage in being conveniently portable, especially for the desktop market. Current activities, such as Mozilla's work on the mobile browser, aim to facilitate mobile application development inside the browser. Improvements include a JavaScript/browser interface to local sensors on the phone, like the GPS, camera and motion detector units. Over time, these will minimize the need even further for native application development.

Native clients also introduce a set of platform dependencies. Although frameworks like Nokia QT attempt to overcome this hurdle, development often requires custom libraries and (specifically mobile) extensions, which can also make the application expensive to support and maintain. These restrictions further cement the case for web-based delivery.

However, at this point in time, not all applications are suitable for the browser. Native clients adhere to a traditional usage model that is very familiar to developers and users. It can be optimized for the platform in terms of performance and usability. And it is not limited to browser technologies.

Over the last few years native applications have become very popular especially among mobile users, due to the unique constraints of the devices. Specific requirements for local interfaces and resources, rich user interfaces, high performance and complex computation may be difficult or impractical to accomplish within a browser.

Desktop Applications

Before diving into mobility, let's take a look at the desktop. Historically, in terms of the Internet timescale, most applications have been targeted to a relatively homogeneous set of user desktops. Even though several operating systems are available, it is possible to reach a high percentage of all users with a handful of base platforms and hardware configurations.

Cloud computing doesn't fundamentally change the nature of desktop use. However, the intention of most cloud-based applications is to be able to scale to a huge number of users. The larger the number of users, the more diverse is the set of access devices that are likely to be connected. As such, it is vital to identify and maximize any commonality that the application can leverage.

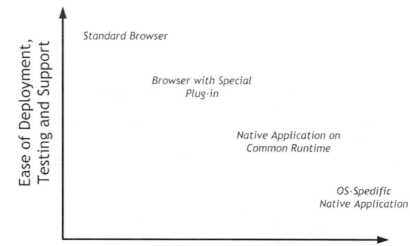

Figure 10-1: Desktop Delivery Vehicles

As seen in Figure 10-1, there are multiple delivery vehicles for desktop applications. They represent different points in a trade-off between standardization and access to native functionality. The former eases deployment, testing and support, while the latter leads to efficient use of resources, maximizing performance and optimizing the user experience.

Since desktop user environments are very similar, they lend themselves well to browser development. Nonetheless, there are situations where users require desktop specific functionality that cannot be easily achieved in the browser. For example, most real-time applications such as video conferencing, IP telephony, desktop sharing, or desktop virtualization are still more commonly implemented and used out-of-browser rather than in-browser. Similarly, if you have a need to directly access and control devices over USB, IEEE 1394, TWAIN or MIDI interfaces, you may find it difficult to achieve all required functionality through the browser.

This doesn't automatically mean that you cannot create a portable application. You can still code to the Microsoft .NET Common Language Runtime (CLR) or

Java Runtime Environment and enhance the visualization with a cross-platform rich internet application framework such as Flex or Silverlight.

If you are able to leverage these technologies, then you benefit from the fact that the frameworks are already widely installed on client computers and, where not, they are easily accessible for download. You still have a significant dependency that you need to communicate to potential users and the support burden will increase over a standard browser application. However, the application distribution and cross-platform support still make it attractive for special purpose applications.

As a last resort, it may be necessary to tailor the applications to the operating systems such as Windows, Linux or Mac OS X. In this case, you need to cater not only to all the supported operating systems, but to all versions and hardware configurations. Ideally you would also be able to test the application in environments where various patches and updates have been applied. Clearly, the combinatorial possibilities quickly lead to a very large number of scenarios, making testing and support very difficult for applications expecting a large and diverse user population.

Mobile Applications

Now, let's expand the discussion to a wider set of end-user systems, where we have even more challenges. Browser technology has largely focused on optimizing the desktop user experience. The idea behind most web sites and applications is that the user has a keyboard, pointing device and at least a VGA screen. Mobile devices often lack a full keyboard and may be restricted to a significantly smaller display.

The newest generation of smartphones and tablets have managed to partially compensate the machine interface with a suite of gesture and touch interaction that consider speed, direction and duration of taps with one or more fingers. However, the applications need to accommodate these facilities in order for them to be useful.

Because the devices are far from being optimized to the typical browser usage pattern, mobile users need applications that differ fundamentally from those commonly found on a laptop or desktop. Currently, native mobile applications are often rewrites of rich browser applications optimized to bring the most important visualizations and control points right to users' fingertips.

A new type of application development model has also developed for mobile devices. Instead of feature-loaded applications, like Microsoft Office, the user may install several targeted applications that do 'just one thing'. For example, if you are a musician, you might look for a guitar-tuning application, a metronome, or a tool for guitar chords. Often, these devices are supported by some cloud

Chapter 10: Native Clients

computing based back-end that offloads computation and storage in an effort to support online behavior.

Mobile Platforms

There are a number of mobile platforms (not to be confused with cloud platforms) that are currently vying for market leadership. From the perspective of cloud computing, there are two considerations surrounding mobility. It is obviously important to decide which mobile devices that a particular cloud application should support. More often than not, each platform involves an additional development stream that leads to increased costs in engineering, testing and support. It is therefore vital to carefully consider which user populations to target.

A second intersection with cloud computing involves the deployment and life-cycle management of the application. Mobility vendors are increasingly adopting the idea of an application store to help build and grow an ecosystem around their platform. In some cases, it is difficult to distribute the application in any other way. However, there may be instances where the application store merely links to the application or the platform facilitates distribution outside the store. In these cases, it is worthwhile considering a hosting provider or cloud service to simplify application distribution.

Before making any decisions, you probably want to go through the list of candidate platforms to determine which might be suitable for your application:

J2ME MIDP: The Java 2 Platform, Micro Edition (J2ME) running an implementation of Mobile Information Device Profile (MIDP) is the most widely available mobile platform, other than a standard browser, or possibly a Wireless Application Protocol (WAP) stack.

MIDP applications, called MIDlets, typically run a subset of Java determined by the Connected Limited Device Configuration (CLDC). This subset is not a proper subset of Java 2 Standard Edition, since it does also include some classes that are unique to mobile devices.

MIDP development tools are only available for the Windows environment. Sun Java Wireless Toolkit for CLDC is a miniature IDE, automating tasks for building and testing MIDlets, for example through the use of a mobile phone emulator. The process entails JARing the MIDlet suite class files and the resource files, and putting some extra information in the JAR manifest. The .jad and .jar files for the MIDlet suite will be generated and placed in the bin directory of the project, which can be transferred to the mobile device.

For those who prefer to code using Eclipse, there are some plugins that assist in developing J2ME MIDlets by connecting Wireless Toolkits to the Eclipse development environment. One popular environment is EclipseME, which has now been replaced by Mobile Tools for Java (MTJ).

RIM Blackberry –Research In Motion's Blackberry devices support J2ME as the primary application development environment. Rather than developing a proprietary platform, they have extended the tools and services available for J2ME to facilitate development for the Blackberry.

The device itself supports a proprietary RIM API in addition to all the J2ME functions. The API supports Bluetooth and the BlackBerry "push" architecture. It also enables integration with the native e-mail, texting, browser and organizer applications.

Developers can download a Blackberry Java Plug-In for Eclipse along with a Blackberry Widget Software Development Kit (SDK) that includes a handheld simulator. Application deployment can follow several paths. If the device is tethered, the user can install it via the Desktop Manager. It can also be downloaded and installed over the air from a web site. Corporate administrators may choose to push applications through a Blackberry Enterprise Server. Alternatively, to target a wide population of consumers, the developers can distribute the application through Blackberry App World.

PRESENTATION

Symbian: Symbian is a very popular operating system that powers a range of Nokia phones as well as some devices from Ericsson and Motorola. It is a descendent of Psion's EPOC operating system and was originally architected by an alliance of Ericsson, Motorola, Nokia and Psion, but was later bought out by Nokia.

While there has always been significant market potential for the platform, the task of developing applications based on Symbian has been somewhat onerous for many programmers. Not only are there different SDKs for each manufacturer but also for each Nokia Series (60, 80, 90) and specific version.

Furthermore, the tools aren't available in bundled form but need to be assembled from different sources. In addition to the SDK, it is necessary to install a JRE and a set of Windows development tools as well as ActivePerl. Developers can choose between Borland, Metrowerks or Microsoft IDEs, or forego an IDE and use the command line. The code itself implements the MVC in three respective classes, and the SymbianOS also exposes APIs for MMS, Bluetooth, Graphics, Networking, Messaging and WAP.

A Symbian GUI Application, when compiled and installed on the device, is comprised of (at least) three files. There is an .app file containing the logic of the application. A .rsc is the compiled resource file, containing the description of the GUI. The .aif contains the icon bitmap and some runtime information about the application. These files can be packaged into a .sis file that can be deployed to the device, for example by loading it onto an SD card or downloading it from the web.

While Symbian is still one of the most common mobile operating systems, it is unclear how its future will look now that Nokia has announced plans to license Windows Phone 7 on its devices.

MeeGo: Meego is an Open Source platform that works across any Atom-based device. Technically, it is the merger of Intel's Moblin and Nokia's Maemo, both of which were open-source Linux distributions. As such, it reflects a joint effort between Intel and Nokia.

The MeeGo SDK includes a chroot environment, which contains a simulator for MeeGo applications based on Xephyr, some scripts to start/stop a MeeGo desktop inside Xephyr, and tools to deploy to remote MeeGo devices. At the heart of the SDK is Qt, which provides a set of cross-platform APIs as well as Qt Creator, a cross-platform C++ integrated development environment. It includes a visual debugger and an integrated GUI layout and forms designer. The editor's features includes syntax highlighting and auto-completion.

The standard package format is a Linux RPM file consisting of a signature, some metadata (name, version, architecture, authors) and an archive of files to be installed on the destination file system (e.g. executables, images, documentation).

At this stage it appears that the preferred App Store for MeeGo will be Intel's AppUp store. However, the future of MeeGo is currently just as doubtful as that of Symbian, given Nokia's agreement with Microsoft.

Windows Phone: Windows Mobile never gained the same market penetration as Microsoft's desktop operating systems but Windows Phone 7, the most recent release, is still a major player in the mobile space, particularly for corporate users. It has received even more credibility since the joint agreement between Nokia and Microsoft, mentioned above, was signed February 2011.

Development requires a recent version of Microsoft Visual Studio to author, debug and package applications. There is also a Windows Mobile SDK containing the API header and library files to access Windows Mobile functionality as well as documentation, sample application projects, and emulators to deploy and debug your application without a Windows Mobile device.

Programming Windows Mobile applications is relatively straightforward for any developers familiar with Microsoft Technologies. Visual Studio includes a template called "Smart Device" that takes care of the unique mobile requirements. The toolbox and code are very similar to those used for desktop applications.

In order to test and deploy applications on a device, the programmer needs to download ActiveSync (or Windows Mobile Device Center). The user then connects the device to the desktop, and can launch the project from Visual Studio. It is possible to package the installation file for manual deployment via a file copy or web download. Alternatively Corporate customers and telcos may use Microsoft System Center Mobile Device Manager (SCMDM) for bulk and policy-based distribution.

HP Palm webOS: Palm webOS is Hewlett-Packard's mobile operating system running on a Linux kernel. After selling PalmOS to ACCESS, Palm had licensed Windows Mobile for their devices until announcing webOS as the primary platform in 2009. It is currently available on the Pre and Pixie.

As the name implies, the intention of webOS is to leverage standard web technology (HTML, CSS, JavaScript as well as the Prototype framework) for all its functionality. In keeping with modern development methods, the operating system runs an MVC framework, which is called Mojo. If you trace the code you can see that the homepage starts with index.html and enters Mojo through a JavaScript call.

PRESENTATION

The SDK includes an emulator and a Palm plug-in for Eclipse to handle debugging, packaging and installing. The emulator runs as a virtual machine in VirtualBox. Alternatively, the SDK can deploy to any USB-connected webOS device.

Palm's orientation toward the web is also apparent in its Project Ares, claimed to be the first mobile development environment hosted entirely in a browser. Using this model, developers don't need to install an SDK. Even the emulator is embedded in the web application.

iOS: iOS is Apple's mobile operating system comprising the technologies necessary to run applications natively on devices, such as iPad, iPhone, and iPod touch. It shares some underlying technologies with Mac OS X but has been enhanced to meet the needs of a mobile environment with new features such as multi-touch interface and accelerometer support.

The development environment for iOS runs only on the Apple Macintosh operating system. The iPhone SDK contains the code, information, and tools to develop, test, run, debug, and tune applications for iOS. The Xcode tools provide the basic editing, compilation, and debugging environment for the code. Xcode also provides the launching point for testing applications on an iOS device or in the iPhone Simulator.

The iOS services are exposed through a four-layer model. The Core OS and Core Services layers contain the fundamental interfaces for iOS. These include access to files, low-level data types, Bonjour services and network sockets. The Media layer contains the fundamental technologies used to support 2D and 3D drawing, audio, and video. This layer includes OpenGL ES, Quartz, Core Audio and Core Animation.

The most common interface is the Cocoa Touch layer. The Foundation framework provides object-oriented support for collections, file management and network operations. The UIKit framework provides the visual infrastructure including classes for windows, views and controls. Other frameworks at this level provide access to the user's contact and photo information as well as to hardware including the accelerometers.

It is possible to develop iOS applications in other languages, such as Python or Ruby, but Apple's documentation concentrates on Objective-C, making it the easiest starting point. Objective-C defines a set of extensions to the ANSI C programming language to facilitate object-oriented programming. It is the native language for the Cocoa frameworks and most standard applications.

Xcode's graphical debugger provides a means to debug and test code in a simulator. It is also possible to plug the iPhone or iPad into the Mac to check the application on the target device. Once development is ready for beta-testing, it can be distributed in "Ad Hoc" mode to up to 100 other users who are able to install the software through iTunes.

The final stage of distribution involves uploading the tool to Apple's App Store. Once it has been checked and released by Apple, it can be downloaded by any iPhone user. If the software carries a price tag, then Apple will provide billing and collection services in addition to deploying the software.

Android: Android is an open-source operating system targeting mobile devices. It was originally developed by Android Inc, which was acquired by Google. Although it is officially endorsed by the Open Handset Alliance, a consortium of leading mobility vendors, it is still primary maintained and supported by Google.

The operating system is based on Linux and features an object-oriented application framework supporting most components of Java 2 Standard Edition (except Abstract Windows Toolkit and Swing). It runs a Dalvik virtual machine that is optimized for mobile devices. For example, it offers enhanced garbage collection and just-in-time compilation of Dalvik-specific executable code (.dex rather than Java bytecode). It also compiles XML to binary for efficiency in processing and storage.

Some of the libraries include relational database, speech, telephony, mapping, locations, security, 2D and 3D graphics and several wireless interfaces such as Bluetooth, WiFi and GSM.

Development typically involves an Eclipse plug-in called ADT (Android Development Tools) although it is possible to use the command line to develop and deploy applications. The Android SDK also includes an emulator for testing applications. Just like most other emulators, it has some limitations, for example in testing USB connections, camera, video, headphones, battery and Bluetooth. However, for most common purposes it works just fine.

The installation package involves an APK file that users can install directly from SD card or through a file copy. The Android Market lends itself well for wide distribution – by some estimates (AndroLib, 2011), it currently holds over two hundred thousand applications and has delivered almost four billion downloads.

It's not the intention of this book to give an in-depth perspective on the various mobile platforms. The important points to realize are that, on the one hand, there is some commonality in what they all offer to developers. They typically provide an SDK, which might include an IDE or IDE plug-in. There is some means of testing the application, which often includes an emulator. And there are mechanisms to deploy the application, with most either providing a marketplace or giving a clear indication of their plans in that direction.

PRESENTATION

On the other hand, there are some distinctions that you need to observe. To begin with, your choice of supported devices will depend largely on the size of the user base, which varies greatly between platforms. You may want to consider the level of standardization and opportunity for code-portability between device types. Furthermore, there is some variation in the ease, or difficulty, in assembling development tools and publishing applications.

Common Data Transport

Although native applications may seem inherently different from web browser applications when you look at them from a display perspective, this doesn't mean that the entire presentation layer is necessarily distinct. While the visualization is closely tied to the operating system frameworks, the underlying processing may be very similar across platforms.

More specifically, native applications may use the same communication techniques as web applications, including real time feeds with HTTP push or JSON interfaces to pull data. This means that the same techniques used on the infrastructure side to optimize data transport to web browsers are directly applicable to many of the native client scenarios.

Practical Recommendations

In order to maximize use of your applications, consider some suggestions related to mobile users:

- Don't ignore mobile users! Even if browsers seem ubiquitous, mobility is growing in size and importance.
- Leverage applications stores for reach, sales channel and visibility!
- Keep in mind that the mobile application doesn't need to be identical to the desktop or browser version!

PRESENTATION

Chapter 11

Presentation Optimization

At the end of the day, the success of any application is determined by user acceptance. Even the best software is worthless if nobody wants to use it. More specifically, one of the most important factors influencing customer acceptance is perceived performance. Applications that appear unresponsive will generally frustrate users and may eventually be abandoned.

Cloud computing complicates the optimization process because it is tightly associated with a federated service-oriented architecture that consumes granular services from a variety of sources. These function calls are often opaque to the user and may rely on many additional network requests. When the program logic is sequential, the risk of additive latency being exposed to the user is quite real. At the same time, the lack of transparency makes it difficult to identify the root causes. You therefore need to look at the architecture very carefully.

Although presentation performance is most directly related to the client device, whether it be a browser or native application, delays and bottlenecks from other sources have a significant impact on the user experience. We can identify three general performance areas: client, network and server.

Client: If the client is asked to perform computationally intensive operations that exceed the capabilities of the device then there may be delays that ripple up to the user. On the other hand, intelligent caching of information can actually accelerate the perceived performance of the application.

Network: If the application transfers huge amounts of data between the client and server while the network connection is not sized for this traffic, then bottlenecks may delay the transfer. Likewise, high latency between nodes through geographical separation can slow down an application, particularly, if numerous synchronous operations execute sequentially.

Server: Any delays in processing on the cloud servers will ultimately slow down the application on the client. If the processing is asynchronous, then it may be possible to mask some of the delays; but if the operations are synchronous, they can have a devastating effect on the user experience.

In practical terms, it is critical to understand all performance components before redesigning the solution. For example, if a native application is using HTTP with JSON as a data feed (e.g. a Twitter client running on the iPhone), then the bulk of the time on the phone may be spent waiting for the server to respond back to the requests. In this scenario, it isn't sensible to squeeze every millisecond out of the client application. The effort would be much better spent in reducing the data transport times with a binary JSON format, optimizing the server with Memcached or prefetching and caching client-side data.

PRESENTATION

In order minimize any performance problems and improve the user experience, we follow three steps: Measure, Analyze, Optimize. First, we need to measure the application to determine how well it is performing and, ideally, compare it to some benchmark. Second, we analyze our results to identify the source of any performance issues. And third, we try to find a way to minimize any delays that we have found.

Measuring the Presentation Layer

Regardless of whether it's native software or a browser application, client instrumentation helps to understand how widely the application is used and whether the performance is acceptable. Based on the results, you can decide how to measure and do split (A/B) testing with your user population.

There are several services that can assist in this process, such as Google Analytics, Pingdom and Chartbeat. For all of these, a typical deployment model is:

1. Create an account with SaaS provider.

2. Customize a few web pages that the provider is hosting to match your service and customize the look and feel.

3. Integrate the service in your website by typically dropping 10-20 lines of JavaScript inside your website templates.

Google Analytics

Google Analytics is a free service that provides a range of visitor statistics about any participating website (Figure 11-1). Although it is mainly intended for marketing activities, it also provides useful information for managers and developers. In addition to showing aggregate counts of visiting users, it displays where they come from and how they came to the site. It is also possible to gain some insight into user activity on the site and identify poorly performing pages by visualizing the conversion funnel and monitoring the time users spend on the site.

Figure 11-1: Goolge Analytics

PRESENTATION

Pingdom

Pingdom is another network monitoring tool that tracks uptime, reachability, responsiveness and performance. The service monitors servers (public and password-protected websites, FTP servers, email servers) from multiple locations on the Internet, making sure that they are working. It also has a means of sending SMS, email or Twitter alerts when there are problems and has an API to facilitate integration with other monitoring tools.

PRESENTATION

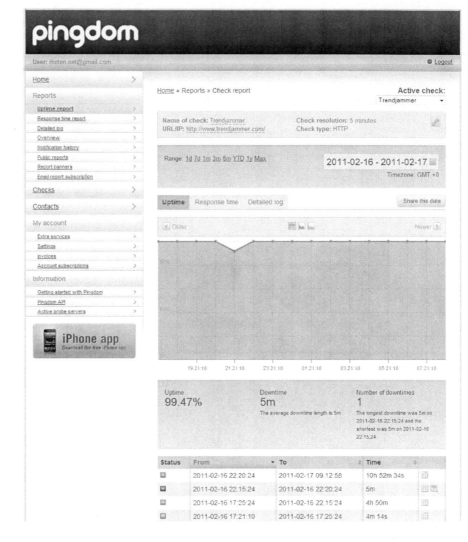

Figure 11-2: Pingdom Uptime

Pingdom keeps reports of all errors it detects, and makes them available via the control panel (Figure 11-2). It shows when the error/downtime happened, how long it lasted, what kind of error triggered it, and for each outage, Pingdom also performs an additional error analysis. Depending on the kind of error, this extra error analysis may include DNS lookups, traceroutes to locate network problems, saving of the actual HTML page at the time of the error, and the header response from the server,

It also performs regular performance checks and keeps track of the response time so that you can gather a composite view of how well the application performs over time (Figure 11-3). These statistics can be helpful to diagnose errors or identify performance bottlenecks.

Figure 11-3: Pingdom Response Time

Chartbeat

Chartbeat offers a dashboard that gives you an overview of the traffic to your site. The summary shows you the number of active visitors along with the minimum and maximum daily counts. It breaks the active number down in terms of new and returning visitors.

You can also identify the top pages of your web site and analyze the traffic sources by referring sites as well as by geographical location.

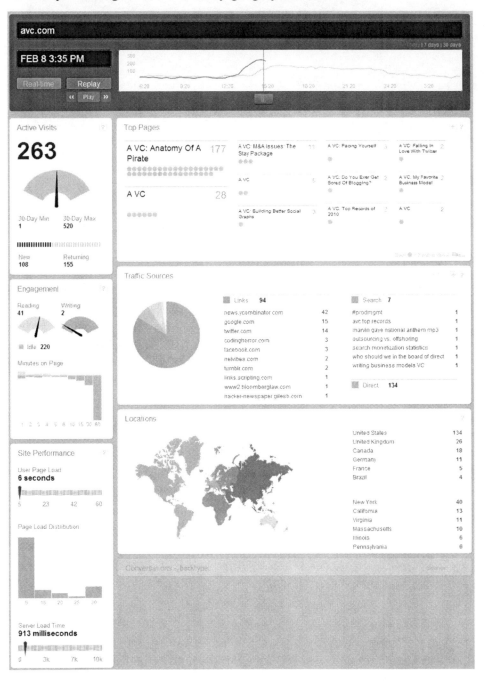

Figure 11-4: Chartbeat

A/B Testing

As you consider functional and cosmetic changes to your web site, it is vital to assess the impact, so that you can roll back unpopular updates and refine your strategy to extend customizations that are most accepted. The least intrusive way to compare a new version of a web page with an older baseline is through A/B testing.

This means that the server directs a small percentage of incoming requests to a staged version of the application, and then measures the differences in usage patterns between production and staged versions with something like Google Analytics.

For example, if the base page is www.myservice.com/index.html, the URL routing of the application could transfer 10% of the incoming HTTP requests to www.myservice.com/newversion/index.html. These two versions would show up under Google Analytics as different pages and would be separately trackable.

Server / Client Performance Measurement

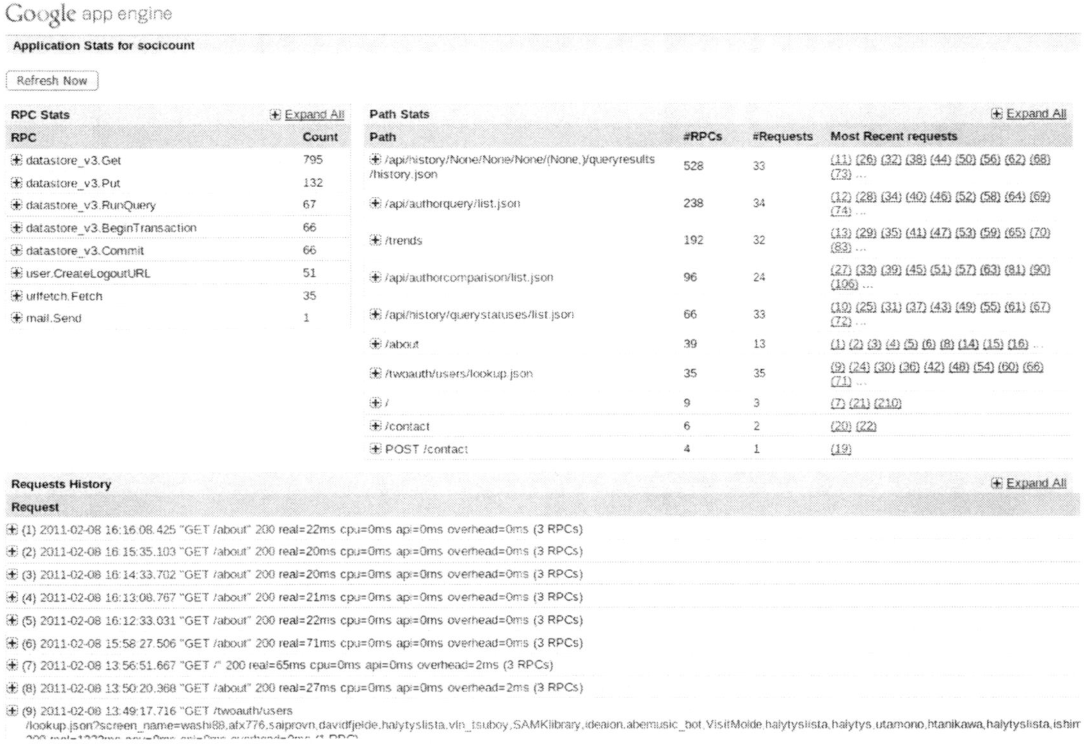

Figure 11-5: Google AppStats

Chapter 11: Presentation Optimization

For services running on Google App Engine, the AppStats (Figure 11-5) capability is an excellent example of a measurement tool. Appstats provides server-side performance profiling for all the request handlers in an App Engine application. It lists the request times and also offers a breakdown of how many, and which, database calls each HTTP request has triggered.

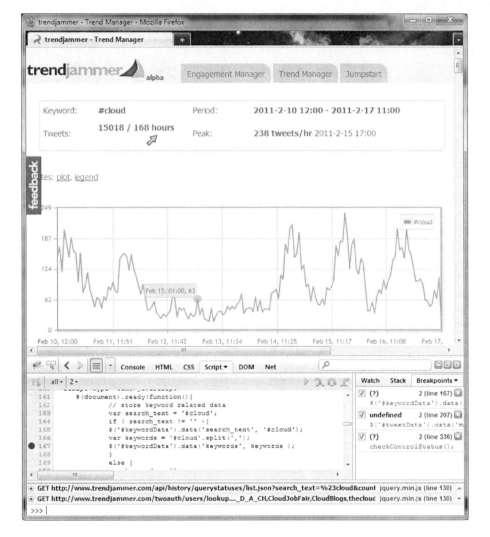

Figure 11-6: Firebug Client-side Debugging

AppStats together with FireBug (Figure 11-6) as the client side test suite can be a really powerful combination for measuring and debugging performance in the application.

Presentation Optimization Techniques

In addition to using available tools to identify and refine the performance of your sites, Souders (2007) and others have compiled best practices that apply to most web-based applications. We have loosely grouped these guidelines into five categories: reduce network requests, minimize downloaded content, distribute the information, organize the sequence and tune the application logic.

Reduce Network Requests

One way to speed up the application is to minimize the number of requests that slow down the application. Each DNS lookup or HTTP request increases traffic and processing. If it is synchronous, it also introduces additional latency. You can reduce the number of HTTP requests by combining scripts, stylesheets and images, or by avoiding unnecessary redirection. By the same token, DNS lookups are required for all unique hostnames on the page. If you can reduce their number, you can decrease their lookup time.

Minimize Downloaded Content

Assuming that you have pruned your calls to the most essential, the logical next step is to ensure that each request is as concise as possible. Most image formats (e.g. JPG, PNG, GIF) have already compressed the files, so there is little point in trying to squeeze any more out of them. However, you can reduce network traffic if you compress any sparse data sets (e.g. text files), such as stylesheets, XML or JSON on the server, and decompress them on the client.

In addition, there are several tools, such as JSMin and Packer, which minify JavaScript by eliminating any unnecessary white space and comments. They tend to make the source code less readable, so they can be a mixed blessing during debugging. However, once the software is stable, they have their place in maximizing performance.

Distribute and Cache

In addition to minimizing the amount of data that is passed over the network, you can save time by decreasing the distance of the traffic. You may want to use a CDN, like Akamai or Limelight, to get the content as close as possible to the end user. However, before you go down that path, find out what your provider offers. Amazon CloudFront is a CDN service that may appeal to EC2 customers. Other providers, such as Google, replicate content by default, and thereby reduce the need for a separate CDN.

If some of your pages are largely static, you can reduce unnecessary network requests by adding an Expires header to them. After the initial visit and download of the page, the browser will serve the page from local cache until the time indicated in the header elapses.

ETags (entity tags) are a more advanced cache control mechanism used by client browsers to determine whether a resource is still valid based on parameters such as last-modified date, version number or checksum. It differs from the Expires mechanism above in that it requires an explicit HTTP request. However, if the content has not changed, then the client can reuse the old version rather than re-questing a full retransmission of content. There are some disadvantages of using ETags, particularly for websites served from multiple servers. Nonetheless, as long as they are used judiciously, they can reduce network traffic.

Prefetching is the most sophisticated form of caching. If you are able to predict requests before the user or application makes them, you have the opportunity to issue the calls ahead of time. You may increase the overall network traffic (since some requests will be unnecessary), but you can reduce the latency and make the content appear to render more quickly.

Optimize Sequence

Another consideration is the order in which the content is presented to the browser. Browsers cannot render all the elements on a page accurately until they have received the prerequisite stylesheets. As a result, it makes sense to place them at the top of the page, so they are loaded early.

On the other hand, scripts tend to delay rendering of other elements once they start to download. In order to display the page to the user as soon as possible, it is a good idea to put the scripts at the bottom of the page.

Tune Application Logic

The last area to look at is the computational side of the application. Even after you have eliminated all network-related delays, the client and server both will require some time to perform their functions. Generally, the server is more of a bottleneck than the client (and it is also costlier to the service provider), so you will want to move as much work as possible to the client, in the form of Java-Script. However, beyond this simple tradeoff, you will still want to optimize both the server and the client in the tasks they perform.

On the server side, having separate infrastructure for caching allows for more efficient treatment of static content. Effective use of Memcached can also mi-nimize database queries. If you consider that Google App Engine can respond to a Memcached query in roughly one fiftieth of the time of a database query, you can appreciate that it is worthwhile to cache what you can.

On the client side, there is also plenty of advice available on how to tune Java-Script (Greenberg). Some of it is obvious: limit processing inside loops, minimize repeated expressions, and eliminate unnecessary variables. Other advice is not so intuitive: use a switch statement rather than if-then-else, count loops down rather than up, and use JavaScript math functions. Beyond optimizing Java-Script, you can also look at minimizing processing, for example by avoiding CSS expressions. We won't attempt to repeat all the guidance here, but instead refer you to the experts in the subject.

Another important area revolves around offline access to browser applications. The historical challenge for web applications running in disconnected mode was the absence of any persistent storage. To address this obstacle, the W3C has standardized software methods and protocols as part of the Web Storage specification. It was initially a component of HTML5, but has since been decoupled and defined on its own. An obvious implication of offline access is that it will generally reduce the server load if you can process content independently. However, you need to consider the performance impact of synchronization when all changes are reconciled.

Practical Recommendations

In addition to the techniques just described, make sure you keep the broader picture in mind as you fine-tune the presentation layer:

- Measure and optimize the presentation layer both on the client and server! Just because some parts are not running on your systems doesn't meant they aren't critical to your success.
- Avoid any unnecessary synchronous calls! If they are needed, try to make them asynchronous.
- Minimize the amount of information that is sent across the wire and compress its size!
- Distribute content to the network edge! The closer the content is to the users, the better will be their experience and the higher their satisfaction with your service.
- Optimize performance in the browser with JavaScript minification and performance debugging to identify/optimize the slowest JavaScript calls.

Chapter 12

Real-Time Web

With the rapid growth of Twitter and the popularity of status updates on Facebook and other social networking sites, Real-Time Web has moved to the front and center of technical progress. If you're writing a cloud application without a real-time component you're missing an opportunity to excite your users about the service that you're building.

In some ways, it represents an evolutionary next step in a trend from static to dynamic web content. However, the implications are far-reaching. The ultimate ambition in fine-tuning a user experience is to include all relevant information available on the web, which may include such areas as collaboration, analytics, search and eCommerce (e.g. pricing) (Moon, 2009).

As a wave of web applications moves towards providing users with information about something that's happening right now the challenge breaks down into three components:

- Push any recent information to the user immediately

- Aggregate and present all relevant recent information

- Expose useful information externally

The first task is to ensure that any dynamic content in the service is delivered to the user as soon as possible. Unfortunately, browser technology and standards were not originally designed with this interaction model in mind. As a result, the transition to an information-push paradigm is not simple, particularly when it needs to reach a broad audience of users.

The second task is to determine what relevant fast-paced content might be available externally, as well as how to retrieve and deliver it. It is likely to come from a variety of sources, whereby the largest ingredient of newly created information is user-contributed (tweets, blogs) and data feeds (newsfeeds, blog feeds, twitter feeds), both of which are volatile and widely dispersed.

The last area of opportunity involves fostering the ecosystem of the application. This means that any information that might be useful to related services should be made available to them in a form that they can consume. This exposure comes at a cost. When users bypass your offering, you have no tangible benefit even though they consume your resources. However, most successful sites today have focused on growing reach and recognition, coupled with a compelling proposition for direct site visits.

We will look at these three tasks separately.

Delivering Real-Time Information

As described in Chapter 9, simple HTML pages are static. The only way to update them is for the user to press the refresh button of the browser. It is certainly possible to automate this process with an HTML meta refresh, but it is still very disorienting to the user. JavaScript can address the disruptive visual impact of a refresh. However, it was originally used for processing local data only and therefore had no access to dynamic data on the server.

As a result, web sites that were built ten years ago had very little ability to send new data without confusing and irritating the users. Fortunately, a few techniques have emerged since then that attempt to address these challenges. They include Ajax, Comet and Web Sockets.

AJAX / REST

Ajax (Asynchronous JavaScript and XML) is a set of methods used to create interactive web applications. As the name implies, the approach is typically asynchronous and relies on XML. However, neither of these requirements are mandatory. The essence of the approach is that, once the page is presented to the user, client-side JavaScript continuously retrieves data from a server transparently to the user and can use it to update the screen.

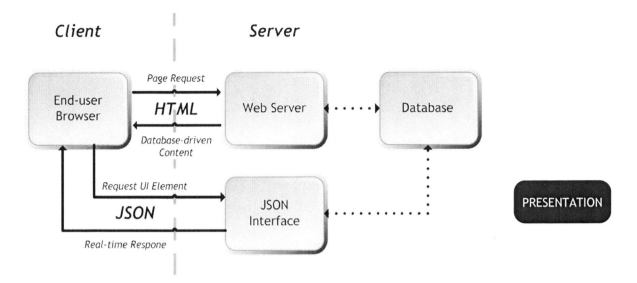

Figure 12-1: Real-time Browser Updates

In the prototypical example, client-side web applications asynchronously retrieve data from the server using the XMLHttpRequest object (XHR). Although Ajax was initially based on XML, there is increasing use of JSON as the data transport. JSON has recently become very popular for many web applications, since it is easier to parse with JavaScript and often seen as a more lightweight, human readable data format. Furthermore, JSON as the data format, and RESTful interfaces as a way to represent resources in the web, often go hand in hand.

As user works through the UI elements, JavaScript in the browser consumes required information over a JSON interface, either from the same or from a different server, and uses the retrieved information to update elements in the page (Figure 12-1). For instance, stock trading web sites often display near real-time information about the recent offering price and trades that have occurred. With the use of clever JavaScript and other plug-ins, a page can present itself to the user just like any native application.

However, behind the scenes, Ajax still suffers from one disadvantage in its request model. The browsers have the responsibility of constantly polling the servers for potential new information, whereby the length of the polling interval marks a tradeoff between latency of updates and resource utilization. Irregular polling leads to delays in the propagation of new information. On the other hand, frequent polling is an inefficient use of server and networking resources. There is usually no new information between polls, so the requests just return the equivalent of 'no changes'. Overly aggressive polling can even lead providers to defensive reactions, such as throttling traffic, blocking requests, or blacklisting the site.

Comet

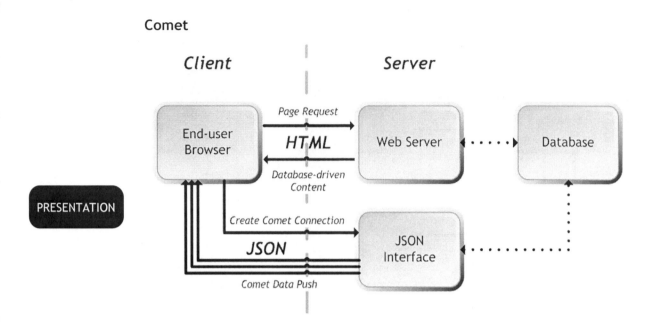

Figure 12-2: Comet Data Push

In web development, the term Comet describes a web communication model in which a long-held HTTP request allows a web server to push data to a browser, without the browser explicitly requesting it (Figure 12-2). Comet is an umbrella term for multiple techniques that achieve this interaction.

Methods of implementing Comet fall into two major categories: streaming and long polling.

Streaming: In an application using streaming Comet, the browser opens a single persistent connection to the server for all Comet events, which is handled incrementally on the browser side. Each time the server sends a new event, the browser interprets it, but neither side closes the connection. Techniques for accomplishing streaming Comet include the following.

- A hidden Iframe HTML element (an inline frame, which allows a website to embed one HTML document inside another). The Iframe is sent as a chunked block, which implicitly declares it as infinitely long. As events occur, the Iframe is gradually filled with script tags, containing JavaScript to be executed in the browser.

- The XMLHttpRequest (XHR) object, the main tool used by Ajax applications for browser–server communication, can also be pressed into service for server–browser Comet messaging in a few different ways, such as using the content type multipart/x-mixed-replace or multipart responses to XHR.

PRESENTATION

None of the above streaming transports works across all modern browsers without causing negative side-effects in any—forcing Comet developers to implement several complex streaming transports, switching between them depending on the browser.

Long Polling: XMLHttpRequest long polling is easier to implement on the browser side, and works, at minimum, in every browser that supports XHR. The client makes an asynchronous request of the server. The response can contain encoded data (typically XML or JSON) or Javascript. After processing the response, the browser creates and sends another XHR.

A long-polling Comet transport can be created by dynamically creating script elements, and setting their source to the location of the Comet server, which then sends back JavaScript (or JSONP) with some event as its payload. Each time the script request is completed, the browser opens a new one, just as in the XHR long polling case. This method has the advantage of being cross-browser while still allowing cross-domain implementations.

Comet represents a significant improvement over Ajax in enabling true "push" communications. However, it also has a couple of limitations. Each upstream request requires an additional HTTP connection. It is possible to configure bidirectional communications, but these require two connections and therefore imply a certain amount of overhead.

A second challenge with Comet is its lack of standard implementation for either XHR or iFrames, which makes development difficult. A few frameworks (such as Cometd and Jetty) are available that provide abstractions for these transports, implementing the Bayeux protocol. Bayeux seeks to reduce the complexity of developing Comet web applications by allowing implementers to more easily interoperate, to solve common message distribution and routing problems, and to provide mechanisms for incremental improvements and extensions. However, it also introduces further message transformation overhead and complexity.

WebSockets

The HTML5 WebSocket is a technology providing bi-directional, full-duplex communications channels, over a single Transmission Control Protocol (TCP) socket. It is designed to be implemented in web browsers and web servers and addresses the same use cases as Ajax and Comet. However, it avoids the connection and portability issues and provides a simpler and more efficient solution.

The WebSocket API is being standardized by the W3C and the WebSocket protocol is being standardized by the IETF. Since ordinary TCP connections to ports other than 80 are frequently blocked by administrators outside of home environments it can be used as a way to overcome these restrictions and provide similar functionality with some additional protocol overhead while multiplexing several WebSocket services over a single TCP port.

For the client side, WebSockets are implemented in Firefox 4, Google Chrome 4, Opera 11 and Safari 5. On the server side, there is an initial handshake over HTTP that is required in order to upgrade an existing HTTP connection to a raw TCP/IP connection. Kaazing Gateway, an open source project, represents the first server to provide this support. It is also supported by Tornado (python), Sprocket, Mojolicious (Perl), em-websocket (Ruby), and Node (server-side JavaScript).

Google Channel API

The Google Channel API is written to be client-compatible with Comet and WebSockets. It provides a server-side interface built on the XMPP real-time chat protocol. The interface opens a server client push channel for real time like information. The server initializes the channel, and then the client side web page opens a web socket connection to listen to the push messages coming in via that channel. A callback function presents the user with any data that is received. The Channel API might be useful for collaborative applications, such as conferencing whiteboards, concurrent document editing, multi-player games, or chat rooms.

Aggregating Real-Time Information

As you try to put together an exciting web site, you are not limited to content that you are producing yourself. The Internet is full of interesting information, which you can leverage as long as it is relevant to your users. One important prerequisite in assessing whether it will be well received is whether it is new, or whether your viewers may already have seen it elsewhere. You don't want to give the impression of simply repackaging and duplicating stale information.

There are at least two areas where you have an opportunity to present dynamic information: news feeds and social networks. These change frequently, so if you can channel the data stream to your web site in real time, you are likely to be seen as adding value.

Feeds

A web feed is a data format that describes structured, but frequently updated content, intended for wide distribution. We will look at feeds in more detail in Chapter 16 as they are a useful technique for integrating applications at the data layer. For now, it is important to consider how they provide a means to incorporate external information streams into a web site.

The two most popular feed technologies are RSS and Atom. Unfortunately, on their own they do not lend themselves well to real-time updates since they would require a constant connection between the client and server. One approach that we will also describe in Chapter 16 is PubSubHubbub, which offloads the feed content distribution from a website itself. It is agnostic to the format of data feeds extending both Atom and RSS. The standard is an open, server-to-server, web-hook-based publish/subscribe protocol. Its objective is to provide near-instant notifications of change updates to subscribed topics rather than relying on periodic client polling.

The most intuitive approach for including RSS / Atom feed information on your web page would be to use JavaScript. However, the logic of processing a feed is non-trivial and the performance impact can be significant so most sites use a server-side component to parse the content. If you do want to retain processing on the client, you might consider a Jquery-based tool, like jFeed, to simplify the application logic.

Another alternative is to use a popular RSS-to-JavaScript transformation service, such as:

- RSS-To-JavaScript

- Feed2JS

- RSS2HTML

- FeedSweep

- Google Dynamic Feed

For example, with the Google Feed API you can download any public Atom, RSS, or Media RSS feed using only JavaScript, so you can easily mash up feeds with your content.

Unfortunately, depending on a free external service is somewhat risky since it is unlikely to come with a strict SLA. When it is unavailable, your web pages won't render properly, and if there are other problems you are unlikely to receive immediate support.

To avoid these problems, you can implement your own feed reader within your service. Depending on the programming language you use, you will probably find source code available that you can use to get started. You can check out SimplePie for PHP; Universal Feed Parser or PyRSS2Gen for Python; and RSSLib4J or JswingReader for Java. If you are coding in Ruby, then you are even luckier since it has built-in support for RSS.

Social Networks

The largest volume of information that doesn't require complex authentication or authorization is from Twitter. You can use the Twitter search API to present recent tweets, which you will want to narrow down by username or keyword (usually a hashtag, such as '#cloud').

When it comes to implementation, some of the same discussion applies to Twitter as to news feeds. You can code almost anything in JavaScript. You can often write it more easily using a framework like Jquery. However, it is most efficient to run it on a server. If you want to make use of an external service, you can look at TwitStat.us or look at Twitter's Search widget.

Other social media services, such as Facebook, Flickr and LinkedIn, may have content that is of interest in users' status updates, as well as photo and video links. However, you will need to request authorization from the users in order to extract and share any protected information. We will look at this process in Chapter 13. If your site is oriented around social networking, and is geared toward building a strong community spirit, then you might want to explore the APIs of any related social sites.

PRESENTATION

Expose Information Externally

Exposing your information externally is the inverse of the previous section. As part of your marketing strategy, you have an incentive to maximize your presence and grow the population not only of your direct but also indirect users. As other sites leverage your content, they increase your rank with search engines and your visibility to consumers.

The practical implication for your service is that you should try to publish as many of your programming interfaces as possible. If you have content that may be relevant to other related services, then you should consider packaging it as an embeddable component, such as a feed, that others can consume. To ease the load on your own infrastructure, you may want to make them available via PubSubHubbub.

Salmon

The Salmon protocol is a standardized mechanism to distribute user-contributed content, such as comments, ratings and reviews, to other consumers. The background problem is that a significant amount of social activity is syndicated but that this aggregation flows only in one direction. Any downstream updates or additions are invisible to the original source.

Salmon lets aggregators and sources unify the conversations. It is a bi-directional protocol, focused on public conversations, which specifies a mechanism for additional content to "swim upstream" to the original content sources and thereby trigger more commentary. It is interoperable with PubSubHubbub, which can be used to send notices in real-time.

Practical Recommendations

Real-time web is an exciting new area that will require rethinking in how to design a successful user experience. Some ideas to consider for your service:

- Enable Twitter and Facebook to help drive traffic and support your business.

- If you support feeds, make them available via PubSubHubbub – to ease the load on your own infrastructure.

- Enable sharing of content from your site to real-time services, such as Twitter, Facebook, consider using something like: sharethis.com.

- Aggregate comments in both directions with Salmon.

- Take advantage of other real time feeds in your service: show latest tweets, recent stock quotes, etc.

- Detect presence of your users in the service. Let your service show which users are active and present in real time.

- Follow the real-time web principles in your own service design and let users contribute content with comments and reviews.

- Extend your ecosystem by publishing part of your service as an embeddable component that other sites can use.

Identity

Most applications have a need to distinguish between users in order to optimize the experience with customized, highly relevant content and enforce any access controls on sensitive and personal data. Typically, the data related to individuals is stored in a directory, which needs to scale to very large sizes in order to accommodate multi-tenant enterprise applications and global consumer-oriented services.

Scalability is not the only challenge. There is also a requirement to simplify the user experience with minimal manual re-authentication between services, which is difficult in a distributed multi-vendor architecture and leads to a need for federated identity management for which there are new standards that have yet to converge. Due to the dispersed nature of cloud services, a high level of security is mandatory in order to protect credentials and any personal information.

In addition to security there is also the potential to leverage user-based preferences, context and history to maximize accessibility; improve the efficiency, clarity and aesthetics of the experience; and generate custom content that is tailored to the user's geographical location and social networking environment.

Chapter 13

Authentication

Unless a service provides anonymous access exclusively, it needs to manage its users. The service will need to identify each connected user in order to analyze and personalize the user experience. There may also be a need to correlate usage to an identity in order to bill for a service or provide differentiated access to personal and other sensitive information.

This chapter examines several approaches to managing identities and associated credentials in order to provide secure and efficient authentication across an ecosystem of cloud-based services.

Background

In the past, many applications approached these problems in isolation, leading to a proliferation of user management stores and systems. This fragmented approach to identity management has contributed to a variety of problems:

- Users must battle with an overwhelming number of accounts and credentials that they need to remember and manually reenter.

- The additional burden on the user often leads to weak passwords or reuse of credentials across security domains. As a result, the sensitivity of any data may be compromised.

- Users may balk at the prospect of creating additional accounts resulting in poor visitor-registration and conversion ratios.

- Application providers need to redesign and manage an identity management system. This involves considerable work in an area often outside of the core competency of the web developer.

- Compliance to regulations such as Sarbanes-Oxley, FDA 21-CFR-11, HSPD-12, Gramm-Leach-Bliley, HIPAA, Canada's PIPEDA and the

EU Privacy Protection Directive 2002/58/EC often imply sophisticated identity management, making it difficult for small web sites to enter the market.

- A silo approach misses an opportunity to leverage common site requirements and share acquired information (e.g. browsing history and analytics) as authorized by the user.

Directory Synchronization

The earliest attempts to deal with this problem involved synchronization of user data between security domains. Users could then provide the same identity (username) and credentials (password) to multiple applications. It was also possible for an organization to establish a directory synchronization mechanism with another organization or between applications.

IDENTITY

This approach reduces some problems but creates others. The user is not burdened with duplicate credentials, but the implementation requires establishing, coordinating and monitoring a number of point-to-point connections between multiple systems. Furthermore, since most synchronization occurs periodically as a batch job, there is a propagation delay in provisioning and de-provisioning. Not only does this present a challenge in supporting users who require immediate access to a resource, but it also presents a security risk when access needs to be revoked with urgency.

Nonetheless, directory synchronization is still very widespread and may be the only viable option for some organizations. Cloud providers recognize this and often provide some means to support the process. Google Apps Directory Sync provides a means to synchronize Google Apps users accounts with an enterprise LDAP server (such as Microsoft Active Directory or Lotus Domino). It supports sophisticated rules for custom mapping of users, groups, non-employee contacts, user profiles, aliases, and exceptions. Similarly, Microsoft Outlook Live Directory Sync pulls user, contact, group, and dynamic distribution group data from an on-site AD DS or Active Directory and replicates and synchronizes it with the corresponding Outlook Live domain.

Real-time Lookup

In order to optimize the user experience, it is necessary for service providers to standardize on on-demand mechanisms for sharing Authentication, Authorization and Accounting (AAA) information with each other and releasing other personal information upon request.

In this context, *Authentication* describes the process of verifying an individual's identity. Typically the users supply credentials that are associated with their digital identity. These credentials are often classified into:

- What you know (e.g. personal identification numbers or alphanumeric passwords)

- What you have (e.g. digital certificate or cryptographic token)

- What you are (e.g. fingerprint, iris scan)

Each of these has its strengths and weaknesses, so strong authentication systems will usually combine at least two mechanisms to overcome the most apparent vulnerabilities.

Authorization refers to the mechanism to establish if the authenticated entity is permitted to execute a particular activity or access a given resource or service. In addition to the user's identity, the criteria may include a combination of physical location, time of day and previous access history.

The *Accounting* system tracks access and use of network resources by authenticated and authorized users for billing, capacity planning and security purposes. In addition to the identity of the user and time of access, an AAA system may also record more granular auditing that is specific to the actual service.

RADIUS and its successor Diameter have had significant success in AAA federation for network access, however they are not ideally suited for web access, where a separate set of initiatives has gained traction.

Federated Web Identity Solutions

Fortunately, there is no lack of standards relating to identity management. Web federation technologies such as OpenID, Security Assertion Markup Language (SAML), OAuth and Information Cards typically provide some combination of authentication, authorization and personalization services. In fact, one of the biggest obstacles to widespread adoption has been the rivalry between competing approaches. It is further compounded by the flexibility of the standards, which leads to discrepancies in their implementation.

Nonetheless, federated identity solutions ultimately benefit enterprises by allowing them to perform better logging and audit functions, while decreasing the costs associated with password reset and secure access to existing heterogeneous applications (Ping Identity, 2009). Similarly, they reduce the risk of orphan accounts, thereby preventing application access from former employees who have left the company. They replace spreadsheet-based reporting with a comprehensive view of access rights that provides a clear understanding of security posture and helps in implementing centralized, enterprise-wide controls.

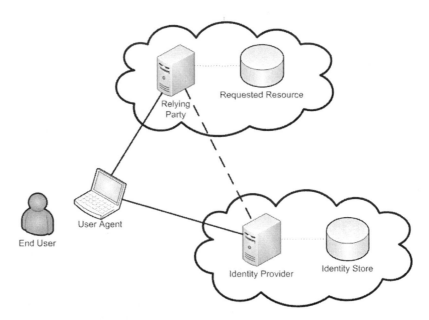

Figure 13-1: Federated Identity Management

As shown above (Figure 13-1), the fundamental premise of a federated identity management use case is that the requested resources reside in different management domains than the identity stores holding the users wishing to access the resources. Therefore there is a need for the entity managing the resource (called the Relying Party) to validate the user's identity through the Identity Provider. This means that the client application (User Agent) obtains credentials from the End User and passes them to the Identity Provider, which validates them. The Provider then informs the Relying Party that this User Agent has been authenticated. While it may be possible for the Identity Provider to communicate directly with the Relying Party, it is more common to provide the validation via the User Agent in the form of a secure token that has been digitally signed by the Identity Provider.

Single sign-on (SSO) is the term used for facilitating user identification, authentication and authorization. In an enterprise, it is typically based on a primary identity store such as Microsoft Active Directory or Sun Identity Manager. In a cloud-based world, it has become increasingly desirable to also use application-based user-stores such as Salesforce.com or Google Apps as the primary directory.

These can be linked to other identity stores through standards such as Liberty Alliance Identity Federation Framework (ID-FF), Web Services Federation (WS-Federation) or the Organization for the Advancement of Structured Information Standards (OASIS) Security Assertions Mark-up Language (SAML). In some cases, OAuth, OpenID and information cards are also being used to authenticate users for off-premise applications.

While granular application authorization is still relatively immature, the federation standards themselves are robust enough to be deployed in many enterprise scenarios including those with SaaS requirements, assuming that the SaaS providers implement a mechanism for federated SSO.

The current trend in preferences appears to be toward SAML-based SSO complemented with eXtensible Access Control Markup Language (XACML), which describes both an access control policy language and a request/response language for the policies ('who can do what when'), accommodating queries for specific authorization.

OAuth is also gaining popularity due to its simplicity. It provides a means for one application to access data (e.g. images, documents, contacts) stored with another service provider without revealing the credentials to the consuming application. Usually, a new browser window appears that allows the user to supply credentials directly to the data source. For example, if an application needs access to Google Contacts then it would first redirect the browser to a secure Google URL. After successful authentication, the storage provider (e.g. Google Contacts) would release the requested data to the consuming application.

Identity Architecture

Before we dig into the practical implications of Identity Management it is worth pointing out a key distinction between applications that cater to enterprises and those that target consumers.

Consumer Applications

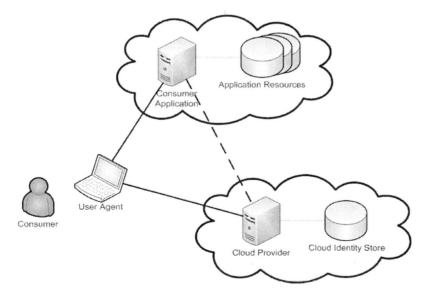

Figure 13-2: Consumer Identity Management

Chapter 13: Authentication

Applications that provide consumer access need to be able to handle huge numbers of users, but generally only store simple information and provide limited access control (Figure 13-2). In the most common scenario, the relying party is any web application. The identity could be provided anywhere but it is easiest to achieve large scale and high interoperability by leveraging cloud providers and using their usernames, often in the form of an email address.

If you are thinking of designing a new web based service and building a proprietary user authentication system just for your application, then you have an opportunity to simplify your solution through federation, by tapping into Google, Yahoo, MySpace, Twitter or others as user providers.

However, federated identity often needs to be complemented with an application-specific user store that manages individuals' specific details, such as their service profiles. The local application store, which includes user logs and preferences, links to the authentication and authorization system through the user identification (such as an email address).

IDENTITY

Enterprise Applications

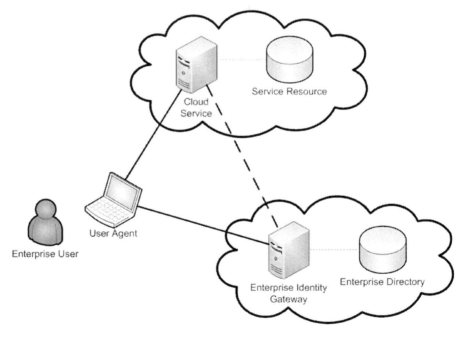

Figure 13-3: Enterprise Identity Management

Enterprises may more commonly adopt the reverse form of federation (Figure 13-3). Instead of tapping into a global identity store from a cloud provider, they manage their own users. However, there is an increasing demand for incorporating cloud-based services into their corporate architectures and making these applications accessible to their users without sacrificing any control over authorization.

Keep in mind that even large enterprises usually have relatively small identity stores (less than a million users), but they have much more sophisticated requirements including additional user attributes, refined authorization, workflow, privileges, access controls and advanced auditing capabilities.

As a result, it makes sense for the enterprise directory (e.g. Microsoft Active Directory, Lotus Domino or any other LDAP directory) to remain the authoritative source of identity information. Web and cloud applications (whether custom-built on IaaS/PaaS or commercial SaaS offerings) need to find a way to interact with the enterprise directory and share authentication, authorization and accounting information.

While real-time lookups always have the benefit of providing current information, there may be scenarios where they are not appropriate. In the consumer context described above, there is no feasible way to synchronize user information given the size and rate of change that cloud-scale identity systems need to accommodate. However, in an enterprise environment replication is a very real option and should be considered.

IDENTITY

Earlier in this chapter, we mentioned Google Apps Directory Sync and Microsoft Outlook Live Directory Sync as examples of LDAP directory synchronization options. While these are possible, they do carry disadvantages related to propagation delays. On the other hand, provisioning standards, such as SPML, make it possible to immediately replicate important changes to identity stores with little or no latency. As these standards evolve they are likely to replace batch-oriented directory synchronization.

Identity in Practice

Regardless of whether you are targeting consumers or enterprises, the overall approach is the same. The key is to determine which information is needed and then decide which stores are likely to have both the candidate information and a suitable (e.g. multi-factor) level of authentication.

While you may have reason to limit yourself to one particular back-end store, the more flexible your solution is, the more customers that you can potentially reach. In many cases, the login page is, in fact, an identity provider discovery page: the users choose which external identity they want to use for logging in.

A choice of heterogeneous authentication leads to the decision of which federation standard(s) to support in your application. In the consumer market, OpenID and OAuth are prevalent, whereas in the enterprise market it is more common to use SAML and/or SPML. However, these are not cast in stone. You can use any of the standards for any type of customer as long as all they are supported by the services that you use.

For example, App Engine applications have three supported options for authenticating users: Google Accounts, accounts from Google Apps domains or OpenID identifiers. Applications can detect whether a connected user has already signed in and can redirect the user to a sign-in page. While a user is signed in, the application can access the username (user's email address or OpenID identifier) and can detect whether the current user is an administrator.

Next, we will look at some of these options in more detail.

OpenID

IDENTITY

OpenID provides a framework for establishing an account with one provider (e.g. Google Apps) and providing sign-on capabilities to other web sites accepting OpenID authentication. More technically, OpenID is a federated identity system used to authenticate users across disparate web services. It offers the ability for users to log into one website (an OpenID relying party, such as Facebook) using credentials from another website (an OpenID identity provider, such as Google).

In practice this means:

1. The user creates an account with an OpenID identity provider (such as Verisign, Google, Yahoo or MySpace).

2. The user visits the site of an OpenID relying party (such as Facebook or a Google Apps hosted domain).

3. The site offers multiple login options including a link to the OpenID identity provider.

4. The relying party refers the user to the identity provider for authentication.

5. The user authenticates with the identity provider.

6. The identity provider confirms the user identity to the relying party supplying a token (persistent opaque identifier).

7. The user can visit the relying party website without providing a password.

Open ID gives you one login for multiple sites. Each time you need to log into a site using Open ID, you will be redirected to your Open ID site where you login, and then you will be referred back to the original site. In some cases, the authentication may even occur transparently. For example, you can link your Facebook account to your Google account and then log into Facebook automatically whenever you have already signed in to Google.

If you set up your App Engine service to use OpenID for signing in, your app becomes an OpenID relying party. In other words, your app does not provide OpenID identifiers, but it requires them for sign in. Note that App Engine does not provide a user interface API for OpenID sign-in. This is the responsibility of the developer.

The OpenID sign-in user interface must allow the user to enter a URL that serves as an OpenID identifier. The application might include a pop-up menu listing the domain names of popular OpenID providers, along with a box for the user to type the unique part of the URL.

Because OpenID identifiers are provided by a large number of popular websites and services, including Google, supporting OpenID is an effective way to integrate your service with Google App Marketplace and make it broadly accessible to users.

OAuth

OAuth specifies a standard authorization protocol that allows users to grant granular access to resources managed by other services. In the past, you would have needed to provide the resource credentials (e.g. username and password) to all websites needing access. This approach entails two disadvantages: the password could be compromised and it provides no restrictions on what can be done with the password.

OAuth solves this by:

1. Allowing resources to be shared between websites without exposing the user's password

2. Providing fine-grained access to resources and services across websites.

In the simplest terms, OAuth provides a mechanism to authorize one website – the consumer – to access data from another website – the provider. For instance, you may want to authorize a social networking service, such as Facebook, to access images from a photo repository, such as Flickr. In this case Facebook would be the consumer and Flickr the provider.

There are countless other scenarios where one service leverages the content of another. A printing provider might require access to a photo storage service. Value added Twitter services will require access to a user's Twitter stream and private messages. Social networking sites often try to seed their address books with contacts from other sites.

In these cases, the user will log into the provider (or have previously logged in). The provider will indicate that the consumer would like to access specific content and ask for authorization after which it will refer the user back to the consumer for further action. How the provider authenticates the user is beyond the scope of OAuth. It might require a username and password or a physical token. Or it might authenticate with Open ID.

OpenID with OAuth

In fact, OpenID and OAuth are often used together even though they are two distinct and independent standards, focusing on authentication and authorization, respectively. The main objective of OpenID is to reduce the number of identities users need to maintain online. On the other hand, the purpose of OAuth is to provide a simple and secure mechanism for one website to access user-owned resources on another website.

IDENTITY

Each standard has its place. If you build a website and use OpenID, then you do not need to authenticate users or manage their identities. However, you do not automatically have access to all of their web-based resources since you never actually receive their credentials. On the other hand, if you use only OAuth, then you can receive access to a user's external resources but you do not automatically know the user's identity. While you may only have the need for authentication or authorization, it is very common to require both.

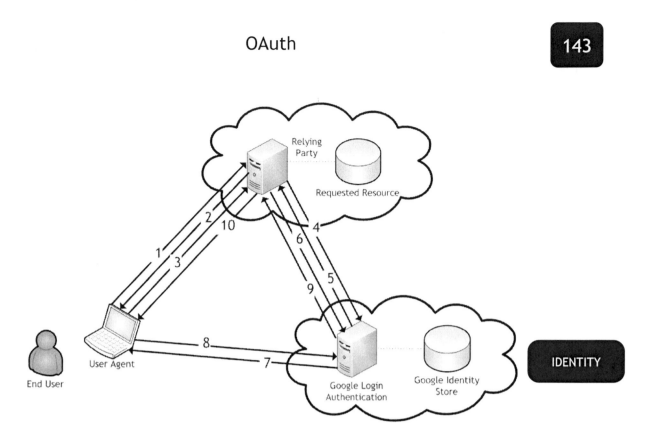

Figure 13-4: Google Login Authentication

In order to enjoy the benefits of both OpenID and OAuth, it is necessary to combine them. A good example of this approach is a web application that leverages Google Apps (Figure 13-4)[1]. In this scenario, the web application is the relying party and Google acts as the identity provider.

1. The user requests a web page offering protected content.

2. The web application asks the end user to log in by offering a set of log-in options, including Google Apps accounts.

3. The user chooses to sign in using a Google Apps account.

4. The web application performs discovery to find the location of the XRDS (eXtensible Resource Descriptor Sequence) document. XRDS is an XML format providing metadata about the resource, such as the location of the user's OpenID service provider.

5. Google returns an XRDS document, which contains the Google Apps (hosted) domain endpoint address.

6. The web application sends a login authentication request with OAuth parameters to the provided endpoint address.

---

[1] As documented by Google: code.google.com/apis/accounts/docs/OpenID.html

7. This action redirects the user to a Google Apps account Federated Login page.

8. The user signs into the Google Apps account. Google Apps then displays a confirmation page and asks the user to confirm or reject a set of authentication requests by the web application. The user is also asked to approve access to a specific set of Google Apps services.

9. If the user approves the authentication, Google returns the user to the web application, and supplies a persistent, opaque OpenID identifier that the application can use to recognize the user as well as an OAuth request token.

10. The web application uses the Google-supplied identifier to recognize the user and allow access to application features and data. The web application uses the request token to continue the OAuth sequence and gain access to the user's Google Apps services.

IDENTITY

SAML

The Security Assertions Mark-up Language is another Federated Identity Management standard. Similar to Open ID, it allows a Service Provider to offer a service without implementing its own authentication system. Instead, the service providers trust another entity (the Identity Provider) to provide authenticated users to them.

The technology used to implement this functionality is XML-based. It competed initially with WS-Federation, which is part of a joint Microsoft & IBM initiative called WS-Security. However, SAML appears to have been more widely adopted for SSO (single sign-on) and WS-Security eventually joined OASIS so that the standards have grown to be more complementary than competitive.

At the same time, there is still a wide area of overlap between the use cases for OpenID and SAML. They are difficult to compare since they specify to different levels of abstraction. Some argue that it would be better to compare the SAML Web Browser SSO Profile rather than the SAML "core" itself, to OpenID Authentication for a side-by-side comparison of capabilities.

SAML is an abstract framework specifying the definition of assertions along with protocols for obtaining and transporting these assertions. Most importantly, the SAML core specification does not define any end-user visible behavior. The background reasoning is that end users should not be encumbered with the underlying trust relationships and security assertions involved in SSO. It should occur automatically, and execute as transparently and invisibly as possible.

SAML-based Web SSO provides the tools to meet such a requirement, while OpenID defines a specific Web Single Sign-On protocol prescribing a particular "end-user identifier format" as well as a particular form of "identity provider discovery".

In summary, both standards are similar. SAML is more flexible but also more difficult to implement. OpenID caters to Web SSO where it defines a specific user interaction. If web-based single sign-on is the objective, then it is the simplest solution. For other use cases, such as transparent authentication to a back-end identity store, SAML offers more options.

A good example of SAML is provided by Google for Google Apps hosted services that are linked to a customer's identity store. In this case, an application (such as Gmail) is hosted by Google and represents the relying party, but the customer provides a SAML-based user authentication service and is therefore the identity provider.

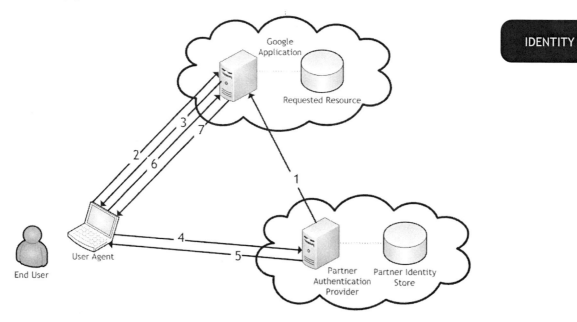

Figure 13-5: SAML Authentication to Google Apps

Figure 13-5 illustrates the following steps[1].

1. Before any authentication can proceed, the partner provides Google with the URL for its SSO service as well as the public key that Google can use to verify SAML responses.

---

[1] As documented by Google:
code.google.com/googleapps/domain/sso/saml_reference_implementation.html

2. Each authentication process begins when the user requests access to a hosted Google application, such as Gmail.

3. Google generates a SAML authentication request. Google then redirects the user's browser to the Identity provider. It embeds both the SAML request and the URL of the requested Google application in the URL for the SSO service.

4. The identity provider decodes the SAML request and authenticates the user. They could authenticate users by either asking for valid login credentials or by checking for valid session cookies.

5. The identity provider generates a SAML response that contains the authenticated user's username. This response is digitally signed with public and private DSA/RSA keys. The identity provider encodes the SAML response and returns it to the user's browser along with a forwarding mechanism for the browser.

6. The browser forwards the information to Google's ACS (Assertion Consumer Service). For example, the SAML response and destination URL might be embedded in a form with JavaScript on the page that automatically submits the form to Google.

7. Google's ACS verifies the SAML response using the provider's public key. If verification is successful, ACS redirects the user to the destination URL and logs the account in to Google Apps.

Microsoft

As mentioned above with regard to WS-Security, Microsoft has been a major participant in various federated identity management activities for many years. They do support some of the standards described above in their products and services, so even organizations that have a heavily Microsoft-oriented software portfolio have no absolute need to use proprietary Microsoft services and technologies for Identity Management.

Nonetheless, it is worth at least mentioning two Microsoft identity systems in the context of cloud computing. The first is Live ID (formerly Microsoft Wallet and Microsoft Passport), which caters to consumers of public services. And the second is the Windows Identity Foundation of Windows Azure, which might be of interest for enterprise-based authentication.

Given the reach of Microsoft, it is useful to cover the service-consumer and service-provider perspectives for both consumer-oriented and enterprise-oriented use cases.

Consumer: Microsoft has announced that Live ID will eventually support OpenID, making it possible for cloud-based services to easily leverage the

Microsoft identities in the same way they connect to other public identity stores. However, in the interim, it is also possible for ASP.NET applications (or Windows Azure) to obtain WebRole and delegate authentication to Live ID through the .NET Framework.

In the other direction, Windows Azure, or other cloud-based applications running on Microsoft technologies, can implement OpenID, OAuth or SAML in order to tap into a wide variety of alternate user repositories with large user populations.

Enterprise: Enterprise customers have different requirements as we have already discussed. Those who use Active Directory will probably wish to use the directory as their authentication mechanism for any cloud-based services they consume. This could entail enabling WS-Federation or SAML on Active Directory Federation Services (ADFS) and exposing the directory to an identity provider or it could simply mean providing a one-way trust to an Active Directory hosted by the Identity Provider.

There will also be requirements for cloud-based applications that target enterprises authenticating users from a range of sources. The Windows Identity Foundation of Windows Azure is an extension of the .NET Framework that allows the application to decouple its authentication. It implements a claims-based identity in which security tokens (e.g. SAML tokens or X.509 certificates) contain claims (such as group membership) that are digitally signed and passed via the browser. These claims allow the application to implement more advanced authorization schemes in addition to authentication.

Force.com

Identity Management support is a constantly changing function of most cloud providers, so we won't cover each one of them in detail. Many offer partial support of the standards already mentioned or have announced plans to include them in future releases.

Salesforce.com illustrates this point. Force.com provides single sign-on to Active Directory or any other LDAP directory as well as SAML 1.1. A simple configuration setting indicates the location of the SSO Web service and Force.com offers code stubs that can be used by anyone building their own service.

It is also possible to grant access to Force.com data through OAuth with a Remote Access Application. To ensure security, the developer can generate a consumer key and secret that will be embedded in the external application.

Identity Service Providers

As mentioned above, Identity Management is still an evolving technology. There are several different standards and proprietary protocols in operation, whereby many cloud providers haven't even begun to consider any of them. This can make life difficult for an application developer who wants to be able to offer universal SSO connectivity but isn't prepared to implement a dozen different interfaces.

Amazon, Google, and Safesforce.com support the Security Assertion Markup Language (SAML). But they are the exception rather than the rule. Only about 5% of the estimated 2,200 service providers in the cloud-computing market publicly support SAML and even fewer have committed to the other standards (Messmer, 2010).

IDENTITY

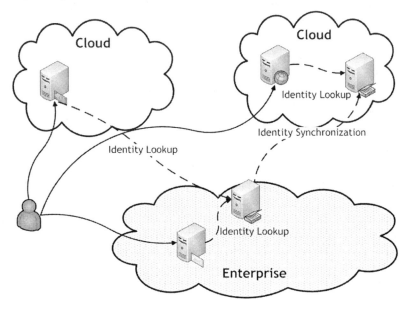

Figure 13-6: Identity Management

One alternative is to connect with trusted external parties that securely manage the identity of your users. Novell's Identity Manager works with Salesforce.com and Google Apps, as well as Microsoft SharePoint, and SAP applications to support a federated identity structure in the enterprise. Outsourcers, such as IBM, offer hosted options for enterprise identity management. The external parties could also be IDaaS (Identity as a Service) providers (e.g. PingIdentity, Tricipher/myonelogin, Symplified, SSOCircle, Janrain/myOpenID), or alternatively, identity services of your partners (suppliers, customers or affiliated organizations).

Identity-as-a-Service providers, which are often cloud-based themselves, may also be helpful in federating identity management (Figure 13-6). For example they may help to abstract and manage complexity between versions (e.g. SAML 1.1. vs SAML 2.0) and frameworks. But, in including them in the solution, it should be clear that they become critical cloud providers with all the drawbacks of vendor lock-in, service level negotiation and single point of failure.

While interoperability and standards are a critical part of the identity management challenge there are other considerations as well, such as the supported authentication mechanisms, provisioning and precautions for identity theft. Where security is a concern it is vital that, in addition to robust password policies, cloud providers support strong authentication either natively or via delegation and support. Even strong passwords can be compromised and, in the case of a breach, a hacker can automate attacks involving compromised credentials with relative ease.

It is much more difficult to circumvent biometric or token-based authentication or secure combinations of multiple factors. Identity solutions, such as TriCipher myOneLogin, provide a variety of authentication mechanisms such as SMS-delivered one-time-passwords, browser certificates, smart cards, security questions, biometric scans and secure tokens. An organization can combine these to achieve its preferred balance of usability and strong security.

Example: myOneLogin

Identity Management is usually considered very complex, often requiring substantial custom code and advanced configuration to make it work. Understandably, this discourages most people who don't have an immediate need to see it in action. If you would like a quick sample of a brokered identity service you can find a free and quick sample at myOneLogin (at least at the time of writing).

myOneLogin offers free demo domains that you can use to broker a SAML authentication profile with a list of identity providers. With the code that myOneLogin supplies added to your website you can automatically enable Google Accounts as an OpenID provider.

Provisioning

Another consideration is provider support for provisioning/de-provisioning. Provisioning should be rapid to expedite on-boarding new employees and changes in roles and responsibilities. De-provisioning is even more critical. In cases of identity theft or contract termination there must be a facility for immediate de-provisioning.

The primary standard for provisioning is the OASIS Service Provisioning Markup Language (SPML). SPML is not yet widely implemented across cloud services. However, it is still possible to achieve a certain degree of centralized provisioning. For example, SinglePoint Sync, coupled with a set of SPML gateways, can automate user account management and integration across many services in the cloud.

Access Controls

Authentication and authorization focus on determining who users are and which resources they can access. However, even if this information can be derived securely, it doesn't automatically mean that it will be enforced.

In a traditional, on-premise environment, it is possible to implement physical access controls. Applications and information may be confined to a location that is protected by a surveillance system with hardware authentication systems. Many enterprise services also assume a degree of trust toward employees. Those who have network access are not expected to abuse it.

IDENTITY

Neither of these two approaches, physical or trust-based, work very well in a cloud environment. It is impossible to create physical controls when the location of the data is outside the control of the owner. Likewise, a trust-based attitude is not prudent when anyone in the world can gain access to the information. Therefore it is critical for the software to regulate access to sensitive information according to stringent criteria. It is also vital to audit and validate the algorithms that provide this protection.

Multi-tenancy

One of the biggest benefits of cloud computing is the increased utilization that results from sharing of resources through multi-tenancy. However, it also introduces significant risks since it implies that tenants of the same system may share access controls and information.

The first concern is that a common access control system may be susceptible to cross-authentication if it is not properly isolated. In this case, authentication through a co-tenant may allow a user to access an organization's resources. Similarly, a model that relies on the lowest common denominator may not provide multi-factor authentication required by security-conscious enterprises.

A second concern relates to co-mingled data. If the data of multiple tenants is shared in the same repository it will maximize the efficiency of the system. However, this means that any software bugs or vulnerability exploits in the application could expose sensitive information to co-tenants.

In order to address these concerns, the application needs to be equipped with solid and flexible access controls. However, it is also necessary to rigorously enforce isolation and to take a vigilant and proactive stance in applying patches and monitoring anomalous activity.

Application Exposure

Putting together all the pieces to make a service work is only the first step in maximizing its potential. At some point, it is necessary to think through a full business model with all of its options. There are often multiple channels that you can use to deliver your value to consumers and receive some reward for doing so.

The most obvious is for users to directly access your application through a web browser or a thick client. However, you will reach a much larger audience if you also expose significant parts of your service programmatically. Some customers may integrate your offering into their application; but the biggest benefit comes from other service creators who are able to multiply the reach of your service.

Few services launch with a fully developed ecosystem in mind. Nonetheless, when they are carefully managed they have the potential to create significant internal synergy. It is not difficult to design services from the onset so that the endpoints can be exposed when the business decides that the time is right. It is therefore worth at least creating a foundation with maximum flexibility to leverage as many technical channels as possible.

IDENTITY

Practical Recommendations

Integrated identity management is one of the biggest challenges of cloud computing. As you take on these challenges, consider some suggestions:

- Don't build your own identity management solution! Leverage other stores with OpenID or SAML!
- Expose your service via OAuth to maximize your reach!
- Enrich your service's user experience by tying in features from other providers via OAuth!
- Ensure your service is multitenant-capable from the beginning!

Chapter 14

Personalization

The value proposition of electronic media over printed media includes the concept of personalization. There is no need for the user experience of every user to be identical. Instead, it can be customized and fine-tuned to the individual.

On the one hand, personalization may be based on explicit user actions such as defining preferences or entering payment information. On the other hand, it may also be implicitly derived from the user's location, device type or past interactions with the system.

Another way to look at personalization is that it may serve any of at least three objectives. It may help to make the content accessible to a certain use case or geographical market. It could also be used as a means of enhancing the user experience, making the customer more efficient and increasing satisfaction. Or, it could provide a means of introducing custom content and enlarging the user interaction.

Accessibility

At the risk of stating the obvious, there is a need to make sure your application will be available to all target users in whatever way they are likely to use it. The key word here is 'target'. It's a business decision which markets to pursue. Over-ambition may not lead to the highest profit margin.

There is significant incremental effort in developing a multilingual system over a single-language service. So you will want to make sure you really need it. Start by identifying the markets where the service will be relevant. Who is the target user population? Do they need support for multiple languages? Or is just a single language interface sufficient?

Usually, multiple languages are designated with a series of national flags or language dropdowns that take the user to parallel sets of web pages. The architectural challenge is to segregate all the language-specific components from the application logic. To visualize the problem, imagine that you have a number of

AJAX routines in your HTML pages and you cover twenty different languages. Whenever you need to update the code you also need to replicate it to all the pages. If you can separate the language specific components into separate modules, they will be less affected by code changes.

Other user-specific factors are support for different font sizes (varying precision of nearsighted vision) and potentially multi-modal input/output using combinations of text, graphics and sound.

In addition to user-based criteria, another important dimension is the device type. Users may be accessing the site through mobile devices and suboptimal network conditions. Screen sizes and bandwidth can span a very large range of values. Ideally the application can optimize the user experience based on the device characteristics and optionally also provide support based on the machine interfaces that are supported (e.g. ranging from voice to keypad and keyboard to stylus and mouse).

User Experience

Broadly speaking, there are three aspects of the user experience that may be personalized: Efficiency, Clarity and Aesthetics.

Efficiency

Efficiency relates to minimizing the mechanical effort of the user. There are several ways to reduce the number of clicks and keystrokes required in order to achieve the desired result, including optimized navigation, smart defaults, auto-completion, synchronization and network tuning.

Optimized navigation begins by determining the appropriate landing page for the user. You may have a top-level home page that serves as a base for all your activity. But, particularly for returning users, this may not be the optimal place to locate them each time they visit the site.

Optimization also involves determining the most common user actions and ensuring that they can be easily reached from the landing page. This might mean putting links on the home page itself or even in the menu structure that are visible on all the site pages.

The location on the page may also be significant. If users need to scroll to see a button or hyperlink then it increases the user effort. The top left of the page is generally the best place to put important links for left-to-right languages since it is most immune to browser resizing. However, if the focus of the page is elsewhere there may be a compelling reason to relocate, or duplicate, the navigation links.

To a large extent, optimized navigation is a universal requirement that does not differ from one user to another. However, there are also often user-specific tendencies to exercise certain options more than others. If the application monitors the user behavior, and tracks the most frequently used and most recently used actions, it can ensure that these receive preferential placement in the navigation structure.

Smart defaults assist the user by defining initial configuration and settings that are most likely to reflect the user choices. Again, there is a universal aspect of pre-loading these properties to optimal settings for the entire user-base. However, there may also be an opportunity to ascertain these with finer granularity by looking at the location (and locale), the device or even by drawing inferences based on personal details or user behavior.

There are some obvious ways that some of these properties may be used. The physical location (or the geographical locale specified by the user) may be used to provide a default language or regional formatting (currency, date, time). The device may influence the display characteristics or image resolution.

IDENTITY

But beyond these logical implications, there is also the opportunity to mine usage information over a larger array of factors. Over time, you may discover that female teenagers with smartphones tend to specify a very different configuration than male retirees using desktops. If you can anticipate the configuration based on a small set of automatically discovered properties, then you can preset the defaults accordingly.

Auto-completion takes the idea of smart defaults and applies it to content rather than configuration. The simplest implementation involves caching all user input and providing it as an option to the user for subsequent interactions. For example, it is common to retain payment methods and details as well as billing address and shipping information so that the user needn't re-enter the specifics with each order.

If there is only one possible set of values, it is easy enough to pre-fill the form with them. When there are a few sets of values (e.g. credit cards, shipping addresses) they can be listed as alternate options from which the user can choose. However, it is challenging for a static page to supply a vast number of values, such as search terms.

A browser cache may be able to partially address the problem but it can only access content that the user has supplied. A more common approach today is to use AJAX to connect to an Internet-based service that correlates partial entries with popular requests across the entire user base and proposes real-time auto-completion based on the most likely candidates.

Synchronization of devices provides another means to streamline the user interaction. Taking the counterexample of multiple isolated devices, the users need to re-enter all relevant data in each device. This can include configuration preferences as well as content such as contacts and personal data.

Synchronized devices, on the other hand, automatically replicate initial data and propagate changes thereby relieving the user of a tedious burden. Furthermore, particularly when one of the devices has a restricted machine interface (such as would be the case for entering text on a keypad phone) the user has the flexibility to optimize the entry to the most suitable device available.

Network tuning doesn't impact the amount of effort of the user. However, it does have a noticeable impact on the duration of the effort. It ensures that the bandwidth and latency (as well as quality and cost) of the network are optimized within the range of options available. The most logical first step is to prioritize the performance and pricing characteristics of the connectivity options of the device. For instance, WiFi and Ethernet may be subscription-based or free with significant bandwidth while 3G may be volume-prices and offer less reliable and slower connections.

Unfortunately, while there is significant opportunity for optimization in this area, most web-based applications are unlikely to have access to the information required and lack the authorization to manipulate the network interfaces. The main network-related capability of cloud-computing is only to optimize worldwide delivery by distributing the service geographically and associating the user with the nearest edge node. The most sophisticated approaches involve using a content delivery network. However, for smaller scale applications it may be a significant improvement to split the service into two or three regions and redirect the user to the appropriate server through DNS.

Clarity

The previous section makes some aggressive recommendations to optimize steps in user interaction. It's important to keep in mind that these are not guidelines to pursue at all costs. There should be a balance between user effort, intuitive feel and predictable behavior.

As an illustration of the dilemma, imagine an application that continuously re-structures the menus according to the most recent user actions. While there may be some efficiency gains in terms of fewer clicks needed, it is very likely to confuse the user who needs to search through an apparently random list to find each link. To minimize this nature of disruption there is a lot to be said for keeping the application stable and placing commands and buttons predictably, maintaining consistency with other tools while respecting user-specific custom definition.

It is also important to avoid cognitive overload of presenting users with an over-abundance of rarely used options. One approach is to allow users to provide a simple navigation scheme by default and allow users to advance to a more complete menu structure when they are ready.

The key is to carefully plan all levels of the user experience potentially beginning with anonymous access to a simple authenticated menu system that gradually evolves into a fully functional environment. This migration needs to retain some continuity in the browsing experience and consider the granularity of user configurability at each level.

Aesthetics

One last aspect of the user experience relates to the preferred appearance of the service. While there is some overlap between aesthetics and clarity, we use this category to relate primarily to the non-functional items of the user interface, such as fonts, colors and backgrounds.

Even though you can't expect a great productivity improvement in allowing the user to customize the service appearance, you still have a significant incentive to consider it in order to improve your application's stickiness. If the users invest effort in personalizing the user interface, and are pleased with the result, they will more strongly identify with it and are likely to foster that attachment.

A simple example of these settings might be the option that you get from a Twitter account to select your background or Gmail's choice of theme. Your application can expand on the granularity of configuration to your heart's content but, again, you want to make sure you don't overwhelm the user. One technique is to packages a consistent set of settings into skins and allow the user to select (and potentially further customize) these. Skins also often go beyond simple colors and fonts to modify the window shape, menu structure and other significant parts of the UI.

Custom Content

The experience relates to the personalization of configuration settings and streamlining user input. Beyond these, it is also possible to leverage a variety of external content that will vary depending on the user's identity and attributes. We'll look specifically at location-based information, social networking content and then generally comment on other sources of content.

Location

A tremendous amount of information derives its relevance from its proximity to the user's location. The technique to derive the geographical coordinates of the user usually involves an IP lookup for stationary devices and triangulation for mobile users. The conventional approach is for the server-side code to check the detected user IP address against the IP2Location database.

Mobile devices can use either GPS or wireless triangulation. The technique isn't that different in either case. GPS provides a triangulated position based on a precise clock and the latency from three or more satellites. Wireless (cellular or, in

Chapter 14: Personalization

some cases, WiFi) relies on precise positioning information about the transmitters and uses signal strength to triangulate a position. Devices that have both a GPS receiver and a cellular radio will often use a combination of both to achieve the fastest and most accurate results.

While it might technically be possible for a cloud-based application to query a mobile device for its position, there are so many possible mechanisms to identify location that it would be difficult to implement. HTML5 is a great help in this regard. It offloads this work to the browser so that the application doesn't need to worry about device-dependent features. HTML5 provides functions to determine the current location with parameters such as timeout, maximum age and accuracy, after which it can also show a map in the browser.

Location information can have far-reaching consequences on the content of an application. Market offerings and news, for example, are often only relevant to a specific territory. You may also need to consider licensing issues for content that you do not own. As an example, Netflix, an American company that offers on-demand video streaming over the Internet, doesn't allow international users full access to its service as this would infringe on its license from the copyright holders.

One of the most obvious applications of geolocation is mapping, which is particularly useful for navigation systems. There are several providers of cartographic information you may want to leverage in your application. Google Maps, for example, has APIs that let you embed its functionality into your own website and applications, and overlay your own data on top of them. You can use Web Service URL requests to access geocoding, directions, elevation, and places information from client applications, and manipulate the results in JSON or XML.

OpenStreetMap is the Wikipedia of cartography. It is a community led project that offers similar functionality to Google Maps, with one exception: it allows community members to update maps and upload additional layers of mapping information. As a result, their database appears to be growing at a substantially faster rate than Google's. Google, on the other hand, provides an excellent StreetView and offers other innovative user-oriented features. So, it is really a question of looking at the application needs before making a design decision.

Navigation goes beyond the simple visual display of a map and assembles a directed graph of street vectors to derive a path from the point of departure to the destination. Unfortunately, this is a relatively complex task and there are few public APIs available at present. There are rumors of interfaces being made available on some of the mobile platforms but unless you can be sure your customers only use this platform they are of limited use. It is an item worth tracking, but you may need to rely on manual intervention in the short term.

While flat mapping information is interesting and can be very helpful, it is only the tip of the iceberg of what is possible through overlays. From points of interest, to community-provide photos, ratings and blogs, it is possible to associate a significant amount of content with particular locations and then visualize it in a way that reflects our spatial sense of structure.

Geosocial networking services, such as Foursquare, Gowalla, Qype and Yelp, combine location information with geotagged information, such as restaurants, and user-contributed content, such as ratings and reviews, to provide targeted and highly relevant information to mobile users.

Cloud computing lends itself particularly well to these multi-layer systems. Location information can be assimilated from a variety of sources and contributed by individual users, but it is then aggregated in the cloud where people can share their information. Cloud-based services can then mine knowledge from these location datasets of large-scale users to generate advanced analytics and further fine-tune the user experience.

IDENTITY

The biggest challenge in designing such a system is simply the volume of data than needs to be collected in order to generate useful information. As we shall see later in this book, SQL databases are not necessarily the best choice for this use case. Some of the newer projects such as CouchDB, MongoDB and Tokyo Cabinet may lend themselves better.

Social Graphs

Another vast area of content that is extremely user-specific is based on social networking. The simplest instance of this network is an address book with links (email addresses) to another group of individuals. It may also store other attributes such as telephone numbers, addresses, birthdays and other personal information.

Social networking services, such as Facebook, Twitter, Plaxo and LinkedIn combine these into a graph that you can traverse so that, for example, you can more easily find individuals with common friends or followers.

This content is highly personal and may be somewhat confidential. Therefore, it is typically restricted to the social networking application. However, using some of the standards we covered in the previous chapter, such as OAuth, you can retrieve and leverage the data to enhance your users' experience.

An emerging standard called XAuth may help to makes this sharing process even more automatic. As service providers, such as Google, Microsoft or MySpace begin using XAuth they will inform XAuth of which users are signed into their services (without passing the credentials, obviously). This alleviates the need for the user to inform another application how it wants to sign in and which services it would like to share. XAuth enables service providers to extend authentication across sites more efficiently. It also gives users the ability to see and manage what is being extended as users can visit xauth.org to see how services are using XAuth.

Other Services

In addition to social networking there are many other services that may be shared between sites. Automatic payments might be effected when a payment method is entered, for example. The key is to ask which services make sense to integrate with this application. Are there per-user integration points that will impact personalization? Which service components need to be personalized?

Practical Recommendations

As you optimize the stickiness of your site, consider taking a few steps to facilitate a highly personal user experience:

IDENTITY

- Engage the users in customizing the site to their preferences! Once they have invested effort, they are more likely to remain and return!
- Leverage location and social networks to provide high-value custom content!
- Ensure a clear and efficient user experience by optimizing navigation and data entry!

Integration

Cloud computing features a high level of scalability, such that processing cannot always take place on a single machine. A high degree of service decomposition for a granular service-oriented architecture also allows providers to achieve maximum efficiency and flexibility. Since the core functionality of the application is not completely self-contained, there is a need for an integration framework that simplifies federated data transfer and task processing.

INTEGRATION

In order to leverage widely distributed applications, systems and services, you need to achieve network connectivity across physical links and security boundaries and to optimize these connections for performance. A second step is to ensure compatibility of the application end-points and include suitable synchronous and asynchronous mechanisms to integrate with legacy applications. At a higher level, the application decomposition may need to be revisited to impose loose coupling and avoid single points of failure or performance bottlenecks.

Chapter 15

Network Integration

Cloud applications tend to be highly distributed. This means that multiple components collaborate in order to complete the requested tasks. In some cases, all components may be hosted by the same provider. In other cases, the services may be dispersed among several data centers and cloud providers. In order to orchestrate their interactions, it is necessary to develop interfaces between instances running in separate environments.

INTEGRATION

There is often a requirement to integrate with legacy components, which will typically come with a set of predefined interfaces. When there are dependencies, the choice boils down to which one of the existing interfaces to use (if there is more than one). On the other hand, if the system is being designed from scratch, then all options are on the table as the interfaces can be designed with connectivity in mind. In addition to ensuring that all integration end points are addressable and reachable, it is necessary to verify that there is secure, reliable and cost-efficient connectivity between them.

These basic requirements hold for both the deployment and the production phases, but the data traffic and security policies may be different between the environments. Integration during the introductory transition from another computing environment to the cloud may be particularly complex since it may also entail data migration with special connectivity. In some cases, the ongoing operation may function with a lesser level of integration. It is therefore important to look at both scenarios, the migration and the production environment, separately.

This involves examining the connections and assessing bandwidth charges, bandwidth limitations, latency (location to the extent it can be established) and any potentially unreliable components or links along the path. It also involves ensuring reachability (common address space, firewall permeability) and protecting the connection (SSL, VPN) particularly when components need to connect between clouds.

Network Connectivity

Required Connections

A starting point of the assessment would be to address how to provide network and transport connectivity between each of the end-users and back-end systems, as well as all services and their dependencies. You can begin by determining which end-points need to interact with each other.

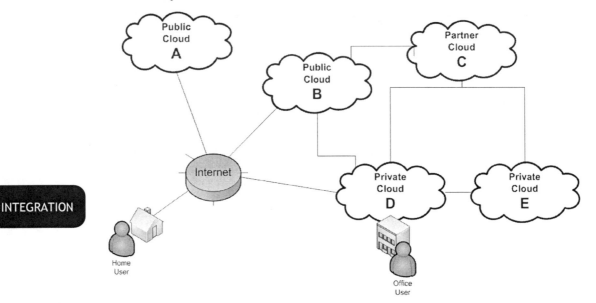

Figure 15-1: Basic Cloud Connectivity

It may not be necessary to create a full-mesh network architecture. For example in Figure 15-1 the network design shows that services from Public Cloud A are accessed via the Internet regardless of where the users connect. Public Cloud B, on the other hand is accessible from the Internet for remote users. But there is also a private connection to the internal network Private Cloud D. Partner Cloud C does not offer any Internet access at all. Users and services from Private Cloud D and E can access C, and C can interact with services on Public Cloud B. There are also two private networks, which might be used for disaster recovery and/or load-balancing. Office users can connect to these directly, whereas a Home user would connect via the Internet over a secure channel.

Given the diversity in enterprise architectures, the actual implementation will vary significantly from the example. A real deployment may be considerably more complex, but the basic principles are the same. The first step is to identify and classify all the required connections. Some of these may already be in place, but they should still be included in the design since there may be potential impact on them from the shifting of services and network traffic.

It is also important to consider internal connectivity within cloud providers. If a given cloud is geographically dispersed, then it may be useful to break it apart as in the example above with Private Cloud D and E. But even if the (private) cloud is confined to one data center, it is critical to understand the routing topologies and bandwidth utilization on each of the links. If the data center is approaching capacity constraints, then it may be necessary to re-architect the network or upgrade some of the links.

Connection Requirements

The next step will be to describe the requirements for each connection.

- What applications and traffic will run over it?
- How critical is the connection to the business?
- Are there any bandwidth/latency constraints?
- Who can access the connection? Is it secured?
- How reliable is it?
- Can you implement any fail-over or redundancy?

Some of the main categories are bandwidth and latency. You may also have specific requirements related to Quality of Service (QoS) and security.

The bandwidth requirement you specify will range from your average bandwidth to your peak load, depending on the criticality of the data that goes across it. Anything less than your average requirements will create a bottleneck that isn't sustainable. Allocating above your expected peak load (including some margin for error and growth) will not present a technical problem but is generally uneconomical.

Within that range, it is important to understand the impact of some amount of data loss during peak usage. If you are likely to lose major transactions, or even violate some laws, then you will want to err on the side of caution and overcapacity. On the other hand, if the loss can be easily sustained and the traffic resent at a later time, then you may be able to save costs by allocating resources more stringently.

In some cases, you may be able to influence your bandwidth requirements through the selection of your data format. As we will see in the next chapter, JSON is generally leaner than XML for encapsulating structured data and has become increasingly popular among cloud services. A binary format is typically even more succinct but may be difficult for humans to read and debug. Where large amounts of data are involved, it may even be worthwhile to compress the data prior to transmitting it. If data format size is critical, a common practice is to use JSON during development for ease of debugging and readability and convert to a compact binary format for production.

Latency is largely independent of bandwidth and represents the delays that occur between sending a packet from the source and receiving it at the destination. It is one of the most critical factors affecting the user experience and speed of transactions. The TABB Group estimates that more than half of all stock exchange revenues are exposed to latency risk (2008). A brokerage can lose up to $4 million per millisecond of latency. Google estimates that an additional 500 milliseconds of latency result in a reduction of 20% of traffic to its sites. And Amazon is calculated to lose 1% of sales for every 100 milliseconds of latency (James & Stolz, 2009). Given such drastic financial implications, it is wise to consider the geographical placement of any key distribution points.

QoS includes considerations of latency but also the percentage of dropped packets and jitter (or variance in latency). Browser-based HTTP access is largely resilient to minor transmission problems. The upper layers in the protocol stack can recover errors without the user noticing a difference. However, interactive streaming media, such as Internet Telephony and Video over IP, tend to expose network glitches and variability much more awkwardly to the user.

If the connections carry any sensitive traffic, then it is also necessary for them to be secured. This doesn't necessarily mean they must be encrypted at the Network or Transport Layer. The applications may use the Secure Socket Layer (SSL) which will provide a similar level of protection. Nonetheless, the requirement should be documented, so that it isn't inadvertently lost if the application provider assumes network-layer security.

Connection Options

After considering the requirements for each of the connections, comes the task of examining the possible options that meet the needs. There may be multiple telecommunications providers that offer network links between two end-points. In some cases, it may just come down to a financial decision on the costs (fixed and variable) that both demand. However, it is also worth looking at the service-level agreements, ability to expand and redundancy capabilities too.

You may also have additional options. For example, if you discover that one application is responsible for a high proportion of network activity, or cannot cope with the link latency the providers can offer, then you could look at restructuring the topology. One possibility would be to choose an alternate cloud provider but you may also be able to displace some of your internal infrastructure to improve the network performance too.

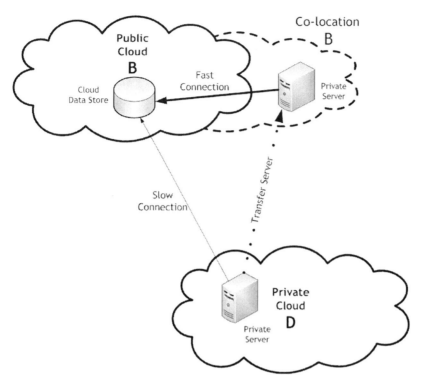

Figure 15-2: Transfer Server to Co-location

Imagine that you have a latency or bandwidth problem with link BD above (Figure 15-2). You might be able to move a server that interacts heavily with a data store in Public Cloud B from Private Cloud D into a co-location with Public Cloud B. This will have ramifications for connections that the server initiated with other internal systems, but if they are not as network-intensive or network-sensitive, it may be the better option.

Note also that you may not have control or responsibility over all the links that are critical to your business operation. Link BC, in Figure 15-1, would be administered between your partner and cloud service provider. You may also depend on links between cloud service providers that are not contractually your responsibility. Nonetheless, it is in your best interests to verify that these links exist, that they meet your requirements and that they are governed by service-level agreements.

Finally, you need to look at which mechanisms you will use to secure the connections. It may depend on how you are connecting to the cloud service provider. If you have a dedicated connection (e.g. through an MPLS network) you may not feel the need to further protect it even though it is not encrypted. On the other hand, if you are leveraging a shared Internet connection or are not comfortable with the security precautions of your ISP then you may want to protect the connection with IPsec or an SSL VPN.

Connectivity Configuration

Each network configuration involves some largely manual tasks to ensure that all configuration settings match at each end. Presumably all your cloud providers, including your own business, have experts who can make these happen.

At a network design level, however, there are some considerations that are good to verify early.

Addressability: How will the connection end-points locate their communications partners? You may choose to request static IP addresses, which will simplify connectivity issues. You may also want to register the servers in the global Domain Name System, so that the address space can change at a later point in time without disruption to the applications.

Firewall configuration: All clouds will probably have one or more firewalls that separate them from the Internet and other security domains. If your applications need to connect through firewalls, you need to ensure that the protocols and host IP addresses are registered in the firewalls. Your connections may also pass through HTTP proxies, which rewrite headers and/or present their own IP addresses to the firewalls. There are countless possibilities. The bottom line is that you need to test your application through the firewall to ensure that it works.

Routing: IP traffic needs to be routed from each end-point to the other. In a globally routable address space, this is not ordinarily a challenge. Your network administrators will have ensured that all external traffic is funneled in the right direction. However, if the service provider uses Network Address Translation to create private address space, then you may need to update your routing tables in order to be able to communicate with the correspondent.

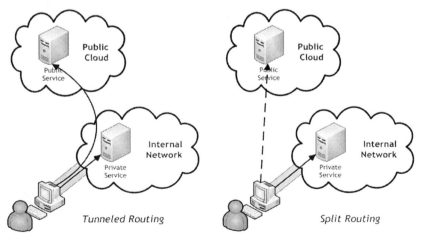

Figure 15-3: Tunneled versus Split Routing

Split Routing is another potential area for consideration. The most common use-case is a remote client connecting through a VPN to access corporate resources. If the tunnel is exclusive, all the traffic from the user's PC goes through the corporate network - even the traffic that is destined for the Internet. This routing is inefficient but it also allows the enterprise to more closely monitor traffic and enforce policies. The tendency today is to split the tunnels so that traffic is directed along its most efficient path. But this is not necessarily the best solution for enterprises with tightly enforced network filtering.

Unfortunately, it's impossible to enumerate all the configuration pitfalls you may encounter. Each case is unique in its requirements. The key consideration is not to underestimate the complexity, which new delivery models entail. Let us illustrate with a non-intuitive example of a problem we encountered:

INTEGRATION

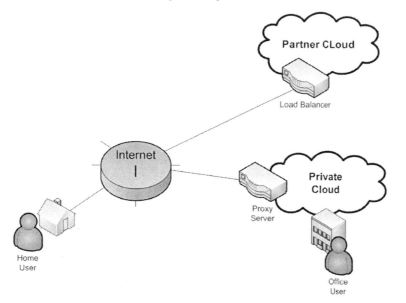

Figure 15-4: Proxy-channeled Traffic

Figure 15-4 is a simplified version of our previous topology. In this case, the private cloud (internal LAN) connects with the partner's cloud via the Internet. Users can also access the partner resources remotely, which presents an elegant and versatile solution. The challenge is that all outgoing traffic is routed through the internal firewall via a proxy server. This means that all outgoing traffic presents itself with the same IP address. That is not ordinarily a problem. However, if the Load Balancer receiving the connections is only expecting one IP address per connection, and one connection per user, then it may diagnose the incoming traffic as a denial-of-service attack and reject further connections leading to unavailability of the service.

Virtual Private Cloud

As alluded to above, establishing secure connectivity between an enterprise data center and components is not trivial. When you compound the complexity of discovering network resources, addressing them and ensuring all traffic is protected as it passes through public networks, the result is a challenge some organizations choose to forego.

One means of facilitating the task, and thereby seamlessly extending legacy applications into the cloud is through the use of a so-called Virtual Private Cloud (Figure 15-5).

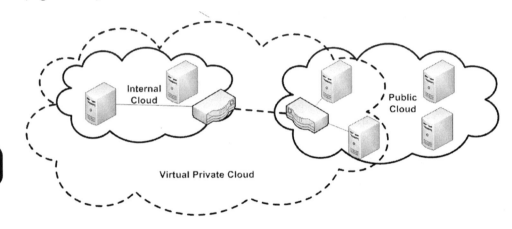

Figure 15-5: Virtual Private Cloud

Amazon launched a service by the same name in 2009, which essentially provides secure connectivity into a segment of Amazon's EC2 cloud. Other solutions, such as CohesiveFT's VPN-Cubed, provide similar functionality across cloud service providers. CloudSwitch also offers facilities to migrate virtual machines from the enterprise data center into the cloud. Layer-two bridging ensures that the network environment, including host names, IP and MAC addresses, remains intact thereby making it relatively easy to migrate legacy applications into a secure hybrid environment.

Content Delivery Networks

In some cases, content delivery (or distribution) networks (CDNs) can also help to improve performance and scalability when there are bottlenecks in backbone capacity or if there is excessive latency between two end-points. CDNs are networks of computers that collaborate to distribute content. They replicate content (media files, software, documents, and real-time media streams) to so-called edge servers that are as close as possible to end users.

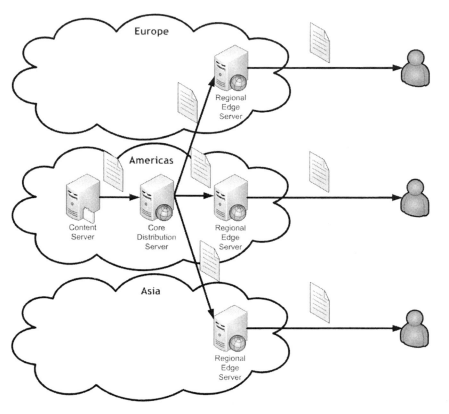

Figure 15-6: Simple Content Distribution Network

Figure 15-6 illustrates a simple content distribution network. Content is created on the Content Server and replicated into the CDN initially through synchronization with a core distribution server. The data is then propagated to multiple edge servers and the user can retrieve the content from the closest distribution point.

To understand the value proposition, imagine that the initial content is created in the United States. It is copied once to a core CDN server then once each across a transoceanic links to Europe and Asia as well as to one edge server in the Americas. The benefit in the Americas is less pronounced. But if thousands of users retrieve the content in Europe and Asia they will only be loading the regional links and the intercontinental traffic is minimized.

Content delivery networks are not simple to build. In order to work effectively they must determine user proximity, for example based on reactive or proactive probing. They may even monitor the connection and redirect users in-session. In addition, they typically employ advanced systems for web caching, server-load balancing and request routing (HTML rewriting, DNS-based). In some cases, they also provide real-time statistics and usage logs to their customers.

They help off-load the traffic on the Internet backbone and along the entire routing path, which equates to decreased bandwidth bottlenecks and end-user latency. They also reduce jitter, packet loss and minimize peak/surge performance degradation. And finally, the additional redundancy of the CDN can ensure higher availability in the face of local outages that might affect individual edge servers.

In summary, organizations that deliver significant volume of content that is sensitive to delivery times and patterns may want to investigate both the content-delivery capabilities of their cloud provider (e.g. Amazon CloudFront) as well as some of the leading CDN offerings, including Akamai and Limelight.

Practical Recommendations

The scale and heterogeneity of cloud services imply a set of complex connectivity requirements. As you try to address these, consider some suggestions:

- Test connectivity with representative loads! What should work in theory often fails in practice.
- Consider data location for any latency-sensitive traffic!
- Protect your connections! You never know where the data will go and who may be able to see it.

Chapter 16

Application Integration

Once the network infrastructure is in place, it is time to move on to the applications, which also need to be connected. As noted in the preceding discussion, application connectivity depends on network connectivity at the application protocol level. In other words, the application must use a transfer protocol such as HTTP, FTP, SMTP or a database-oriented connection protocol such as JDBC or ODBC. It will be the task of the network and perimeter security managers to establish this connectivity through all relevant firewalls and middleware.

INTEGRATION

Beyond establishing protocol connectivity, it is important to verify that business processes will be viable across all the applications that are involved. This means that service levels, reliability and performance expectations of each of the applications must be determined, as well as the impact on other applications that might interact with them.

Legacy and External Applications

Unless you are building a complete system from scratch, you will need to integrate with a number of applications that are outside your immediate control. In order to determine if the components can interoperate where necessary, you need to establish which interfaces/protocols are used between them and whether they are standard, or at least common between the endpoints.

Common integration styles to couple applications include:
- Data-scraping
- File Transfer
- Shared Database
- Message Passing
- Remote Procedure Call
- Web sockets

Data-scraping is one of the oldest, and most primitive, forms of application integration. It refers to a mechanism of parsing the output user interface for application information. Screen-scraping was a popular technique used to upgrade and interface with terminal-based applications. Web-scraping is still often used to extract information from browser applications when no other interface exists.

The challenge of this approach is that the applications are designed for human, rather than programmatic, access. It can be difficult to navigate the user interface without a thorough understanding of the application logic. The data may not always be positioned consistently on screen and may not correspond directly to the stored data. These problems lead to scalability and stability problems and make the approach a case of last resort.

Nonetheless, there may still be instances in a cloud-based implementation where it presents the only connectivity option. In this case, there will be a need to install the client stub (which might be a standard browser in the case of web scraping) on the system running the consuming application. It will also be necessary to deliver application-level connectivity between the client and any servers or databases that it requires. In some cases, it may be possible (and simpler) to relocate the whole application stack onto the same subnet as the consuming application instead of arranging for complex connectivity requirements.

File Transfer is the next option. It is suitable when applications don't expose any programmatic interfaces but do offer capabilities to import and export data, for example through reporting functions. Typical formats might include comma-delimited text files, fixed-field-size reports and, more recently, XML or JSON. If the two end-points don't share a common format, an additional transformation step may also be required.

In the cloud environment, file transfer is one of the simplest mechanisms to accommodate as it only requires a means of copying files from one system to another. This can be accomplished through FTP, HTTP or SMTP, and other protocols. The key requirement is therefore only to enable the relevant protocol between the two end-points, or at least from the cloud application to the drop and pickup point, and to ensure that both applications access the file using the same data structures.

Shared Database allows for tighter integration between applications. They can share data while also leveraging the transactional capabilities of the database management system. The main application requirements will be the use of a common schema by both applications as well as database connectivity between the cloud application and the database repository. Don't forget the operational responsibilities this may imply if the database ownership and management cross organizational boundaries.

A related approach would be to synchronize independent data repositories leveraging the replication capabilities of most relational database systems. This is a simple, low-cost solution. A more sophisticated mechanism would be the use of a transaction processing monitoring such as BEA Tuxedo, Microsoft MTS or IBM CICS, which can guarantee integrity of transactions, while also providing queuing, routing, and load balancing capabilities.

Message Passing is currently the most popular of the asynchronous communications mechanisms (which also includes File Transfer and Shared Database). It passes information in the form of messages, which have a predefined structure (schema) and embed the information as content (data). Very often these messages are queued with a message-oriented middleware (MOM) component. MOM, usually visualized as a bus or hub with spokes, can also structure the information flows in channels, pipes and filters and can transform or route the messages according to business logic rules.

The key considerations with MOM mirror those of database-oriented integration. It is essential that the end-points share a common schema and all applications need to have connectivity to the central MOM component, often called the Enterprise Service Bus.

Cloud-based examples of message passing services include the Amazon Simple Queue Service, Google App Engine Task Queue and Microsoft Azure Queue Service.

Remote Procedure Calls offer a synchronous alternative to message passing. This means that the calling application is blocked until the call completes. The logic of the application is therefore simpler since it is much easier to guarantee data integrity. However, the blocking nature may also introduce delays in processing, particularly if the calls involve large amounts of computation or run over high-latency links.

Some of the most common synchronous communications mechanisms in the past have included OSF DCE and distributed objects such as CORBA, JCA and Microsoft COM. Current web-services architectures more frequently use SOAP (formerly XML-RPC) and REST.

In addition to ensuring connectivity of the transport protocol (typically HTTP for SOAP and REST), it is necessary for the calling application to issue requests that align the published interfaces of the providing application. It may be possible to derive these from a WSDL definition or look them up in a UDDI repository. But most commonly, the developer is familiar with the interface definition and codes the client accordingly.

Internal Integration

Connecting external components is relatively straightforward from a design perspective. It may not be easy to configure a compatible interface, but you do not typically have a large number of options. You must use the interfaces that the external services expose.

On the other hand, a fully self-designed system can be decomposed and interconnected in an almost infinite number of ways. If you are trying to implement a service-oriented architecture, then principles of loose coupling would lead you to create minimal interfaces between modules in order to maximize their independence from each other. In this respect, both queuing and procedure calls are preferable over shared databases and files.

The downside of a granular architecture is that you will have a large number of components with countless interconnections and will need to decide how to implement them. One of the most fundamental questions is whether requests are synchronous or can be asynchronous. Asynchronous calls are preferable in a cloud environment since the process logic can proceed without a dependency over a potentially unreliable and slow network and there are no delays that arise from waiting for other modules to complete. However, the application logic may need to be more sophisticated since it will be necessary to integrate the results of the external module when it does complete.

The asynchronous process is highly encouraged (in some cases forced down) by the PaaS providers (Google App Engine), as their scalability model is based on small asynchronous requests that can be completed quickly and independently. This lets them fire up a sufficient amount of background capacity to serve your resource needs without their server resources being overloaded with a few labor-intensive requests.

On the other hand, the application logic is much simpler with a synchronous call, and it is an easier approach to use when the sub-task is simple, fast and does not involve high latency.

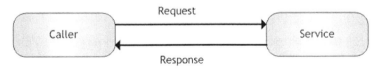

Figure 16-1: Synchronous Call

Synchronous calls primarily conform to two API styles (Figure 16-1). SOAP established itself as the first general-purpose API for web services. It is based on XML and typically involves XML-formatted parameters and responses.

REST is a newer style that is rapidly growing in popularity since it tends to be easier to use than SOAP and is often combined with JSON, a data format that is more succinct than XML. REST also has the added benefit of being usable from any browser, facilitating its use for testing and investigative purposes.

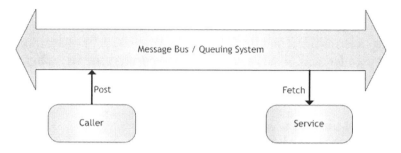

Figure 16-2: Asynchronous Call

Asynchronous access involves a message queue or message bus where tasks and/or data can be stored for subsequent processing by other components in the system (Figure 16-2). Typical queuing services include the Google App Engine Task Queue and Amazon Simple Queue Service (SQS).

Twitter is arguably the largest and best known queuing mechanism in the cloud – even if most people don't think of it in that way. It is designed as a human-to-human message bus but enhancements in the Twitter API now make it attractive for programmatic interaction. Typically, one side of the channel is still human but many applications consume and analyze Twitter data and some may generate tweets for marketing or special purposes, such as voting.

As part of your interface blueprint, you should also keep in mind that the application may be more successful if it exposes its own integration points to other applications. There is an increasing trend for Internet services to expose a RESTful interface to external application developers in order to grow their ecosystems. Many Internet applications now have a developer's section on the website that enables others to integrate with them. The Twitter API is a good example. It was designed for the Twitter web application, but is now published and available to other 3rd party developers as well.

Data Layer

We will look at data components and architectures in more detail in the next chapter. However, it is useful to describe the connectivity that is involved in this section. From a high-level perspective, the data layer provides content to the presentation layer and consumes back-end storage. It may also provide interfaces to the computational layer for information processing. There may be some mashup services, where content is pulled from multiple external data services, but generally the information is internal to the application.

Chapter 16: Application Integration

There are two primary approaches for interfacing the presentation layer with the data layer:

- Framework-specific data transport: e.g. Python/Django passes data to Django templates, which are then rendered for presentation

- Web Presentation Layer: JavaScript that pulls data from Data Layer using Restful Interfaces. In some cases, the internal presentation uses the same interfaces to data as are offered to partners for external access.

Data Feeds

Feeds are often directed at end-users and may be imported into a web page or news reader directly. We briefly touched on end-user feeds in Chapter 12 as part of our discussion on Presentation. However, it is also possible to use feed technologies to encapsulate a flow of semi-structured information. In this case, the information may never even be revealed to the user, or it may be transformed before being presented. As such, data feeds provide an interesting mechanism for application integration.

Let's back up and summarize what we mean by data feeds, also called web feeds, news feeds or syndicated feeds. As mentioned above, the formats for passing structured data between modules are often based on JSON or XML. However, not all information is highly structured. One specific data format that is widely used for data feeds is partially structured and encapsulated in so-called documents.

A web feed is a data format that describes structured, but frequently updated content, intended for wide distribution. A good example of this is Google reader, which consolidates news feeds from multiple sources to a unified interface, so that users can enjoy reading the news from a single site. Feeds offer several benefits: publishers can syndicate content automatically and readers can subscribe to timely updates from favorite websites or aggregate feeds from disparate sites.

Common content that is syndicated through a web feed includes news, blogs and podcasts. It may consist of HTML, links or attachments with digital media. Some web feeds are used only as a notification mechanism of content updates and therefore only include a summary rather than the full content, which is referenced by a link. A feed may also include headlines, excerpts, summaries or other metadata.

Web feeds make it possible for software programs to check for updates published on a website. In a typical scenario a content provider publishes a feed link which end users register with an aggregator program running on the local desktop. The aggregator, or client-side reader, may be a standalone program or a browser extension. Aggregators can be scheduled to poll all feeds periodically and download any new content.

There are two common technologies that underlie web feeds: RSS and Atom.

RSS (Really Simple Syndication) is a family of XML-specified web feed formats that were initially defined in 1999 and have now gained widespread use. An RSS document (which is called a "feed", "channel") includes full or summarized text, plus metadata such as publishing dates and authorship.

The *Atom* format is more recent and was developed as an alternative to RSS, whereby the name Atom applies to a pair of related standards.

- The Atom Syndication Format is an XML language used for web feeds. It was published to the IETF standards track in December 2005 as RFC 4287.

- The Atom Publishing Protocol (AtomPub or APP) is a simple HTTP-based protocol for creating and updating web resources. It was published in October 2007 as RFC 5023.

The proponents of Atom attempted to address some of the limitations of RSS that were at least partially attributable to its need for backward compatibility.

Content model: RSS supports both plain text and HTML but doesn't explicitly label the content. Atom supports explicit tagging of plain text, escaped HTML, XHTML, XML and Base64-encoded binary.

Date formats: RSS uses RFC 822 formatted timestamps. Atom supports the newer RFC 3339 (subset of ISO 8601).

Internationalization: RSS can only indicate the language of a feed but not that of its individual elements. Atom uses the xml:lang attribute to specify the language context for any human-readable content. Atom also supports links to resource identifiers that contain characters outside the US ASCII character set.

Modularity: The elements of the RSS vocabulary are specific to RSS. Atom elements may be reused outside of an Atom feed document.

Atom appears to have a lot on its side. It is an IETF Proposed Standard, contains several functional improvements and is strongly supported by companies such as Google. On the other hand, RSS was the first to market and is already well known and deeply established. Many sites do not even take sides. They simply publish in both formats.

Both Atom and RSS are pull-oriented protocols. They rely on the client to periodically poll for updates. Pull-oriented approaches have an inherent trade-off between latency of updates and resource utilization that is regulated by the polling frequency. In other words, if the client polls very frequently then it will slow down the application. On the other hand, if it polls irregularly it may take a long time for updates to be visible to the end user.

Push notifications can address these problems by having the server trigger any updates on the client. However, in order to work effectively, it is necessary to maintain a constant connection between the client and server. For websites with a very large number of subscribers, these connections can represent an unacceptable load and server-side bottleneck.

As more services become more data centric, especially through the real-time web, the amount of data and the update frequency are growing exponentially. It is inefficient for every service to build its own synchronization mechanism between data providers (who are updating data) and data consumers (who need to check updated data). A scalable framework to address this problem is PubSubHubbub, which caches data feeds and does not burden the original data source with unnecessary traffic.

PubSubHubbub offloads the feed content distribution from a website itself. It is an open, server-to-server, web-hook-based publish/subscribe protocol that extends both Atom and RSS. Its objective is to provide near-instant notifications of change updates to subscribed topics rather than relying on periodic client polling.

PubSubHubbub operates in an ecosystem of publishers, subscribers, and hubs.

- *Publishers* expose their content as traditional Atom or RSS feeds, but with the inclusion of hub references, such as <link rel="hub" ...>. Whenever they publish a new item they also post notifications to all of their hubs, which in turn, inform their subscribers.

- *Subscribers* also consume Atom or RSS feeds as before, by requesting them from the publishers. However, if the feed contains a hub reference then the subscriber can choose to subscribe to the feed on that hub. In this case the subscriber must accept notifications (via webhook callbacks) from the hub when any of its subscribed topics have updated.

- *Hubs* can be run by the publisher of the feed, or can be a community-supported hub open to public use. Whenever the publisher updates a topic, the publisher software pings the Hubs saying that there's an update. The hub fetches the published feed and multicasts the new/changed content out to all registered subscribers.

The protocol is decentralized and free. No company is at the center of this controlling it. Anybody can run a hub, or anybody can ping (publish) or subscribe using open hubs.

Information Connectivity

There is another conceptual level of connectivity that is located above the application and business process layer. All Information Technology has an ultimate purpose of gathering and providing information to its users. It is important for this information to be accessible as an integrated whole even if it is dispersed among multiple providers and distributed across geographical boundaries.

This means that content repositories including portals, collaboration tools, messaging systems and data warehouses need to be aggregated, classified and connected. An advanced archiving system can help to provide enterprise search functionality to company users and can also facilitate compliance for legal electronic discovery requests.

In order to provide these securely and efficiently, it is necessary to consolidate and de-duplicate all the information sources, maintain and enforce authorization and access controls, and ensure that no data is inadvertently leaked. This means enforcing encryption and data destruction policies – both locally on user devices as well as centrally in the data repositories.

As an application designer, it is important to determine at an early stage what enterprise search and archiving requirements you may have for your data. Archiving in the cloud is not trivial since large amounts of data are involved. While cloud storage is convenient in that it is elastically scalable and implies a certain amount of data redundancy it is not typically viable to constantly replicate all data from an enterprise into a cloud service provider for archival.

INTEGRATION

This leads to the question of where to position the archival system, co-located with the storage, or alternatively closer to the data source. Since the archivable information is already de-duplicated and compressed it would usually be efficient to place the archiving system closer to the information source. However, the situation may not be quite as simple in a real scenario which includes multiple distributed information systems and a geographically distributed cloud storage provider.

Application Integration Services

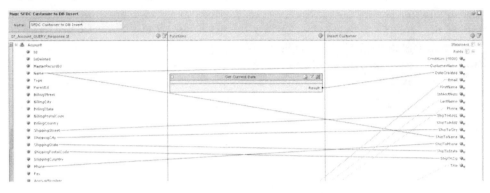

Figure 16-3: Dell Boomi Data Mapping

An interesting area that is currently developing is the emergence of vendors, such as Dell Boomi, IBM Cast Iron, Informatica and Pervasive that provide integration services to connect on-premise, as well as cloud-based, applications at the data level.

INTEGRATION

These integration services allow customers to define data mappings (Figure 16-3) and transformations between a wide range of application sources using web-based portals. Some offer rich sets of templates and packaged integration processes as well as graphic workflow and business logic development capabilities (Figure 16-4).

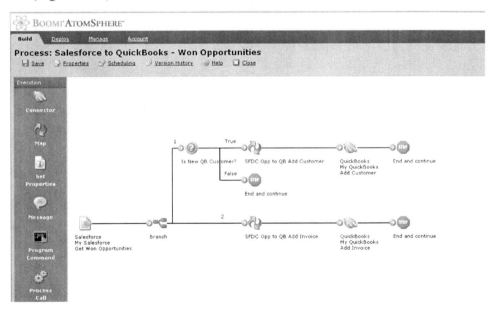

Figure 16-4: Dell Boomi AtomSphere Workflow

Practical Recommendations

Connecting disparate applications and information sources is not always trivial
As you pull services together to build a complete solution, consider a few suggestions:

- Couple loosely for asynchronous operation!
- Use PubSubHubbub and data feeds to connect semi-structured information!
- Publish your own end-points and try to build an ecosystem that multi-
  plies your presence!

INTEGRATION

Information

The Internet, and therefore by implication also the cloud, are becoming increasingly data-centric. Applications usually consume or provide data to data stores external to their native platform, whereby the specific solutions may vary in using structured, unstructured, static, and volatile data with or without transactional restrictions. The biggest challenge again is size. Large datasets frequently require partitioning, which leads to a trade-off between availability and transactional integrity.

While SQL still governs the interaction of the majority of transactions, there is an increasing need for other data architectures. Graph and tree structures lend themselves for some applications, such as social networking. Furthermore, there are many initiatives to abandon SQL for large tabular data due to its scalability constraints. Unfortunately, the alternatives imply a loss of many rich and useful features and a lack of compatibility with legacy code. However, in some cases they appear to be the only viable options.

INFORMATION

While scalable information presents a challenge for cloud-based applications, there are also many advantages to a service-based model. For example, the developing area of storage services helps to address elasticity challenges while at the same time abstracting both the physical and logical implementation and often exposing new data architectures.

Chapter 17

Storage

As the name implies, Information Technology is largely about data. The value proposition of IT systems hinges on the content in can provide to its users. In some fashion all cloud services revolve around this purpose. However, not all data is necessarily destined for direct consumption by the customer and, in fact, there is quite a diversity in the requirements and characteristics of cloud storage.

For example, we might classify the information into these categories:

- **Content**: Application data that is either directly visible to the end user or can be analyzed and transformed into useful data for the customer.

- **User information**: Information about the end users and customers. This might include billing and usage information as well as attributes and access rights.

INFORMATION

- **Application**: Executable code along with configuration information and potentially versioning, auditing and logging data.

There is also considerable difference between persistent storage and working storage: The former represents the data that directly characterizes and shapes the service over time. It needs to be durable and highly resistant to any loss. The latter is a means to an end. It is used internally by the application in order to produce the required functionality. It is usually possible to recover from losses in temporary data, but there are high performance requirements of working storage, in particular with regard to low latency of access.

More generally, you may want to consider a certain degree of storage tiering, or hierarchical storage management, depending on the ways in which the information is used. For example, it makes sense to equip the presentation layer with the most efficient storage possible in order to optimize the user experience. As we shall see, Memcached addresses performance on this layer. For long-term archiving, on the other hand, performance is less the issue than cost and durability.

Staging is another dimension of the storage architecture. It may be desirable to run test systems on sample data rather than jeopardizing the production environment. This is not always trivial. For instance, Google App Engine supports multiple application versions. However, at the present time, all of them must use the same production data and segregating the data requires significant effort.

Storage Requirements

A few key questions may help to gain a high-level picture of the type of storage to be used in a cloud environment / application:

- What type of data is to be stored? Is it structured (database) or unstructured (e.g. text, rich media)? If it is structured, is it tabular? If it is relational, how complex are the relations and queries?

- How large is the data set? Does it fit on a traditional database server / cluster with all of the required indexes or would you need to distribute the information across multiple servers?

- How often does the data change? What percentage of the data changes per day? What is the ratio of reads to writes?

- What types of transactions are performed on the data? How frequent are the queries? Are they ad-hoc or repetitive requests? Do you run regular comprehensive analytics through the whole data set?

- What are the performance requirements to the queries? Should users expect to see results of their queries within two to three seconds (the usability limit of an "instant" experience), or is it sufficient to return the results via another channel (e.g. email, instant messenger notification) when they're ready.

- What are the application requirements for scalability, load balancing, consistency, data integrity, transaction support and security?

- How susceptible is data to loss? Is it costly to obtain? Can it be reconstructed from external and archived sources in the event of a user error or system failure?

Architectural Choices

As you assess storage requirements, such as latency, recoverability, availability and confidentiality, as well as external constraints, such as network connectivity and the costs of bandwidth and storage, you need to keep in mind which architectural options that you have at your disposal, so that you can align the requirements with a feasible implementation.

For example, you may have some discretion over the medium of storage. Random Access Memory, Solid-State Disks and Hard Disk Drives, not to mention the different makes and models of each, have varying performance characteristics with regard to persistence, latency, throughput and cost.

The current trend is for storage to become cheaper while I/O speed becomes relatively more expensive. As you plan for the future, you may need to put more weight on an efficient internal topology. However, storage will never be free so it is critical to allocate it effectively.

The physical placement of the data is also very important for end-user performance. The location of the data has a direct impact on the latency since highly localized data can travel between systems faster. However, it is important to consider not only where the consumers are located but also how the internal systems are organized so that latency is minimized on those links that carry the most time-sensitive traffic.

Geographical dispersion of data can be useful in terms of ensuring availability and reducing last-mile latency. However, it also creates a problem in ensuring integrity unless the information is naturally segregated. The degree of susceptibility to compromised integrity differs substantially between applications. An inventory control system would be almost useless without transactional controls to ensure it is accurate. On the other hand, search and analytics are far more tolerant to stale or partially inconsistent data.

As we will address in more detail in Chapter 21, regardless of the application, massive scale will eventually exceed the capacity of any given system. This is true even in a High-Performance Computing (HPC) environment, but particularly relevant in cloud services, which frequently run on commoditized servers. It therefore becomes necessary to partition loads horizontally (across servers) rather than only vertically (by adding computing capacity to a single server).

INFORMATION

One approach to geographical segmentation that maintains reliability and accuracy without sacrificing latency or performance is data replication. However, designing replication across multiple systems is not a trivial task as it also involves data propagation latency and can generate significant data traffic, which may have performance and cost implications.

Lastly, it is vital to consider the nature and sensitivity of the data involved. If it is confidential, and potentially covered by legal restrictions, as is the case with much personal information, then there need to be sufficient precautions to protect the data while it is at rest and when it is in motion. In other words, the storage must either be encrypted or encapsulated in sufficient access controls. Data communications, both internally and to the end user, will typically also need to be encrypted using a secure key exchange since it is virtually impossible to protect the medium in a public cloud scenario.

Local Implementation Options

The local storage options will be strongly influenced by the service delivery model and platform architecture that has been selected.

Level	Access	Method
SaaS	Explicit	Build
PaaS	Implicit	Connect
IaaS	Limited	Rely

Table 17-1 : Resource Access Requirements

Infrastructure Services can accommodate seemingly explicit access to all local resources. In other words, the application is able to directly allocate memory and leverage the local file system without any significant constraints other than the capacity of the system. These resources might be virtualized (e.g. through VMware or Xen), but from a software perspective they look like explicit access.

Platform Services do not typically support operating-system-level calls to internal memory or any attached storage devices. However, for the most common use cases, it is possible to achieve similar functionality through the use of application variables and working files or databases. There is no strict need for the platform provider to implement these locally; but, in order to maintain a given service level, they will at least be designed to equivalent performance criteria.

When Software is delivered as a Service, there is no inherent need for any application development at all. There are, however, some software services that allow customizations and extensions that may be added programmatically. Since the objective of the SaaS model runs contrary to large development projects the platforms are usually limited and, at most, would offer non-transparent storage access to variables and local files similar to platform services.

In light of the preceding discussion, only an infrastructure service is able to accommodate a custom-built, scalable memory or file system internally, and is the focus of this chapter. Platforms may be able to connect to service components that achieve the same objectives. Software services, however, must rely on the functionality that is available to them, and therefore have only very limited options to organize data storage.

Memory

Random Access Memory is necessary for working memory and can be very helpful for any data that requires high throughput or low latency. At the presen-

INFORMATION

tation layer, user-visible response time will be directly correlated to query latency, so there is a strong incentive to implement as much as possible in memory. This might include in-memory databases that cache frequently accessed information. For instance, a database-driven application may cache objects to minimize the number of queries to external data sources or large databases.

If your application is running in a standard virtual machine, then accessing memory on a small scale is very straightforward. There is no particular difference related to cloud computing. The distinctions arise when the application needs a high level of horizontal scalability that is common in the cloud.

In a private data center, tightly coupled clusters may facilitate a pool of shared memory. However, in a cloud environment running on commoditized hardware it is necessary to segment and synchronize distributed memory with additional software.

The most common approach in use in the cloud today is Memcached, which was originally developed by Danga Interactive for LiveJournal, but is now used by many other sites, including Wikipedia, Flickr, Twitter and Youtube. Google App Engine also offers a Memcached service through an API.

Memcached is an open-source distributed memory caching system running on Unix, Windows and MacOS. It is technically implemented as a hash table distributed across multiple machines. The system is accessed with get and put functions, using a unique key for each entry.

INFORMATION

It is popular for database-powered web sites where is it often used to cache results of expensive SQL queries, such as counts and aggregate values. Usually applications implement multi-layer requests which first address the Memcached APIs before falling back on a slower backing store, such as a database.

In addition to Memcached, there are other distributed caches available, which may be of interest to specific applications (North, 2009):

- Ehcache is an open-source Java-based cache developed and supported by Terracotta. It is relatively simple to use and is reported to be very fast, especially for in-process requests. It features memory and disk stores, cache loaders, cache extensions and cache exception handlers.

- JBoss Cache is another Java cache and a key component of JBoss Application Server. Technically, it is replicated, rather than distributed, so all information needs to be synchronized between nodes, which can result in significant overhead, but helps to improve read performance.

- Microsoft provides a distributed, in-memory cache as part of the Windows Server AppFabric. It supports retrieving data by key or tag, optimistic and pessimistic concurrency, and it includes an ASP.NET session provider. A cloud service version of the technology is available with the Windows Azure AppFabric.

- Quetzall CloudCache is also an on-demand caching solution that targets developers who don't want to run their own caching infrastructure. CloudCache supports OAuth authorization and uses a REST-style API with bindings for Ruby, Java, PHP and Python.

There are also products, such as GigaSpaces eXtreme Application Platform (XAP), Oracle TimeTen and IBM solidDB, that couple an in-memory cache with a disk-resident SQL database.

File System

Memory is fast but it has a couple of drawbacks. It is relatively expensive to scale into the terabyte range, and it lacks persistence – if the systems fail then the data is usually lost.

If memory isn't suitable then the first port of call is a local disk. It's the simplest option. However, as is the case with memory, a disk may not have the capacity needed for a cloud-scale system. If you are just barely over the threshold you can add some remote file shares and manually distribute the data across a set of systems.

INFORMATION

For example, if you are running on Amazon EC2, you can also add block level storage volumes with Amazon Elastic Block Store (EBS). These volumes are persistent, off-instance storage up to 1 TB that can be mounted as devices by Amazon EC2 instances. Storage volumes are exposed as raw, unformatted block devices. Users can then create any file system on the EBS volumes.

EBS volumes are placed in a specific Availability Zone, and automatically replicated to prevent data loss due to hardware failures. Further resilience is possible with snapshots of volumes, which are persisted to Amazon S3. These snapshots can be used as the starting point for new Amazon EBS volumes, and protect data for long-term durability.

Network storage will allow some amount of elasticity beyond direct attached storage, but it also has its limitations. Difficulties arise for very large data sets, which may be petabytes in size and require thousands of servers. The first documented solution to this problem was Google BigTable (Chang, et al., 2006), developed to index the Web and run complex cartographic functions for Google Maps and Google Earth.

BigTable is the underlying technology for the Google App Engine datastore and lends itself to projects that analyze large collections of data. The framework has also served as the theoretical basis for many of the cloud-based distributed file systems in use today.

As we shall see in Chapter 21, Hadoop is an open source project that emerged after Google released papers on BigTable and Google FileSystem. It consists of two components: HDFS, its Distributed File System (block manager) and MapReduce (distributed processing framework). We will return to MapReduce, but, at this stage, we are mainly interested in the file system.

HDFS stores large files across multiple machines. It is built from a cluster of nodes, each of which serves up data over the network using either HTTP or a block protocol specific to HDFS. The file system achieves reliability by replicating the data across multiple hosts. Member nodes communicate internally to rebalance data and keep the replication of data high. Therefore, there is no requirement for additional hardware or software redundancy, such as RAID storage, and single points of failure can be minimized. For example, with the default replication value, data is stored on three nodes: two on the same rack, and one on a different rack.

There is something to be said for using HDFS for many applications beyond MapReduce. In its native mode, it is only accessible through special APIs and shell commands. However virtual file systems, such as Filesystem in Userspace (FUSE) allow it to be directly mounted by an existing operating system, thereby facilitating the use of standard Unix utilities. HDFS therefore lends itself well as a fully replicated and highly scalable file system.

External Interfaces

Rather than relying on a block-based file system that requires at least some amount of local mapping, another approach is to use an external storage service, usually exposed through a RESTful API. Examples of these would be Amazon Simple Storage Service (S3), Windows Azure Blob Storage or Google Storage.

Amazon S3 provides a web services interface that can be used to store and retrieve terabytes of data. It gives any developer access to the same infrastructure that Amazon uses to run its own global network of web sites. The functionality is exposed through REST and SOAP interfaces, and a BitTorrent protocol interface is provided to lower costs for high-volume distribution.

S3 is intentionally built with a minimal feature set. Each object is stored in a bucket and retrieved via a unique key that can be used to write, read, and delete an unlimited number of objects containing from 1 byte to 5 terabytes of data each. Some of its key features include regionalizing, rights and versioning:

> Objects can be stored in a *region* to optimize for latency, minimize costs, or address regulatory requirements. They never leave the region unless they are explicitly transferred out.

> *Rights* can be granted to specific users and authentication mechanisms are provided to ensure that data is kept secure from unauthorized access.

Amazon S3 also offers *versioning* to preserve, retrieve, and restore any previous instance of every object stored in an Amazon S3 bucket. Customers use versioning to recover from both unintended user actions and application failures.

S3 is extremely robust; however this reliability comes with a price-tag. For those who are storing non-critical, reproducible data, Amazon offers a Reduced Redundancy Storage (RRS) option within Amazon S3 that provides lower levels of redundancy than standard storage at a reduced cost.

Google offers a comparable service called Google Storage for Developers, which is a RESTful service for storing and accessing data. The service combines the performance and cloud-level scalability with security and sharing capabilities, including:

- Fast, scalable, highly available object store

- All data replicated to multiple data centers

- Read-your-writes data consistency

- Objects of hundreds of gigabytes in size per request with range-get support

- Domain-scoped bucket namespace

- Key-based authentication

- Individual- and group-level access controls

As described in Chapter 6, Microsoft also offers an opaque storage service called Azure Blob Storage. A blob is simply a stream of unstructured data. It can be a picture, a file or anything else the application needs. There is a four-level hierarchy of blob storage. At the highest level is a storage account, which is the root of the namespace for the blobs. Each account can hold multiple containers, which provide groupings (e.g. similar permissions or metadata). Within a container can be many blobs. Each can be uniquely identified and may hold up to 50GB. In order to optimize uploads and downloads (especially for very large files) it is possible to break a blob into blocks. Each transfer request therefore refers to a smaller portion of data (e.g. 4MB) making the transaction less vulnerable to transient network errors.

Data Lifecycle Management

As you evaluate different storage options, it is important to consider management of the full data lifecycle. In other words, there will be a need to initially load the data and finally retire or archive the data, in addition to the ongoing requirements of reading, writing and cleansing the data.

Many cloud vendors have data import/export mechanisms and APIs. With respect to the lifecycle, there is an obvious need for data import in order to support the initial deployment. And an export option should be available in order to ensure an exit path should the need ever arise. Beyond these requirements, the transfer services may also be of interest for content distribution, offsite backup, disaster recovery and general application connectivity.

Infrastructure and platform services generally provide simple ways to upload machine images and applications. Storage services expose SOAP and RESTful APIs for storing and retrieving information. Additionally, there may be some service-specific options. Amazon provides an AWS Import/Export that bypasses the Internet with portable storage devices for transport.

The Google App Engine Bulk Loader library supports uploading and downloading datastore entities using CSV and XML files. Keep in mind, however, that if you have specific needs for making your data searchable, are performing data validation (using with App Engine ListProperties) or will be moving data between App Engine applications, then you will probably need to add some custom coding.

Practical Recommendations

It can be difficult to balance the requirement of cloud applications for both data size and speed. As you investigate the options, consider some suggestions:

- Use a caching solution to improve database performance!
- Avoid data lock-in! Always make sure you have an exit path.
- Make sure all critical data is backed up independently – in-house or with another provider!
- Consider location! Try to position storage as close to computation as possible!

INFORMATION

Chapter 18

Relational Data

In the preceding chapter, we approached storage as a simple service that was agnostic to the data required. In such a scenario, it is up to the application to model the information and implement any necessary data structures. This is a logical course of action if you have either very simple data (e.g. small flat files) or else data that is so complex that it requires custom-built schemas and internal logic to process regardless of the storage.

However, a significant portion of use cases involve data that is primarily tabular in nature and may include cross-references between tables. For instance, most programming today involves some object orientation, where similar objects have corresponding attributes and may link to other objects.

In these cases, an alternative to opaque storage services, with all structure in the application, is the implementation of value-added services to facilitate information processing. Strictly speaking, there are major differences in the models underlying hierarchical, network, relational and object databases. However, the focus of this book isn't to explore database theory. We look at these collectively as they represent options to implement some of the most common use cases.

INFORMATION

Scalability versus Integrity

SQL (often referred to as Structured Query Language) is a query language, based on relational algebra, which has established itself as the de facto standard for relational database management systems. It includes functions to insert, update and delete and has the ability to interpret complex multi-table queries that may involve grouping, sorting and filtering operations. The language also defines management functions, such as schema creation and data access controls.

Given its widespread adoption and rich feature set, SQL is a first choice for any application built on a relational data model. SQL provides time-proven methods for complex queries for transactional, normalized and uniform data. However, the management overhead involved in ensuring data integrity and enforcing schema consistency make it difficult to handle unstructured, rapidly evolving or widely distributed data structures efficiently. Stated simplistically, the data is changing too fast for the management systems to process if all relations and constraints need to be fully implemented.

This limitation presents a problem in a cloud scenario where there is a need for systems to manipulate and analyze huge amounts of data without impacting system availability, performance, or throughput. Most relational databases can scale up and down on a single system (by adding storage and processing capability) but are not optimized to scale out (to run on many commodity boxes). When data demand grows bigger than a typical relational database server can handle, alternative solutions are needed. As we shall see later in this chapter, this need has triggered a big push to a movement called "NoSQL", specifically by Google with BigTable, because many people are reading the data simultaneously.

NoSQL is a leaner approach that has the potential of scaling much higher but brings with it a whole new set of scalability challenges (such as overloaded keys or heavy use of indexes). More importantly, the database doesn't enforce any logical constraints, which means an increased burden on the application and much more custom development for custom queries.

A heated debate is ongoing among cloud architects as to the relative strengths and weaknesses as well as future prospects of noSQL. Our intention is to present some objective perspectives on the two options so that you can choose which makes most sense in a given solution, or indeed, if you need to combine elements of both.

INFORMATION

Some of the factors you will want to consider are the degree of transactionality and schema integrity that is required. The overall scale anticipated and the ratio of reads to writes are also critical factors.

Query Model	Software-based Examples	Service-based Examples
SQL	LAMP/MySQL Windows/SQL Oracle	Amazon RDS Microsoft SQL Azure Zoho CloudSQL
PseudoSQL		Amazon SDB Google GQL Datastore Microsoft Azure Storage
NoSQL	Hypertable Hbase MongoDB CouchDB	

Table 18-1 : Cloud-based Relational Options

In this chapter we will look at three options that are relevant for largely relational data (Table 18-1):

- You can use a strict SQL database.
- There are also options to implement a subset of SQL that maintains conceptual familiarity but does not implement all SQL features. The technical community usually also calls this approach NoSQL; however, we have introduced the term PseudoSQL to illustrate its similarity to SQL and differentiate it from the third option.
- In the final category, the data may not have a strict tabular structure. Often, there is no query language, so all access is conducted through programmatic interfaces. In these models, there is little resemblance to traditional SQL databases.

INFORMATION

Theoretically, you also have the choice of two delivery mechanisms. You can acquire the software and implement the database on your own (e.g. within your own virtual machines that may be running on infrastructure services). Alternatively, you can call on external database services. There may still be some gaps in the market (Table 18-1), but the potential exists for all combinations of delivery and query models.

SQL

SQL has been around for a long time. It was developed at IBM in the early 1970s and was eventually adopted as a standard by the American National Standards Institute (ANSI) in 1986 and International Organization for Standardization (ISO) in 1987.

In addition to its rich feature set, it offers a number of advantages. It is a mature language that relies on a tried-and-proven data model. The market-leading commercial and open-source implementations of SQL are robust and highly tuned.

There is a wealth of legacy code that is based on SQL. Even if there are minor differences in vendor products, it is much easier to integrate these with a SQL database than to rewrite the code. And if you are designing an application from scratch, you will more easily find someone proficient in SQL than in any of the other database approaches described in this chapter.

SQL is Not Dead

Despite the prophecies of some SQL-critics, there is no reason to dismiss SQL prematurely. There have been challenges to SQL in the past and it has braved them successfully. There may be some validity to claims that the current platforms lack the ability to scale, which you may need for cloud-oriented applications.

However, there are also very famous examples of huge SQL databases (North, 2009):

INFORMATION

- UPS runs an IBM DB2 database with a table that contains more than 42 billion rows.

- eBay's Teradata system contains 5 petabytes of data.

- LGR Telecommunications feeds a 310 TB Oracle data warehouse.

- Microsoft has 300 million Hotmail users hosted on a 10,000 server farm running Microsoft SQL Server.

Self-managed SQL

There are two approaches to running SQL in the cloud. Either you can run and manage the SQL server and database yourself or else you can use a cloud-based SQL-as-a-Service.

In the case of the former, you would need to subscribe to an infrastructure service, such as that from Rackspace or Amazon. The most common scenario would be a LAMP application instance running MySQL and other open-source software.

However, you could just as well use Oracle, or Windows running SQL Server. Commercial licensing is more expensive than open source, but if the rest of the application is based on compatible technologies (Oracle Application Server, or .NET) then the integration is much easier.

Within your virtual instances, you could run almost any SQL database. Unfortunately, the most common Amazon EC2 AMIs aren't configured for very high workloads. So you would need to license, install and configure a high-end edition of the software to reach cloud scale. Some of the more scalable options include:

- *Oracle 11g* is the market leader in enterprise databases and also a core part of Oracle's cloud strategy along with Fusion Middleware and WebLogic. Oracle offers EC2 AMIs with Oracle Database 11g Enterprise Edition and WebLogic Server 10g, while Oracle Secure Backup Cloud Module can create compressed and encrypted database backups using Amazon S3. Furthermore, Amazon announced in January 2011 that AWS will offer Oracle 11g in addition to MySQL for high-performance computing.

- Now also owned by Oracle, *MySQL Enterprise* is a platform suitable for cloud computing scenarios, such as scaling out with multiple servers and using master/slave replication. Continuent Tungsten and Sequoia are asynchronous and synchronous replications solutions, respectively, that facilitate scale-out of MySQL clustering on cloud computing services such as GoGrid, Rackspace Mosso, and Amazon EC2.

- *Microsoft SQL Server* is also a very popular enterprise database, particularly for organizations that lean towards Microsoft technologies. It is available as a standard Amazon AMI. Alternatively, SQL Azure provides the equivalent functionality on a utility basis.

- *IBM DB2 Enterprise Edition* is one of the most powerful databases on the market. The Enterprise Developer Edition is available on the IBM Smart Business Development and Test Cloud, IBM WebSphere Cloudburst Appliance, and RightScale Cloud Management Platform. Also, the DB2 Express Edition and DB2 Workgroup Server Edition are available on Amazon EC2.

- *EnterpriseDB Postgres Plus Cloud Edition* includes replication, asynchronous pre-fetch for RAID, and a distributed memory cache. It uses a shared-nothing architecture to support parallel query processing for highly-scalable environments such as grids and clouds.

INFORMATION

SQL as a Service

An alternate approach is to consume SQL services as a cloud service. Examples of these services include Zoho CloudSQL and Amazon Relational Database Service (RDS). The advantages of a cloud delivery model should look familiar.

- *Cost-efficiency*: no up-front investment is required, and you pay only for the resources you use

- *Elastic capacity*: flexibility to scale computational resources and storage

- *Reduced database administration*: automatic patches of the database software and data backups

- *Enhanced availability*: through replication and geographical dispersion

At the same time, SQL services accept the familiar SQL syntax and behave similarly to on-premise deployments. So it is relatively easy to integrate existing applications and leverage the expertise and experience of available programmers and administrators.

Amazon Relational Database Service offers native access to a MySQL database with support for Oracle announced. This means Amazon RDS works with existing tools and applications written for MySQL. For customers already using AWS, it is a natural choice since they can leverage Amazon's authentication and authorization as well as the AWS Management Console to create, delete and modify relational database instances (DB Instances). Some of the other features include snapshots, automatic backups, transaction logs and interfaces to Cloud-Watch for monitoring CPU Utilization, Free Storage Space, and Database Connections.

INFORMATION

For companies that prefer other SQL dialects, Zoho CloudSQL supports ANSI SQL, Oracle, Microsoft SQL Server, IBM DB2, PostgreSQL and Informix in addition to MySQL. It includes JDBC and ODBC drivers for transparent connectivity. Additionally, an HTTP API allows developers to connect to the Zoho services through a Web API, by sending their requests as SQL statements.

Other Database-as-a-Service providers include EnterpriseDB, FathomDB, Longjump, and TrackVia. Microsoft architects will want to consider SQL Azure, mentioned above. Of potential interest to App Engine developers is Google's announcement of support for Hosted SQL. However, as of the time of writing, real life examples of using the SQL option with App Engine applications are sparse, representing one of the most critical hurdles of getting started with App Engine from a data structure perspective.

PseudoSQL (Near SQL)

There are also cloud options that resemble SQL databases but do not strictly adhere to the standard. Although most of the information is tabular, there is typically no schema and the management system may not support joins, foreign keys, triggers or stored procedures.

These differences can present problems for legacy code that leverage advanced SQL options since the programs may need be rewritten to implement the features using alternate mechanisms. The fact that the datastore entities are schemaless means that two entities of the same kind are not required to possess the same properties, nor do they need to use the same value types if they do share properties. Instead, the application is responsible for ensuring that entities conform to any schema required by the business logic.

The absence of a JOIN statement is based on the inefficiency that queries spanning more than one machine might introduce, especially in a geographically distributed topology. The consequence is that it is only possible to issue single table queries and the application is responsible for aggregating and filtering data from multiple tables. On the plus side, the services offer elastic scale and commonly are able to also accommodate unstructured data (blobs). Three of the largest cloud vendors: Amazon, Google and Microsoft, each offer options in this area.

Amazon SimpleDB

Amazon SimpleDB is a distributed database written in Erlang. It is offered as a web service in conjunction with Amazon Elastic Compute Cloud (EC2) and Amazon S3 and is part of Amazon Web Services. It allows regional designations for geographical compliance or latency requirements.

As with other similar options, the Amazon Simple DB (SDB), does not enforce a schema. Instead it defines "domains" with items that consist of up to 256 attributes and values. The values can contain anywhere from one byte to one kilobyte. It also supports simple operators such as: =, !=, <, >, <=, >=, STARTS-WITH, AND, OR, NOT, INTERSECTION, UNION. So, most common queries are possible as long as they are confined to a single domain.

INFORMATION

Google App Engine Datastore

The App Engine datastore is optimized for reading while supporting queries, sorting and transactions using optimistic concurrency control. It is a strongly consistent distributed database built on top of the lower-level BigTable with some added functionality. The datastore is programmatically accessible through Python interfaces, Java Data Objects (JDO) and Java Persistence API.

The database is schemaless, which means that the application is responsible for ensuring that entities conform to any schema required by the business logic. To assist, the Python SDK includes a data modeling library that helps enforce consistency.

Google App Engine's query language (called GQL) is similar to SQL in its SELECT statements with some significant limitations. GQL intentionally does not support the Join statement and can therefore only accommodate single table queries. However, Google does provide a workaround in the form of a Reference-Property class that can indicate one-to-many and many-to-many relationships.

Microsoft Azure Storage

As described in Chapter 6, Microsoft Azure Storage handles three kinds of data storage: Blobs, Tables and Queues. Tables are used for structured data. They hold a set of homogenous rows (called entities) that are defined by a set of columns (called properties). Each property is defined by a name and type (e.g. String, Binary, Int). Despite the conceptual similarity, there are important distinctions to make between Windows Azure storage tables and Microsoft SQL Server relational tables, or SQL Azure. Azure Storage does not enforce a schema nor does it support SQL as a query language. While this may lead to portability challenges for many legacy applications, Microsoft's strategy is similar to that of Amazon and Google and reflects the importance of ensuring the new technology is optimized for the scalability requirements of cloud-based services.

NoSQL

NoSQL is the calling cry of a movement to drop the constraints of SQL in order to implement more flexible and scalable data models that are able to cope with the demands of cloud computing. It usually describes a schemaless, horizontally scalable database with built-in replication support. Instead of using a query language, the applications interact with the database through a simple API.

The data structures involved, such as associative arrays, data dictionaries, hash tables, and directed graphs are not new. However, the advent of cloud computing has given them new life as we have seen an increased emphasis on horizontal scalability and load balancing.

NoSQL is ideal for non-OLTP applications that need to cheaply process massive amounts of both structured and unstructured data but have less need for transactional support or data consistency. Nonetheless, it is not a panacea for all known problems. Rather it is an architectural option that may make sense in some scenarios. If you investigate this area closely, you may also come across the term NOSQL, or "Not Only SQL", which emphasizes this point. NoSQL is neither better nor worse than SQL nor are the two mutually exclusive.

Horizontal Scalability

To understand the concept behind NoSQL, it's worth taking a step back and looking at the bottlenecks that make horizontal scalability difficult. When a single database manages a huge volume information and queries, a first step to increase scalability may be to replicate the data to multiple systems. If you do this effectively, then you can scale the number of concurrent reads almost infinitely.

However, it's a lot more difficult when you try to scale a very dynamic database with many incoming writes. You can still resort to replication, however, you inevitably run into the CAP principle: Strong **C**onsistency, High **A**vailability, and **P**artition-resilience are partially incompatible – you can pick at the most two of these. In other words, if you partition your database onto multiple servers then there will be inevitable latency and link failures, which make it impossible to guarantee both consistency and availability. When there is a partition failure, you can choose to block the transaction (to maintain consistency and forego availability), or else you can use majority voting, or expiration-based caching, to maintain availability while sacrificing consistency.

Sharding, or a Shared Nothing Architecture, can partially address this problem. It refers to a design where rows of a database table are stored separately. Each partition forms part of a shard, which may be located on a separate database server or physical location.

This approach reduces the total number of rows in each table and thereby reduces the index size, generally improving lookup performance. Since each database shard can be placed on a separate machine, it is possible to scale a database horizontally permitting developers to design cloud databases that are multiple terabytes in size. This is not to say that you will have no more challenges of availability and integrity. However, it is possible to implement a degree of load balancing that does not impact the integrity of the system.

NoSQL Data Structures

In a sense, any scalable data structure could be classified as NoSQL including those that have absolutely no underlying relational use case. Some of the most common options usually associated with the NoSQL movement are Key-Value Stores, Tabular (also called Columnar) stores, Document databases and Graphs. We will address the first two here and defer the latter two until the next chapter.

We do not mean to imply that you cannot build a relational data model using a document store or a directed graph. There may even be good reason to do so. However, document databases and graphs depart even more radically from the basic relational approach and lend themselves to very different queries and use cases. You can argue this point, and perhaps you would be right, but the division is merely a superficial convenience so don't let it disturb you too much.

Key-Value Stores

The simplest NoSQL data structure is a key-value store. It is usually implemented as a persistent and fault-tolerant distributed hash table and is unmatched in its ability to scale and facilitate load-balanced applications. However, it is not suited for transactions requiring Atomic Consistent Isolated Durable (ACID) properties.

Most implementations are also limited in their built-in support for ad hoc queries, aggregate operations and complex analytics processing, and therefore require programming to achieve full functionality.

Some of the best known Key-value stores include MemcacheDB, Scalaris, Project Voldemort, and Tokyo Cabinet.

MemcacheDB is a persistent variant of Memcached, with its own distributed key-value database system based on Berkeley DB. It conforms to the Memcached protocol, so applications may use any Memcached API to access a MemcacheDB database.

Scalaris uses a structured overlay network with a non-blocking consensus commit (Paxos) protocol for transaction processing. The combination of replication and majority-based distributed transactions guarantee ACID properties while a direct mapping of keys to the overlay facilitate fast data access. The implementation uses Erlang and exposes both a rich Java and limited web interface. Its biggest limitation is that it lacks persistence.

Tokyo Cabinet is written in the C language, and provided as an API of C, Perl, Ruby, Java, and Lua with both hash-table and B-tree data structure support. Its key features are small size (through Lempel-Ziv and BWT compression), fast processing speed and resilience to database corruption. It was developed by Mikio Hirabayashi and is a successor of GCBM and QDBM made available as open source.

INFORMATION

Voldemort is a distributed key-value storage system that is used at LinkedIn. It is a distributed persistent fault-tolerant hash table, which makes no attempt to support ACID properties. It lends itself for high-scalability storage problems where simple functional partitioning is not sufficient.

Data is automatically replicated and partitioned over multiple servers with built-in data versioning. The system combines caching with persistent storage so that the application doesn't need a separate caching tier. Both reads and writes scale horizontally with facilities for cluster expansion without rebalancing all data. It can also handle server failure gracefully since each node is independent of other nodes with no central point of failure.

Tabular (Columnar) Datastores

Tabular stores are more than simple key-value data stores since they hold multiple properties per key. However, they do not support the full feature set of an SQL database, such as a rich query model based on a non-procedural, declarative query language.

Google BigTable is a distributed storage system for structured data. It is a fast and extremely large-scale DBMS designed to grow into the petabyte range across "hundreds or thousands of machines" (O'Reilly, 2006). Each table has multiple dimensions (one of which is a field for time, allowing versioning). It is used by a number of Google applications, such as MapReduce.

Several open source derivatives of BigTable are available in conjunction with Hadoop of which Hypertable (implemented in C++) and HBase (implemented in Java) are the most popular.

> *Hypertable* is an open source database inspired by publications on the design of Google's BigTable and sponsored by Baidu, the leading Chinese language search engine. It runs on a distributed file system such as the Apache Hadoop DFS, GlusterFS, or the Kosmos File System (KFS).

> *Hbase* also provides BigTable-like capabilities on top of Hadoop. Data is organized by table, row and column, similar to SQL databases, but instead of accepting a query language, a programmable interface can retrieve column values for specific keys or iterate through a range of rows.

Even though you don't have direct access to them, it's also worth following the development of some proprietary internal implementations of scalable data stores. Two of the most prominent are Amazon's Dynamo and Facebook's Cassandra.

> *Dynamo* is Amazon's equivalent of the BigTable. It is a highly available keystore that distributes and replicates storage based on hashing rings. While Dynamo isn't directly available to consumers it powers a large part of Amazon Web Services including S3.

> *Cassandra* is Facebook's distributed storage system. It is developed as a functional hybrid that combines the Google BigTable data model with Amazon's Dynamo.

INFORMATION

Both datastores operate via programmable interfaces rather than using a query language.

Practical Recommendations

SQL has become entrenched as the standard for all tabular data access. It has proven to be exceptionally resilient. However, a new set of obstacles appear to be challenging its dominance. As you evaluate the options, consider some suggestions:

- If you have SQL, don't panic! There are many cloud-based solutions that use it to scale to very high capacity.
- Evaluate your long-term needs when you develop your initial design! Do you really need all SQL functionality? What are your scalability requirements?

- Avoid lock-in! If you don't manage your own database, have an escape path prepared, in case you ever need to switch providers.

INFORMATION

Chapter 19

Non-Relational Data

In the previous chapter, we examined data modeling and storage options for scalable repositories handling relational information. To be precise, the models weren't necessarily relational but the technologies were supportive of implementing relational use cases.

In this chapter, we will look at data structures that depart even further from the relational paradigm. We will continue on with some of the prominent NoSQL approaches including document databases and graphs. Then we will look at search options for completely opaque content. We will touch on the exciting area of analytics, which is becoming mandatory as the volume of information explodes, and finally examine options for integrating external data.

INFORMATION

Document Databases

Let's begin with the notion of a document. Lotus Notes is perhaps the best known document database, which supports both structured and unstructured data (e.g. text, graphics or binary data) and has achieved enterprise-level scalability through its replication model.

While the notion of a completely unstructured document is certainly legitimate, it is not typical of this use case, where storage is more typically semi-structured. Using formats such as XML, YAML or JSON, each record may have different sets of fields and the syntax of each record can be determined by the application. There is therefore some degree of structure. However, in relational terms, you do not have a set schema so it is possible for the application to extend the data and/or enforce any constraints that are required by the business logic.

Two of the best known cloud-scale document databases are MongoDB and CouchDB. Both are free open-source document oriented databases. MongoDB is written in C++, while CouchDB uses Erlang, a functional programming language suited to concurrent distributed systems.

Chapter 19: Non-Relational Data

Apache CouchDB is a fault-tolerant data store represented as a collection of JSON documents. There is no schema enforcement; however, there is support for defining views with aggregate functions and filters that are computed in parallel across multiple CouchDB nodes. These views form the basis of the CouchDB query processor, which is accessible through JavaScript.

More advanced processing is possible through a RESTful API for reading and writing documents in both JSON and AtomPub data formats. Several third-party client libraries support additional programming languages. There is also a web-based administration console for management tasks.

Internally, a B-tree index stores the document ID and sequence number of transactions, which helps to ensure ACID properties and data consistency and also provides the ability to generate a version history. CouchDB also offers incremental peer-based replication with bi-directional conflict detection and resolution.

MongoDB is very similar to CouchDB in most respects but there are some important differences:

INFORMATION

- Multi-version concurrency control (MVCC): CouchDB is MVCC-based, while MongoDB performs updates in place. MVCC facilitates intense versioning, synchronization of offline databases and problems that require a large amount of master-master replication. Disadvantages of MVCC include the need for periodic compaction and manual conflict resolution. Therefore MongoDB is a more likely fit when there are high update rates and replication is limited to master/slave or auto failover configurations.

- Horizontal Scalability: CouchDB supports replication as a way to scale. MongoDB is designed with replication as a way to gain reliability/failover rather than scalability. It therefore uses sharding as its path to scalability

MongoDB also implements its own file system to optimize I/O throughput by dividing larger objects into smaller chunks. Documents are stored in two separate collections: files containing the object meta-data, and chunks that form a larger document when combined with database accounting information. The MongoDB API provides functions for manipulating files, chunks, and indices directly.

Whether you look at document databases, like CouchDB and MongoDB, will depend a lot on the type of data you need to manipulate. If it is structured as XML or JSON documents, or would lend itself well to that kind of structure, then the databases can provide very reliable and efficient storage. However, they may not be the best choice for tabular data on the one hand, or completely unstructured data on the other.

Graphs

A graph differs from a traditional database because it describes not only objects, and their properties, but also the connectivity that exists between these objects. The graph defines a topology which reflects human spatial reasoning more closely than flat tables. While both approaches have their place in human cognitive models, graphs lend themselves to different sets of problems, such as social networking, semantic ontologies and navigational systems. For example:

- Navigational graphs have the facility of directing users from one point to another or determining the distance between two locations. Airline reservation systems indicate how many flights you have to take to reach your destination. They may also display direct connections first, or sort the results by the number of connections.

- Social networks like LinkedIn list connections or search results sorted by degrees of separation, and then recommend other connections based on social proximity. Facebook indicates how many friends two members share.

These operations are most easily achieved with a graph, which is a data structure consisting of nodes (vertices), links (edges) and properties. In most cases, the edges also have orientation so it is formally a directed graph. These boxes and arrows go by different names in different disciplines. UML refers to them as instances and links, Semantic Web terminology specifies resources and triples. Others may speak of objects and relationships.

INFORMATION

- Nodes are those objects that can have meaning on their own and don't depend on anything else. This doesn't have any influence on their content. They may be strongly typed or the graph may be indifferent to the object values.

- Edges are not objects themselves but represent a relationship between two objects and therefore depend on them. They are the critical element of traversals which is the most common operation in a graph.

- Traversals are a means of iterating data to derive a set of reachable nodes. They are specified by a starting point and a traversal method (e.g. breadth-first, depth-first).

Graph databases still represent an emerging technology with no clear market leaders. If you are heavily invested in Google technology you may also want to keep an eye on Google Pregel. Pregel is a generalized parallel graph transformation framework. In Google's model, graphs consist of nodes, arcs and properties as with most graph databases. The node also has a logical inbox to receive all messages sent to it.

The whole graph is broken down into multiple "partitions", each containing a set of nodes and representing a unit of execution. Each partition usually has an execution thread associated with it. This approach facilitates horizontal scalability since each machine can host multiple "partitions" to distribute workload.

Some of the other current implementations include:

- Neo4j

- sones

- OrientDB

- DEX

- InfoGrid

- HyperGraphDB

- Infinitegraph

Unfortunately, there is no equivalent to SQL for graph databases. There are no standard APIs, query languages or protocols that might make options interoperable. Many tools offer Java APIs and expose a RESTful JSON interface, but even then, the actual implementations are proprietary.

INFORMATION

Graphs scale well to large data sets that are not necessarily completely homogenous. Their primary distinction is that queries are based on links (and traversals) rather than on common attributes. Consequently, they do not facilitate Join operations but can be partitioned much more easily to achieve horizontal scalability.

Search

Another option for dealing with data is to assume no structure at all and rely on searches to retrieve information. This is particularly appropriate for textual information without any predefined format or layout. But it isn't limited to unstructured data – in fact it isn't limited at all. As long as any viable keys make their ways into the indexes and the searches return all related information, you can conceivably even store tabular data sets. It is then up to the application to organize all information in a format that it is able to parse.

Commercial Enterprise Search

One approach to search would be to use one of the commercially available Enterprise Search products that are on the market. The Google Search Appliance is quite popular but Microsoft FAST, Autonomy IDOL and solutions from Exalead, Endeca and Vivisimo are all viable alternatives.

In practice, it is rare to find cloud-based architectures built on proprietary tools. They do have the advantage that they are usually high quality and backed by guaranteed support lines. However, other than the licensing costs which deter some business-minded developers, there is the fact that large-scale applications often need to add customizations or extensions to the basic search engine which is difficult without complete access to the code base.

Lucene

The most widely used open-source package for search engines is Lucene, originally written by Doug Cutting (who also designed Hadoop) and then submitted to the Apache Software Foundation. It analyzes documents in varying formats and then creates inverted indexes of terms. It also provides a query language that parses queries, searches indexes and returns results. Lucene is often augmented with functionality from Solr and/or Katta to build a scalable, fault-tolerant solution that is easy to integrate into external applications.

Solr

Solr is written in Java and uses the Lucene Java search library as its core for full-text indexing and search. It is an enterprise-grade search service with XML/HTTP and JSON APIs and features an extensive plug-in architecture that enables more advanced customization.

Solr was created by Yonik Seeley for CNET Networks and later also donated to the Apache Software Foundation under the Lucene top-level project with which it eventually merged. Solr's features include powerful full-text search, hit highlighting, faceted (category) search, dynamic clustering, database integration, and rich document (e.g. Word, PDF) handling.

INFORMATION

Searches are done via HTTP GET on the select URL with the query string passed as a parameter. Optional request parameters for sorting, filtering, highlighting and faceting are able to specify what information is returned. For example, you can use the "fl" parameter to control what stored fields are retrieved, and if the relevancy score is returned.

Since humans are generally only looking for conceptual matches rather than precise lexical correspondence, text fields are only indexed after applying various transformations such as stemming and removing punctuation (hyphens), uppercase and plurals. Naturally, the same text transformations are subsequently applied to any queries in order to match what is indexed.

Katta

Solr is highly scalable and provides both distributed search and index replication. However, it is slow if the index is very large and offers no failover or load balancing capability when there is a high volume of traffic.

Katta is a scalable, failure tolerant, distributed, data storage designed for real-time access. It is a search grid that has been built on Apache Hadoop, which is capable of serving large replicated Lucene indexes at high loads and uses Zookeeper to coordinate work between individual servers.

Katta serves the replicated indices as shards optimized to serve high loads and very large data sets. The shards can be stored on the local file system, HDFS or Amazon S3. It also provides a distributed scoring service, allowing search results from multiple indexes to be merged.

Bobo Browse

A key component of most semi-structured data today is a faceted classification system that allows objects to be classified in a multidimensional taxonomy. For example, people in a social network might be classified by location, age and profession; or books by price, author and date.

Faceted search (sometimes called faceted navigation) is a technique for exploring a set of objects organized in a faceted classification system. While Lucene is tailored to unstructured data, Bobo Browse fills in the missing pieces to handle semi-structured and structured data with extensive faceting capabilities.

Beyond the result set from queries and selections, Bobo Browse also provides the facets from the current point of browsing. It supports runtime faceting and offers functions such as facet count distribution analysis and the capability to merge results of a distributed facet search.

You may have come across Bobo as the technology of the LinkedIn Faceted People Search. As you begin typing names, LinkedIn offers an auto-completed list of possible matches. Bobo also powers the advanced search leveraging LinkedIn's vast repository of structured data and automatically detects when a search term is related to a name or to a person's company and position.

Semantic Data Stores

The Semantic Web is the evolution of the Internet as envisioned by Tim Berners-Lee, who played a pivotal role in launching the World-Wide Web. This web of data is similar to the hypertext documents that humans can read but it extends the concept to linked data, which can be easily interpreted by machines and is usually described using the W3C Resource Description Format (RDF). He articulates four principles to implement this vision (Berners-Lee, 2006):

- Use URIs as names for things.

- Use HTTP URIs so that people can look up those names.

- When someone looks up a URI, provide useful information, using standards such as RDF* and SPARQL.

- Include links to other URIs, so that they can discover more things.

RDF data is stored as subject-predicate-object triples. The subject identifies the resource, while the predicate describes the resource and conveys a relationship between the subject and the object. RDF expressions are most easily represented as a labeled, directed graph. The data model is therefore not ideally suited to a relational database and has spawned a need for specialized RDF data stores, such as Franz AllegroGraph RDFStore, JRDF, CubicWeb, Sesame, Mulgara and Jena.

The Virtuoso Universal Server is an open-source middleware and database engine that combines the functionality of a traditional RDBMS and RDF datastore, as well as additional web and file server functionality, in a single system. The server is also available as a pre-packaged AMI for EC2, including RDF Linked Data Sets such as: DBpedia, BBC Music & Programmes, NeuroCommons, Bio2RDF, and the Linked Open Data Cloud.

Analytics

We've seen a number of ways to model, structure and store dynamic data. In making your architectural choices, you should also consider what secondary usage you can glean from the information. We all know that there is an information explosion as the amount of data being processed grows exponentially from year to year.

INFORMATION

Unfortunately, only a small fraction of that volume is actually useful in making decisions. Business Intelligence technologies provide historical, current, and predictive views of business operations with functions such as online analytical processing, analytics and data mining. It is possible to conduct statistical analyses of virtually any data repository but performance will vary considerably depending on the structure of the data.

One major difference between analytical and transactional processing is the optimization for reading versus writing. Transaction processing is most efficient with a high degree of normalization, since it needs to be able to make frequent changes quickly and without sacrificing data integrity. Analytical processing, on the other hand, emphasizes speed of data retrieval, which is easier to achieve when data is denormalized and replicated, so that fewer queries and joins are required for each analysis.

Column stores (which store data by column rather than row) are another approach that is well suited for high-performance analytics applications. A quick and easy way to begin with a scalable business intelligence solution is to take an

Amazon Machine Image with Vertical Analytic Database or Sybase IQ, paying for usage as you build up your service.

Open Source on Cloud Infrastructure

If the commercial products don't suit your needs, a viable approach may be to develop your own data-warehousing solution using cloud technologies. For example, you can install the Pentaho suite of software on a set of virtual machines running on infrastructure services.

The Pentaho BI Project covers software for enterprise reporting, analysis, dashboard, data mining, workflow and ETL capabilities for business intelligence needs. Of particular interest are the Pentaho Analysis Services and Pentaho Data Mining.

- Pentaho Analysis Services is an open source OLAP (online analytical processing) server, written in Java. It supports the MDX (multi-dimensional expressions) query language and XML.

- Pentaho Data Mining is a set of tools for machine learning and data mining with a suite of classification, regression and association rules.

Hadoop Analytics: Hive, Pig, Cascading

INFORMATION

To reach cloud-scale, you can choose from several solutions that rely on Hadoop for workload distribution and horizontal scalability. The best known are Pig and Hive, but Cascading has also received some attention.

The differences between these relate to their levels of abstraction and the tasks for which they are suited (McCarthy, 2010). Pig is a lower-level language (but still easier to use than Hadoop) while Hive and Cascading represent a higher level of abstraction. Pig is suited to data preparation while Hive is optimized for data presentation and Cascading is able to cover both.

Pig targets use cases such as data transformation (with pipelines) and experimental research (e.g. for rapid prototyping). It comes with its own language, Pig Latin, providing developers the ability to write procedural scripts that implement selective and iterative processes.

Hive is a data warehouse built on flat files. It stores its metadata in a relational database management system and the payload in HDFS, using MapReduce for computation. It is relatively easy to use since it presents a familiar data organization (tables, columns, partitions), provides an SQL-like language for queries and comes with both JDBC and ODBC drivers. It is also extensible with facilities to embed user programs into the data flow. Hive enforces a static model of data and offers only limited ETL capability, so legacy data needs to be imported using other tools.

Cascading is also a high-level abstraction layer over Hadoop with an alternative API of most patterns that makes it easy to focus on workflows instead of mapping and reducing functions. It targets use cases such as processing logfiles, targeting ads, and running social media analytics.

It doesn't prescribe a specific syntax but rather provides a collection of functions, filters and aggregators as well as facilities for developers to contribute Java Virtual Machine based language modules (e.g. for JRuby, Groovy, Clojure).

On-demand Business Intelligence

Another option that is certainly also very cloud-oriented is to consume business intelligence and analytics as a service. Offerings include Birst, SAS, Jasper BI and Google BigQuery.

For example *Birst* offers business intelligence of Marketing, Sales, Operations, Finance, HR and Supply Chain as on-demand services that are easy to implement and allow you to pay only for the resources used.

SAS also offers a wide range of BI solutions including Customer Intelligence, Fraud Detection/Prevention, Financial Intelligence, Governance Risk and Compliance. While the primary business model is through licensing, an increasing number are also available on demand.

Jasper BI is also available through a SaaS delivery model. However, Jasper doesn't actually host the service itself. Instead the customer also signs up for Amazon EC2 (cloud infrastructure) and RightScale (cloud management) accounts and then selects the JasperServer template to deploy it to their accounts.

Google BigQuery is a web service that enables you to do interactive analysis of massively large datasets hosted on Google Storage. It is particularly suited for high performance against large data sets and is available on demand. The API includes RESTful and JSON-RPC methods to execute SQL queries against tables and obtain the schemas for those tables. Authentication is accomplished through Client Login, AuthSub and OAuth.

INFORMATION

External Data Needs

We live in what some call a feed era. Rather than building and maintaining your own data store, many applications today aggregate external data from multiple sources.

There are at least two ways to ingest external content into a web-site. You can provide real-time web content and streaming technologies as already described earlier in this book. Alternatively, you can crawl the Internet or a partial web and selectively link to, or import, information as it is needed by the application or user.

Real Time Web Content

Twitter provides an example of the processing of access to 'real time' web content. It exposes two main APIs with respective advantages and drawbacks:

The ***RESTful Search API*** removes the need for a separate search engine. It can perform complex (Boolean) queries and return relevant results. However, it only provides partial coverage, and is expensive to use on a large scale - often, you'll make requests just to find out there are no updates.

The ***Streaming API*** is cheaper to run and involves less waste (since the results are pushed to the caller). It provides better coverage since it can supply all the content meeting the specified criteria, The drawback is that the 'search' rules that can be set are very basic (list of keywords, list of accounts), so the application needs to run its own search engine on the results in order to draw meaningful conclusions from the data.

Web Search

An ad-hoc method of external access that is more suited to isolated and specific requests is the use of web search. Again there are a couple ways you can approach it. You can implement your own crawler and indexer and then lookup information in your system. Alternatively, you can use of some of the search APIs and tap into the indexes of some of the leading consumer search engines.

INFORMATION

The first option makes sense if you have a small domain of web servers to crawl, but need to customize the crawling or indexing in a way that you cannot easily accomplish with commercial software. Nutch is an open-source crawler that builds on Lucene and Solr. It also adds web-specifics, such as a link-graph database and parsers for various document formats including HTML.

Building your own Nutch implementation is a lot of work not only in terms of development and integration but also maintenance and support. It is worth it if you really need the degree of control that Nutch offers, but if you are looking for an easy way to fetch public pages based on search results, one of the search engines APIs may be a less painful approach.

Google, Yahoo and Microsoft Bing all provide programmatic interfaces that make use of their investments in crawling, indexing, ranking and relevancy algorithms. They are conceptually very similar but obviously rely on different indexes and have subtle functional differences.

The Google AJAX Search API lets you put Google Search in your web pages with JavaScript. You can embed a simple, dynamic search box and display search results in your own web pages or use the results in your applications. You can indicate search types of Local, Web, Video, Blog, News, Image, Patent and Book which correspond to similar options on Google's main page.

The easiest implementation is through a Search Control but a Search Form is also provided. One important restriction is that Google expects any users of the API to expose its "powered by Google" branding so that consumers associate the search services with Google.

Yahoo also offers programmatic search through BOSS (Build your Own Search Service). BOSS provides Yahoo!'s web, news, and image search technology. Unlike other search APIs, developers can use BOSS technology with very few restrictions.

Microsoft Bing is very similar to Yahoo in this regard. Although it doesn't require any branding, it uses an AppID parameter to validate that all requests originate from registered Bing application developers. Bing supports source types of Encarta and Spell in addition to Web, Images and News. It exposes HTTP endpoints that provide results in either XML or JSON media formats, but also includes enhanced support for SOAP and an OpenSearch-compliant RSS interface.

Practical Recommendations

Driven in large part by social networking and other new types of applications, the data structures of many cloud applications have veered away from a tabular paradigm and new models are appearing in its place. There are also increased demands to analyze the content and integrate external sources. As you work through the options that are available, consider some suggestions:

INFORMATION

- Look at document databases and graphs for any information needs that can't be handled well with a relational model!
- Leverage as much external content as you can! Much of it is free – or at least much cheaper than it would be for you to create and maintain yourself.
- Move up the stack by analyzing your information for patterns that represent higher value intelligence!

Resilience

Outsourced services can complicate availability guarantees. They require new techniques for monitoring; and recovery usually involves a high degree of redundancy. In order to ensure the availability of the application, it is necessary to look at short-term uptime including reliability of applications and infrastructure. However, it is also important to plan capacity for the long term and ensure that the application is scalable.

Elasticity and reliability may sound like independent objectives but they are related in two ways. Both attempt to address the availability of the service. Reliability relates to the short-term performance of all the components, whereas elasticity ensures that sufficient resources are always accessible whether they are needed suddenly or gradually. The two are also related in their implementation. For both purposes, a common strategy is to decompose the system into modular components that can be scaled up through increased parallelism. They can also serve as redundant failover and hot-standby systems to cover outages and system errors in addition to service growth.

RESILIENCE

Chapter 20

Reliability

Reliability of a service is the most obvious manifestation of resilience. Users expect the system to behave predictably regardless of any external events or influences.

Service level agreements may define key metrics in precise terms that imply significant monetary penalties. However, even when it is free and without contractual obligation, the service is not likely to be successful if it doesn't address key elements of reliability including:

Availability refers to resistance against component and system failures and is often measured in percentage of uptime. It may be achieved through high component reliability, but is usually complemented with redundancy and failover capabilities to achieve fault tolerance.

Usability conveys the idea that the service is not only functional at a minimal level but is also acceptable from a human perspective. This means that the client software needs to be intuitive to use, and that the performance of all elements of the solution must be adequate.

RESILIENCE

Restorability adds a temporal element to the business process requirements. Important transactions and historical data need to be preserved for future access. The system doesn't only need to back up all the information, but it must ensure all versions of the content can be retrieved when necessary.

Continuity designates the ability of the system to sustain a major unforeseeable incident. A complete business continuity plan will contain provisions for redundancy and multi-phase disaster recovery.

Redundancy is a common theme through all these elements since it can help to eliminate single points of failure, provide additional persistence and distribute load to optimize performance. However, there are additional options for each of the objectives.

Availability

There are several strategies to achieve high uptime. Traditionally the focus has been on ensuring high reliability of all components. Where this is not possible, or insufficient, there is an option of pursuing fault tolerance through redundancy and fast failover capability. At the same time, it is worth looking at the overall architecture to ensure that components are loosely coupled and complexity is kept to a minimum. A more recent approach is to accept occasional failures and instead concentrate on expediting the restoration of the service.

Component Reliability

The first approach tries to select the highest grade parts for each component of the solution. In the past, disciplines such as Total Quality Management and Six Sigma have demonstrated that a lot can be achieved through diligence and a commitment to quality throughout the whole system.

There is much to be said for a focus on quality. However, it is not trivial to pursue this avenue in a cloud-oriented solution due to the complexity of the system and the lack of control over all the elements.

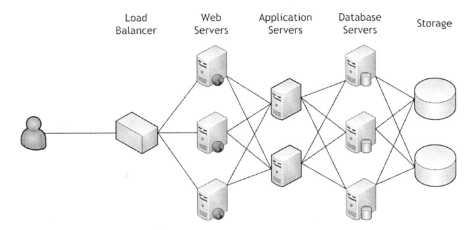

Figure 20-1: Application Components

On the one hand, there are a number of components to consider (Figure 20-1). The applications may run over many different physical and virtual systems with data distributed even more widely. In addition to the three tiers of most web applications, you need to look at load balancers and the entire network infrastructure including the physical links, the routing tables and DNS.

Simply validating the hardware configuration will not be sufficient. The biggest threat to availability is typically software bugs, which are notoriously difficult to pinpoint. You need to ensure that all services perform as expected both in terms of functionality and performance. This guarantee doesn't automatically follow

RESILIENCE

from a collection of error-free components. As the system scales, the number of linkages and dependencies tends to grow exponentially. A second problem is that many of the components are likely to be outsourced. Even in a pure private cloud implementation, there are network links and infrastructure that may be outside the control of the organization.

In addition to these technical obstacles, there are financial considerations. Adoption of premium components and systems runs counter to the principle of cloud computing to minimize costs by relying on standardized and commoditized parts. Even if systematic quality processes are achievable, they may not represent the most cost-effective avenue to reliability.

Fault Tolerance

In the world of Internet, services fail. Servers fail, networks fail, connections get stuck and responses are not sent back to requests in a timely manner. When dealing with massive volumes of compute capacity and complex network connections, it is a statistical fact that some elements will fail.

Given the challenges of ensuring that no part in the system fails, the next logical step is to accept that there may be local failures but strive for the system to be able to hide them. In other words: build the system assuming that things will fail, but ensure users never see outages and data is never lost.

You need to provide fault tolerance for all components at all layers of the architecture including: applications, file systems, CPU, I/O ports, network links, etc. In practice, tolerating faults involves making provisions for common failures or bottlenecks. A cloud-aware application must be able to cope with failures in services and infrastructure that lead to both planned and unplanned downtime.

RESILIENCE

For instance, when building on Google App Engine, the applications are subject to a planned limited functionality period every few months. During this time the applications have read-only access to their data. Also, in case of a catastrophic failure (like we saw in March 2010 with App Engine) services were first recovered to a read only state and writes were enabled later. To minimize impact in these situations, App Engine provides a set of API calls that should be used to detect the availability state of the platform (read/write vs. read-only) and how long the platform is expected to be available in read/write mode (normal) mode (e.g. up to 60 seconds).

Immunity to failures means never expecting the system to be stable. Instead, the application must assume nodes are continuously leaving, joining and failing. The most common technique in achieving fault tolerance is to provide some amount of redundancy along the same principles of Redundant Array of Interchangeable Disks (RAID), which has achieved great success in the area of storage.

By extending this concept to cloud components, we shift the burden from the individual elements to a means of effective synchronization, failover and election. For instance, when building on App Engine, if disks and Memcached are not available then the application might write information in HTTP requests and pass the information further in POSTs until the system is recovered and the data can finally be written on disk. Similarly, if requests to a RESTful/JSON interface don't receive responses in a timely manner, then there may be a need to build polling requests that iterate several attempts before returning a failure.

Reduced Complexity / Loose Coupling

Unfortunately, true fault tolerance is a very difficult objective to achieve. A less ambitious approach to solving the problem in a scalable manner is to reduce the interlinked complexity of the system. By enforcing strong functional cohesion internally, and decreasing external dependencies through loose coupling, you can minimize the impact of local failures and thereby allow the system to continue even when a component encounters major problems.

Werner Vogels, Amazon CTO, has provided copious advice in his blog[1] on how Amazon has been able to maintain high availability of one of the largest Internet storefronts using techniques that follow this methodology. Some points to consider include autonomy, loose coupling and acceptance of failure. It's hard to argue with success so we've drawn on his wisdom.

An autonomous system is able to make decisions based on local state using inferential and probabilistic techniques. It should be able to configure and manage itself as well as diagnose and repair any faults. Full autonomy removes the dependency on other components so that failures remain isolated. This can be partially achieved through effective hierarchical and functional decomposition of workloads into well-understood building blocks.

In most cases, however, some interconnections are inevitable. The objective then becomes asynchrony. By minimizing concurrency, it is possible to reduce the propagation of failures from one module to another. Locking, in particular, is the most dangerous form of concurrency since anything that requires agreement will eventually become a bottleneck.

Where possible it may be sensible to define internal SLAs between web services (from client to services), so that consuming applications can determine the degree of reliance on other services. However, rather than aspiring to an almost perfect availability rate and passing that expectation on to clients, it is safer to consider failure a common occurrence and pass the burden of redundancy and tolerance on to the application, which can manage it most effectively. If nodes

---

[1] www.allthingsdistributed.com

are symmetric (homogeneous), then it is relatively easy for client nodes to fail over when needed and a single failure should not interrupt the service.

At the heart of this guidance lies a trend to weaker consistency where possible. Historically, online transactions processing has used the ACID (atomicity, consistency, isolation, durability) test to ensure that database transactions are processed reliably. This test enforces strong consistency. However, in accordance with the CAP model, it also fails easily, especially in a distributed environment.

An alternate approach called BASE (Basically Available; Soft-state/Scalable; Eventually-consistent) emphasizes availability and offers only weak consistency on a best-effort basis. ACID guarantees are useful, but become costly with scale. BASE, on the other hand, is simple and fast.

In spite of its advantages, weak consistency is not necessarily easier to implement. In fact, it is more difficult to program as it needs to explicitly consider technical details such as quorum, information lifetime, leases, cache and optimistic updating with posterior conflict resolution.

The choice begins at the data design and modeling stage and derives from the basic question of why you need transactions. A two-phase commit will eventually fail in a distributed environment due to locking problems. But you may be able to address it by denormalizing the tables, running the transactions on a single physical node or splitting the transactions with compensating actions for recovery.

Fast Recovery

One final approach to cloud-related failures again assumes there will be problems, but deals with them by trying to minimize the impact through a fast recovery. In its extreme form, this means avoiding all troubleshooting (hence it is often called "lazy") and simply reinitializing the system when there is an incident.

RESILIENCE

The most important activity in this space is called "recovery-oriented computing". It focuses on synchronously redundant and heavily monitored data that is seamlessly partitioned. The underlying premise is that availability is not only determined by the mean-time-between-failures (MTBF) but also the mean-time-to-repair (MTTR). In a highly virtualized system it can be at least as effective to pursue MTTR which involves a focus on (Berkeley/Stanford, 2008):

- Isolation and redundancy

- System-wide undo support

- Integrated diagnostic support

- Online verification and recovery mechanisms

- Modularity, measurability and restartability

Usability

In assessing system reliability, it is easy to become absorbed with abstract metrics and data integrity constraints. These are important, but they may distract from the ultimate purpose of the application. A true measure of availability is not whether the services perform according to a pre-defined functional specification, but rather whether users can consume the services satisfactorily.

On the one hand, this means that the services are easy to use and navigate. They behave not only as the users expect but also in a way that allows the users to achieve their business and personal objectives. We have covered this topic in more depth in earlier chapters, so we will not repeat the discussion here, but want to remind the reader of the context in which the functional capabilities should be analyzed.

A secondary aspect of usability is perceived performance. Graceful degradation should always be a system objective, meaning that a resource shortage should not trigger a sudden system failure when it reaches a given threshold, but instead the capabilities should slowly deteriorate allowing the system to detect and correct problems automatically.

Nonetheless, users will not necessarily distinguish between an application that fails and one that is burdened with an onerous response time. In earlier chapters we have described network and latency optimization, for example through content delivery networks. Where you have control over content storage, you can also improve performance and reliability by caching near the edges.

RESILIENCE

However, even the fastest network won't help if the servers are overloaded. This is where cloud computing shines. A truly elastic service can never be oversubscribed. Nonetheless, just because the capacity is available does not mean that it is being allocated and the load is balanced efficiently across all available resources.

In some cases, load balancing is available from the service provider. Platform services such as Google App Engine and Microsoft Azure include it transparently. Infrastructure services are not sufficiently application aware to provide automatic load balancing, but there may be ancillary services available to customers. For example, Amazon provides Elastic Load Balancing and Elastic IP, which can be incorporated into the application architecture.

Other options range from something as simple as DNS round robin or software load balancers installed on infrastructure services to hardware load balancing, such as those offered by F5 networks for both local and global load balancing. Note that the latter is typically only feasible in a private data center or at least a private virtual cloud.

Disaster

Not all disasters are equal. They can have different degrees of impact from a minor outage to complete destruction of both equipment and facilities. They may also vary according to their geographical scope from an incident in a local data center to a local, regional or even global catastrophe.

This doesn't mean that you need to accommodate full and immediate restoration for every disaster. However, it should be clear which scenarios you intend to address and what your objectives are in those cases. The most common goals are the RTO (Recovery Time Objective) and RPO (Recovery Point Objective). Some also refer to an RLO (Recovery Level Objective).

RTO is the duration within which a business process must be restored after a disaster (or disruption). It includes time for fixing the problem, the recovery itself, tests and the communication to the users. In simple terms, how quickly after a catastrophic failure will you need to be back up and running?

RPO refers to the last state prior to the disaster for which data must be recovered. In other words, how much application data can you afford to lose? Will loss of a week's worth of streaming data lead to bankruptcy? Do you have to maintain copies of every transaction?

RLO is a qualitative rather than quantitative measure. It specifies the scope of the system that needs to be restored immediately after a failure. Rather than attempting to recover the full system it allows IT to focus on the most mission-critical services and processes first.

A Business Continuity Plan (BCP) should be in place that describes the process to back up and recover the data. These may refer to a single RTO and RPO, or it may be necessary to specify a series of RTOs, RPOs and RLOs in order to cover all possible scenarios.

The process can vary greatly depending on the requirements, applications and data. One way to achieve a very quick RTO would be to maintain a set of duplicate instances at another cloud provider's facility and simply redirect traffic to the new site. The main challenge in this scenario would be to continuously synchronize all the data with the alternate provider.

A slower, but significantly cheaper, approach would be to create application instances at a secondary location but to import the data manually (either through a network upload or a physical medium) in the event of a disaster. New transactions might be processed almost immediately, but any queries to historical data would be delayed until the information was uploaded into the new system.

One of the key questions to address is the level of geographical redundancy, which is clearly related to the scope of disaster that needs to be survived. The ability of the application designer to specify locality will depend on the terms of the service providers. Infrastructure providers often let users decide where to position capacity. For example, Amazon offers several availability zones and allows customers to place instances in the zone of their choice. On the other hand, some platform services more commonly rely on shared infrastructure that is opaque to the user. Google App Engine does not reveal to users where their applications are running.

Ideally, the physical infrastructure should be replicated to a geographically removed location, so that it is unlikely to be affected by the same disaster. The more distant the two locations are the better the chances that the second will survive a disaster of the first. A different continent is therefore ideal, but that level of precaution is probably not necessary in every case and may need to be weighed against compliance and performance demands.

An additional level of independence can be achieved if a backup is hosted by a second provider. In this case, an incident (e.g. large-scale intrusion or malware attack) cannot easily affect both the backup and the primary system. However, there are cost implications in distributing the applications, particularly when there is a need to synchronize them. Even within the same provider, there are often charges for data transfers between availability zones. If multiple providers are involved, there will invariably be significant network costs and there may also be an additional effort to integrate the data sources through differing interfaces.

Restorability/Reversibility/Rollback

Disasters are one of the main reasons for maintaining backups. However, they are not the only reason. It may be necessary to restore user information, system configuration, or application code for other reasons, too. Systems fail, users make mistakes and auditors may need to inspect historical data for legal or diagnostic purposes.

A prerequisite for a solid backup plan is a thorough inventory of both business and system data along with an indication of the lifetime and value of the information. You can then proceed to analyze patterns in information usage to identify options and derive a sensible plan.

Some questions to ask are: How valuable is the user data in your application? Can users delete something inside your service or your application? Do you back up user data only as a safeguard against infrastructure failures, or do you also allow users to recover data that they have deleted in error? Can you move user data into a holding area for a period of time, before deleting it?

We will look at three different dimensions of safeguarding information for future use. Backup is the core activity that involves taking periodic snapshots of a wide range of information. Versioning is primarily intended to protect against user error, or at least a change of user intention. It provides a means to revert from the most recent release of a document, program or configuration setting to a prior state that presumably worked better. Archival is concerned with long-term retention of information to provide a basis for historical searches and queries.

Backups

Multiple levels of backups can help to achieve different RPOs. The most secure and reliable are off-site since they are not affected by regional outages and losses. These might be off-site tape backups, disk backups or simply off-site replication (to an auxiliary data center or service provider). In the PaaS world, an off-site backup might mean storing your data from Google App Engine to Amazon S3 or Rackspace on a regular interval.

While off-site backups may be more reliable, there are obvious performance implications related to the additional physical distance and network latency. This may impact the cost and therefore the frequency with which backups are feasible. Given increasingly demanding business requirements for more frequent backups and faster restores, off-line backups may not be sufficient. In order to improve both the RPO and RTO, it makes sense to complement them with more frequent on-site tape or disk backups.

A common scheme would foresee weekly off-site backups in addition to daily on-site backups. It is possible to maintain much more current backups by clustering servers and storage, implementing continuous replication or by taking frequent snapshots and maintaining differential transaction logs.

Keep in mind that backup requirements are changing. Virtualization can help to automate disaster recovery by packaging images and making them easier to deploy. However, it also reduces scheduled downtime, which complicates the backup process. At the same time the demands on backup are becoming more aggressive with rapid growth in information volume and requirements for both encrypted media and long-term readability.

A complete backup/restore plan is likely to include a range of components, ranging from virtual tape libraries to disk appliances, and incorporate a variety of techniques such as disk-based data protection, continuous replications, snapshots and transaction logging. As mentioned above, the tradeoff between better, more accurate information and the higher cost of maintenance need to be evaluated to determine the best mix of backup for any given application and organization.

Versioning

Some storage services, such as Amazon S3, provide facilities for versioning information. The advantage is primarily financial. In theory, it is always possible to implement your own versioning scheme simply by labeling the data with a version number. However, you would be multiplying your storage costs with each incremental version of the data. If you are able to access versioned storage, then you can reduce these charges.

If you are using flat storage and need to version information that is primarily static, you can also look at saving only the differential with each version. There will be some effort in comparing versions and reapplying changes when you need to revert, but it might be more cost effective.

As we shall see in more detail in our Lifecycle section, the application instances typically run through a workflow that relies on versions. However, even beyond the primary stages, you can track progress and provide rollback capability if you maintain a systematic versioning scheme.

In any case, for your application data as well as the application code and configuration you need to decide on the number of versions to maintain and develop a process for storing and retrieving them once needed.

Archival

One of the reasons that backup has become a monumental task in many organizations is that it attempts to simultaneously address a number of requirements. In addition to facilitating both short-term data restoration and disaster recovery, it can be used to ensure compliance with local laws. However, it is a very blunt instrument for achieving these objectives.

Archival provides a streamlined mechanism to comply with e-discovery laws. It also facilitates classification and enterprise search across de-duplicated and compressed repositories of critical information. It doesn't remove the need for backups but it ensures that on-line and off-line data is reduced to its minimum and becomes as accessible and usable as possible.

RESILIENCE

Practical Recommendations

Multi-sourced services are difficult to operate reliably. Many of the conventional approaches to availability break down when they are delivered externally or involve significant geographical separation between components. As you work through the challenges, consider some suggestions:

- Maximize asynchrony! Enforce loose coupling between applications and try to implement non-blocking calls.
- Plan for failure! Ensure you have a comprehensive backup plan and include sufficient redundancy to cope with outages.
- Accelerate recovery when there are failures! If you can't stop failure, minimize its impact.

Chapter 21

Elasticity

Elasticity is another aspect of resilience. The previous chapter looked at how to maximize availability in the face of foreseeable and unforeseeable errors and events. Elasticity ensures that the system has the capacity to handle workload. Unless the system has the ability to allocate and take advantage of resources whenever it needs them, it will not be able to cope with varying demand, either in the short or long term.

The core problem when dealing with Internet applications is that they need to be able to scale in two dimensions. On the one hand, you may have a high volume of users who need to execute independent (but similar) transactions. In this case you have a single code base (which doesn't have to be very complex) that needs to execute in parallel for a large number of simultaneous users.

You may also have scenarios where you want to solve a big problem. It could be related to a large population, but differs from the first problem in that the process is inherently very complex and will not comfortably run on typical cloud-based-infrastructure services.

RESILIENCE

We will look at a few ways that you can address these problems including vertical scaling, application sharding, grid computing and MapReduce. Regardless of the technique you employ to permit high scalability, you also need to look at the resource allocation that will be necessary to achieve flexible and quick elasticity to cope with rapidly changing user demand and computational workload.

Vertical scaling

From the perspective of the application, the simplest approach to adding capacity is through vertical scaling. By adding more powerful processors, additional memory and both network and peripheral interfaces, a demanding application can run unchanged for larger workloads. In the case of Infrastructure-as-a-Service from EC2, this would mean upgrading from a small instance to a large instance.

Vertical scaling bypasses the need to worry about partitioning data and application logic. As we mentioned earlier, the CAP theorem states that this makes it far easier to achieve both high availability and high consistency, so the code needn't include special provisions for either.

Until recently, it was possible to satisfy the increasing appetite of software applications for processing power, memory and storage through advances in transistor density and clock-frequencies, which improved single-threaded performance in an almost linear manner (Kaufmann & Gayliard, 2009). This approach has run into physical limits that prevent further advances without dramatically increasing power consumption and heat dissipation, and are therefore not cost effective or ecologically responsible.

By increasing the number of processor cores, it is possible to reduce per-socket power consumption. However, the job for the software developer becomes all the more difficult in exchange. An application cannot run faster than the aggregate of its sequential components. If an application does not parallelize effectively, then performance will not improve (and may degrade) with additional cores.

The main criteria in evaluating vertical scalability are the relative costs of different server instances and the degree to which they address the performance bottleneck. There may also be instances where a legacy application is not able to scale horizontally at all. In this case, vertical scaling is the only option.

Unfortunately, most public infrastructure service providers are specialized in low-end server instances and offer only limited high-performance virtual machines. However, given the existing need for high-end solutions, some providers have begun to offer high-end hardware configurations and high-availability clusters. For example, Amazon EC2 offers a Cluster Compute Quadruple Extra Large Instance with 33.5 EC2 Compute Units (2 x Intel Xeon X5570, quad-core "Nehalem" architecture), 23 GB of memory, 1690 GB of instance storage, optimal I/O Performance and 10 Gigabit Ethernet interfaces.

RESILIENCE

It may be possible to arrange for high-end systems with other providers through negotiation of special terms. In this case, the only obstacles to using the fastest computers in the industry are the flexibility of your provider and the price you are willing to pay.

An alternative to supercomputers is the consolidation of many low-end systems into virtual machines. ScaleMP, for example, offers a hypervisor that aggregates x86 nodes into larger systems of over 255 virtual processors. It relies on high-bandwidth, low-latency connections between the individual systems that may be challenging to guarantee in an opaque cloud but is worth considering in a private data center or a dedicated segment of a public cloud.

Sharding

Unfortunately, there are limits to the application workloads that vertical scaling can accommodate. Even before the system exhausts all the technical possibilities, the exponentially increasing costs of higher capacity make the approach unattractive.

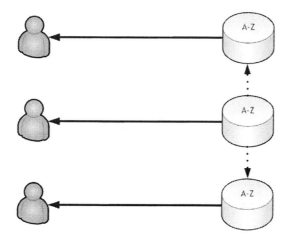

Figure 21-1: Replication

The most common strategy in cloud environments is to scale horizontally when additional capacity is needed. When the majority of transactions are read-only, the task is not difficult. You simply replicate, or cache, the information on multiple systems and ensure that user requests are balanced across all available systems. In effect, you create a content delivery network (Figure 21-1).

The picture changes when you need to accommodate a large number of write requests. You can still install the application in parallel on additional servers. However, you need to ensure that processing is completely independent on each system. We refer to this architecture as "Shared Nothing", which has given rise to the term "shard" or "sharding".

In its extreme form, sharding would imply that there is no common data at all. For example, you might have a set of web servers that are able to perform calculations based only on user input and local data. However, if you expand your interpretation slightly then you can also consider some amount of common static input data as well as external data feeds and repositories.

This is easiest to implement when the same operation is executed on every system, typically using different data. According to Michael Flynn's taxonomy (1972), this is a single-instruction multiple-data (SIMD) algorithm. It works particularly well where bulk data needs to be transformed or web transactions can be processed in isolation.

Sharding isn't applicable to every scenario but where it is feasible it provides a simple solution to scalability. The only technical challenges are to ensure that users are allocated equitably to the available servers and that any stateful information isn't lost between requests.

A load balancer is the simplest way to allocate users to servers. If any data is required, then it needs to be replicated in the background. Most commercial load balancers can also ensure that sessions are sticky, so that users will always be directed to the same server for each request. However, there may be reasons to partition according to a different dimension than the user.

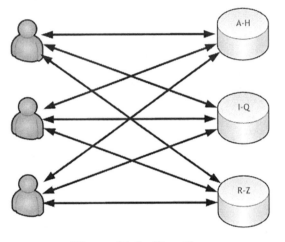

Figure 21-2: Sharding

For example, if requests rely on significant local data then you might want to split the index and shard according to a particular key. As shown in Figure 21-2, this approach means that each shard will only contain a fraction of the database. However, users may need to access several shards in the course of a transaction. To avoid potential contamination, it is advisable to ensure that all requests are stateless and that any intermediate data is maintained by the client.

One last point about horizontal scaling: don't conceal heterogeneity at any cost. Just because you have the same application running on each system, it doesn't mean that it must be tuned to the lowest common denominator. You may be running on different instances and instance types, or even different cloud providers. If systems are configured differently, and have access to different resources or capacity, make sure that they exploit all they can in terms of CPU, memory and storage.

High Performance Computing

While application sharding tries to take a relatively simple problem and apply it to a large number of users or data streams, High Performance Computing (HPC)

RESILIENCE

and Grid Computing attempt to solve very complex problems by decomposing them into smaller tasks that can be distributed on multiple systems.

At a high level, they distribute compute-intensive processing across a cluster of machines. APIs such as the Message Passing Interface (MPI) or OpenMP provide a framework to orchestrate task execution. The approach lends itself to compute-intensive jobs that do not need to transfer large amounts of data between systems. However, some amount of sharing is typically facilitated through the file system, running on a dedicated SAN.

Of the two dominant frameworks, OpenMP is generally considered easier to use. However it comes with several constraints, such as the need for a special compiler and a reliance on shared-memory. Its simpler use may also lead to less rigor, which contributes to application errors. As a result, MPI is more common for solutions with high reliability and scalability requirements.

MPI is the de facto standard for programming high-performance parallel computers. In addition to defining a protocol, it also specifies a set of language-independent APIs and describes an architecture including virtual topology, synchronization, and communication functionality. The software engineer has considerable flexibility, which makes it possible to design systems that scale almost indefinitely. However, the framework also requires explicit management of the entire process from defining and initiating data flow to checkpointing and restarting processes.

There are classes of problems that can only be solved through a complex architecture involving numerous compute-bound modules that collaborate to attain a solution. Although an MPI-based solution is not trivial to implement, it is certainly easier than redesigning an equivalent solution on your own. The challenge in implementing HPC in the cloud is that most providers do not offer infrastructure that is suitable for tight coupling. Without a guarantee of low latency between systems, the approach isn't technically viable. Furthermore, if intra-system bandwidth is expensive, then the costs become a problem.

RESILIENCE

We are now seeing some attempt to fill this need through private virtual clouds with strict service level agreements where the customer also has significantly more control over the hardware and physical placement of their systems. Cluster Computer Instances, such as those available from Amazon EC2 provide another option. They are a new instance type specifically designed for High Performance Computing applications.

MapReduce

One specific technique for processing large sets of data in parallel is MapReduce. It is often associated with cloud computing since it lends itself well to cloud-scale problems and many cloud providers have created offerings that build on the MapReduce paradigm. The main principle behind it is not that difficult to understand, however an actual implementation can become quite complex.

It's beyond the scope of this book to explore the subject in great depth. We refer interested readers to one of the excellent books on Hadoop for more information. In this chapter, we will just look at the main concepts, which we approach through a series of basic questions:

- What is it?

- What is it good for?

- Why use it?

- What does it do?

- How does it work?

- How do you use it?

We will focus on Hadoop. Nonetheless, most of the principles would also apply to other implementations of MapReduce.

What is it?

Google was the first company to publicize MapReduce, inspired by the 'map' and 'reduce' functions from functional programming. They initially invented the technique to build production search indexes, but extended it into a general software framework. Its key attraction was its support of distributed computing on petascale data-sets using clusters of inexpensive computers.

RESILIENCE

MapReduce is also the core function included in Hadoop, an open-source project available from Apache. As we mentioned earlier, it was created by Doug Cutting, who used it for the Nutch search engine project. Since then, Hadoop has become the most popular open-source implementation of MapReduce, with a strong following in the grid and cloud computing communities, including developers at Google, Yahoo, Microsoft, and Facebook.

The Hadoop MapReduce framework requires a shared file system. It typically operates over the Hadoop Distributed File System (HDFS) but there is no absolute dependency for HDFS as long as a distributed file system plug-in is available to the framework.

The model receives its name from the two primary functions it executes:

Map is an initial ingestion step to process the raw data in parallel. The master node reads the input, segments it into smaller chunks, and distributes those to the processing nodes.

Reduce is an aggregation step which collects the output of all the Map functions and combines them to produce the result of the original problem.

There is some similarity to the concept of sharding, described above, in that there is an assumption of effective data partitioning making it possible for each of these two phases to implement a high degree of parallelism.

What is it good for?

MapReduce is ideally suited to processing very large data sets. It is useful in a wide range of tasks and applications including: batch processing, building search index engines, image analysis, distributed grep, distributed sort, graph traversal, web access log stats, inverted index construction, document clustering, machine learning algorithms and statistical machine translation. You may also recall that some of the frameworks introduced in the Data section, such as Hive and Pig, are built on top of Hadoop. They facilitate extracting information from databases for Hadoop processing.

Hadoop includes a set of simple examples to illustrate how MapReduce works (Table 21-1), e.g. computing the maximum of a set of numbers, adding a set of numbers, and counting the occurrences of words in a large text or collection of texts (e.g. The Complete Works of William Shakespeare)[1].

RESILIENCE

---

[1] As documented by Hadoop:
hadoop.apache.org/common/docs/r0.20.1/api/org/apache/hadoop/examples/package-summary.html

AggregateWordCount	Counts the words in the input files.
AggregateWordHistogram	Computes a histogram of the words in the input files.
DBCountPageView	Uses DBInputFormat for reading the input data from a database, and DBOutputFormat for writing the data to the database.
Grep	Counts the matches of a regular expression in the input.
Join	Fragments and sorts the input values over sorted, equally partitioned datasets.
MultiFileWordCount	Demonstrates the usage of MultiFileInputFormat by counting words from several files.
PiEstimator	Estimate the value of Pi using quasi-Monte Carlo method.
RandomTextWriter	Run a distributed job without interaction between the tasks. Each task writes a large unsorted random sequence of words.
RandomWriter	Runs a distributed job without interaction between the tasks. Each task write a large unsorted random binary sequence file of BytesWritable.
SecondarySort	Sorts the data written by the random writer.
SleepJob	Sleeps at each map and reduce task.
Sort<K,V>	Uses the framework to fragment and sort the input values.
WordCount	Counts the words in a set of input files.

Table 21-1 : Hadoop Sample Classes

RESILIENCE

Although MapReduce can help to solve a wide range of problems, it is important to realize that not all use cases are suitable. In particular, interactive applications cannot leverage the framework synchronously as it is intended for bulk processing rather than real-time queries.

MapReduce is appropriate for write-once, read-many (WORM) applications with static data that may be analyzed repeatedly. As such it stands in contrast to relational databases that can handle data being continuously updated. The framework also shines when there is a need to process unstructured data, since it interprets the data at processing time rather than relying on intrinsic properties or schemas.

Why use it?

Just because MapReduce can handle a given problem doesn't meant that it is the best solution. You might even wonder why it is attractive at all since you could implement a distributed processing model yourself without the overhead and constraints of a framework. Where it fits, there are at least three clear benefits to using MapReduce:

Scale: Most importantly, the programming model scales transparently. The developer-written functions concentrate on mapping and reducing without taking the size of the dataset into account. It is the framework that orchestrates the workload, allocating it to the systems that are available.

Performance: MapReduce also offers good performance for processing petascale, data sets which are highly sensitive to latency and bandwidth constraints. Its first step is to co-locate the data with the compute node where possible so data access is local. An inefficient network topology can easily lead to saturated network links so MapReduce explicitly models the physical layout.

Fault tolerance: Fault tolerance is another benefit. The framework detects failed map or reduce tasks and reschedules replacements on machines that are healthy. The programmer can ignore the order of task execution and doesn't need to verify that they run successfully.

These three features are native to the framework. Unless you have very different requirements, it will usually be easier and faster to leverage a mature tool than to reinvent the functionality.

What does it do?

As mentioned above, the MapReduce model is based on two distinct steps for an application. The Map step processes individual records in parallel while the Reduce step aggregates and/or refines the output of many different Map systems. The framework is largely agnostic to the data structures involved, but requires them to be packaged as key-value pairs. The only constraint imposed is that the output of the map tasks must match the input of the reduce tasks.

RESILIENCE

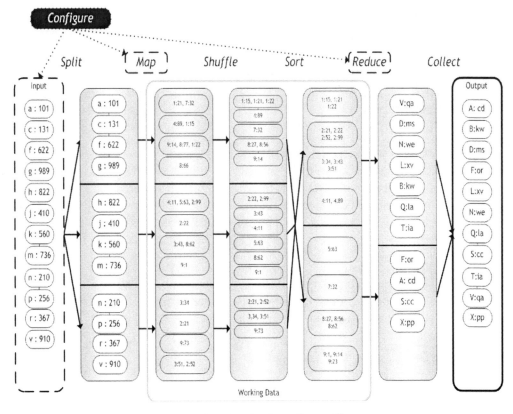

Figure 21-3: MapReduce Data Flow

As shown very simplistically in Figure 21-3, the key-value pairs have three possible data domains: the input data to the Map function; the output of the Map tasks, which also corresponds to the input format for the Reduce function; and the output of the Reduce tasks. In some cases, the input, intermediate and output data will be similar, while in other scenarios, they may be very different.

The steps involved in the MapReduce job include:

- User: Configure
- Framework: Split
- User: Map
- Framework: Shuffle
- Framework: Sort
- User: Reduce
- Framework: Collect

RESILIENCE

Initially the user *Configures* the job by specifying the data locations for input and output and providing the Map and Reduce functions to the Framework.

The framework then aggregates the entire input (which may be spread across several files) and *Splits* it into equitable chunks. It then distributes the chunks to the Map processes that are running on the Hadoop cluster, passing the input in the form of key-value pairs.

The user-written *Map* function analyzes or transforms each data item from an input key-value pair into a set of output key-value pairs.

Each per-map output is then partitioned and sorted as part of the *Shuffle* stage. The output generated from each sorted partition is referred to as a spill. The framework will pull the spill from the output of each map task, and merge-sort these spills.

The entire output is then aggregated and repartitioned according to the number of Reduce processes available. A *Sort* function orders the key-value pairs before passing them on to the Reduce function.

The *Reduce* function again acts once on each input key and returns a set of key-value pairs for each call.

Finally the framework *Collects* all the Reduce outputs and returns them to the user.

How does it work?

To understand how Hadoop works, it is helpful to consider how it is structured and the responsibilities of each component. The master/slave architecture of HDFS is central to the way a Hadoop cluster functions. There are four required daemons in each Hadoop cluster:

RESILIENCE

NameNode: Manages the namespace, file system metadata, and access control.

JobTracker: Delegates tasks to the slave nodes (TaskTrackers).

DataNode: Implements the file system through its locally-attached storage. Each node stores a partial (or complete) copy of the blocks in the file system.

TaskTracker: Executes the map and reduce tasks.

There is exactly one NameNode and one JobTracker in each cluster. However, there can be more than one DataNode and TaskTracker. In fact, a replicated file system implies that you have more than one DataNode. Most clusters run the NameNode and JobTracker on dedicated systems for simplicity and performance reasons. On the other hand, in order to implement data proximity, it is most efficient for the other machines (called 'slaves') to run both DataNode and TaskTracker daemons.

In addition to the four components above, there is a Secondary NameNode that provides a degree of redundancy. It is critical since the NameNode represents a single point of failure in a Hadoop cluster – its absence could make the cluster and filesystem unavailable. The Secondary NameNode prevents permanent loss of state by performing periodic checkpoints of the namespace and putting size limits on the log files.

Hadoop comes with a web UI for viewing information about your jobs. It is useful for following a job's progress while it is running, as well as finding job statistics and logs after the job has completed. The web server on the NameNode reports the status of the DataNodes and capacity of the distributed filesystem. The administrator can also inspect the TaskTrackers and JobTracker.

How do you use it?

If you are expecting to run Hadoop in production, then you'll eventually need personnel with a strong knowledge of Linux and Java. However, you can easily experiment with it using prebuilt images and example programs if your intention is only to familiarize yourself with the technology.

To install Hadoop, you would first download and install all the prerequisite software. This includes Java 6 or higher. For multi-node operation, you will also require ssh and sshd. Although Windows isn't recommended for production, you can run a proof of concept on the platform as long as you install and configure cygwin.

RESILIENCE

If you'd rather not install the software yourself there are VMware system images available on Google Code and Cloudera provides Debian and RPM installer files as well as pre-built Amazon Machine Images.

Hadoop supports three operating modes:

Standalone: The default Hadoop configuration is a single Java process. There is little value in running this mode for a production application but it is helpful for learning about Hadoop and debugging Hadoop applications.

Pseudo-distributed: In pseudo-distributed mode all the Hadoop daemons reside on a single system but each daemon (NameNode, DataNode, JobTracker, TaskTracker) runs in a separate Java process. A functioning Name-Node/DataNode manages the HDFS, which is hosted in a separate namespace from the local file system and stored as block objects in a Hadoop-managed directory. It is possible to extend a pseudo-distributed instance into a fully distributed cluster by adding more machines as Task/DataNodes.

Fully-distributed: In fully distributed mode, Hadoop runs on multiple nodes with distributed NameNode, JobTracker, DataNodes, and TaskTrackers. The simplest implementation involves two nodes, one running all four primary daemons, while the other node only hosts a DataNode and TaskTracker. Clusters of three or more machines typically use dedicated systems for the NameNode and JobTracker, and assign all other nodes as workers (running TaskTracker and DataNode).

As you may recall, the Hadoop MapReduce framework requires a shared file system. HDFS lends itself best since Hadoop is able to leverage its location-awareness in allocating tasks. However, MapReduce is not limited to HDFS. It can also use any distributed file system for which a plug-in is available. Hadoop Core supports the Cloud-Store (formerly Kosmos) file system and Amazon Simple Storage Service (S3) file system. Any distributed file system that is visible as a system-mounted file system, such as Network File System (NFS), Global File System (GFS), or Lustre can also be used with MapReduce.

Complex configurations involving multiple racks of machines can be optimized with HDFS but require special planning. If Hadoop knows which node hosts a physical copy of input data, it can schedule tasks on the same machine as the data. To minimize the possibility of data loss during rack failures, blocks should be replicated on multiple racks. A rack-aware placement policy can be enforced through a script or a Hadoop interface called DNSToSwitchMapping, with which Java code can map servers onto a rack topology.

The heart of a MapReduce system comprises the Map and Reduce functions. Hadoop can run MapReduce programs written in various languages; such as Java, Ruby, Python, and C++. The application developer needs to provide four items to the Hadoop framework:

RESILIENCE

- class that reads the input records and transforms them into one key/value pair per record

- map method

- reduce method

- class that transforms the key/value pairs from the reduce task into output records

To start off the process, the user provides the format and file-location of input and output data as well as a JAR file including the classes for the map and reduce functions.

Unfortunately, we can't go into much more detail on the actual programming in this book but instead refer you to authoritative books on Hadoop as well as the copious online documentation.

Data Association

We mentioned above that Hadoop, in conjunction with HDFS, is able to allocate tasks so that they are in close proximity to the data they are processing. This concept of data locality is fundamental to high-performance distributed computing when large data sets are involved. To illustrate this point, let us look at three different data models (Figure 21-4).

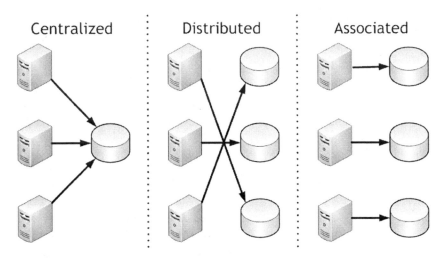

Figure 21-4: Distributed Data Models

In a *centralized* model, the compute instances may be widely distributed, but there is only one information repository, which is shared by all servers. This approach is relatively easy to implement and may be sufficient for services that only require small amounts of data, such as interactive applications or algorithms involving intensive computation.

In a *distributed* paradigm, the volume of information is too great to fit onto one storage device and must therefore be partitioned. The implementation is slightly more difficult since there is a need to partition and balance the data across multiple systems. Nonetheless, it is the logical step to take in order to overcome initial scalability barriers.

Unfortunately, the distributed design makes no attempt to optimize the positioning of data elements. Consequently, there may still be high latency between the servers and storage. For frequent, blocking transactions, high latency will have a direct performance impact. Similarly, for real-time interactive applications (e.g. games), latency will tarnish the user experience.

The *associated* data configuration attempts to minimize both latency and network traffic by placing related information as close as possible to the corresponding compute instance. In many respects, it is the most efficient topology; it is very effective for tasks that perform extensive data processing. However, it is also the most difficult to implement since it is necessary to be able to partition both the workloads and the storage according to the same scheme. As we saw in the MapReduce section, this works well for homogenous operations that need to execute across large datasets. But it is less straightforward for most other applications.

Resource Allocation / Capacity Planning

Designing the software so that it is scalable is only part of the answer. It is also necessary to make sure that the application has access to all the resources it needs – when it needs them. One of the great advantages of cloud computing is its elasticity. It can scale seamlessly up and down as resources are required. However, this doesn't automatically mean that no capacity planning is required. It is much easier and faster to change capacity, but you may still need to intervene to ensure your applications have the resources they need.

There are monitoring systems, such as RightScale, which observe load usage patterns and perform advanced analytics to project future resource requirements. Even if you do choose to use these tools, you should still have a good understanding of what your applications are using so that you can double-check the results and be aware of the costs you are incurring.

A solid capacity plan is based on extensive knowledge of current usage patterns. This includes a trend analysis and examination of any unanticipated spikes and drops to determine cause. Based on these, it is possible to project potential future bottlenecks, which could be along dimensions of CPU, RAM, I/O Read or Writes, Disk Space and Network bandwidth. These metrics need to be investigated, not only for the application servers, but for the database servers, proxies, firewalls, load-balancers and any other nodes that may be part of the overall solution.

RESILIENCE

Note that an impending bottleneck doesn't necessarily mean that you need to increase capacity. It is important to perform a marginal analysis on the additional resources to determine your anticipated costs and revenue both in the case that you expand and the case that you don't. If the resources are required for mission-critical or customer-facing operations, then the equation is probably compelling. In other cases it may not be.

Private Cloud Planning

The notions in the paragraphs above refer primarily to public cloud computing. The challenges are different for private cloud. Capacity planning is more critical given the hard barriers of fixed resources and the lead time in provisioning additional hardware. In some ways, the additional importance is offset by the fact that it is a known art – enterprises have been monitoring performance and using it to project future requirements for decades.

However, it should not be so easily dismissed. Increased virtualization and service orientation have the effect that the internal constitution of services running on hardware becomes opaque to the infrastructure managers. This can make it difficult to manually identify patterns and plan accordingly. It therefore increases the need for analytics that can mine aggregated performance information and correlate it to processes and activities.

Cloudbursting

The most ambitious form of resource allocation exploits all available private assets, but combines these with the elasticity of public resources (Figure 21-5). When it is well designed and orchestrated, cloudbursting can minimize costs and maximize agility. However, while the approach sounds elegant in theory, it is difficult to achieve in practice.

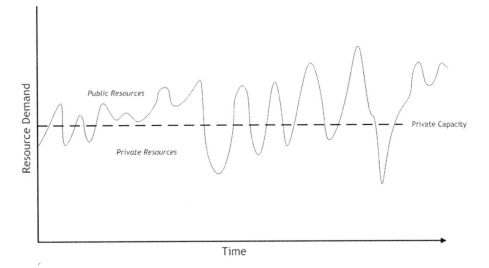

Figure 21-5: Cloudbursting

In order to shift load effectively, three prerequisites are needed: a trigger mechanism, capacity to launch public instances, and capacity to shift associated data.

The first requirement is for a defined means to detect that private resources are close to exhaustion and the launch of public services should be initiated. This implies effective instrumentation of internal utilization. However, unless the launch can be executed instantaneously measurement is not sufficient. You need to be able to project future utilization with sufficient lead time to make the transition. In other words, you must have a good grasp of your load patterns so that you can extrapolate based on current trends.

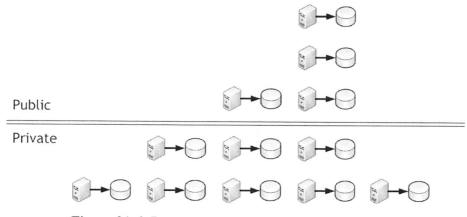

Figure 21-6: Instance Replication for Cloudbursting

The second item on the list is the ability to launch public compute instances (Figure 21-6). Single-server tasks may be simple to start with a call to a public cloud management service. However, complex configurations with many different components should be planned in advance. All relevant parts of the internal infrastructure must be replicated in the cloud environment for the processing to transfer seamlessly. The interaction between any components running in different clouds need coordination, and after processing completes, the results require consolidation.

The last task is generally the most challenging. There is a need to pass all the associated data from the internal services to their external counterparts. In some cases this is not a problem: interactive applications usually involve very little data; other tasks may utilize predominantly static data sets that can be replicated to the public cloud in advance. However, there are many use cases that require large amounts of dynamic data. In these cases, cloudbursting could be difficult to achieve, especially with the speed required to be effective.

Even if it is possible to address these three technical issues, it may not be financially attractive. The costs of a parallel infrastructure and shifting data between services need to be weighed against the additional benefits they provide. Nonetheless, it is wise to design any service with flexible sourcing options in mind. The economics may change in the future, but rebuilding agility after the fact is likely to remain an expensive proposition.

RESILIENCE

Practical Recommendations

Cloud computing automatically implies resource elasticity. However, it doesn't directly lead to application elasticity. As you design your service so that it will scale on demand, consider some suggestions:

- Focus on horizontal scalability first! Try to decompose the business logic into parallel elements that can run autonomously.
- Look for options to maximize data locality! Where possible adopt an associated data model by partitioning the workload and storage using the same scheme.
- For complex, data-based problems, investigate MapReduce! If you can leverage the framework, it greatly reduces the effort you need to invest in orchestration and management.

RESILIENCE

Monetization

A key requirement for most applications is for them to deliver value that justifies their costs. Externally facing applications need a mechanism for charging usage and collecting payment. Even internal applications require instrumentation to establish usage and allocate costs effectively. These demands are not necessarily unique to cloud. They are mandatory for all profitable applications. However, the cloud presents new services and is usually associated with flexible and ad hoc payments that are difficult to achieve with traditional payment systems.

After building it, the business task for a successful application is to ensure the application is recognized and used. Marketing techniques may include paid placement or active optimization of appearance on the most visible related pages. In the cloud, this usually means increased appearance on search engines and social media.

The payment involves a few steps. The first is to decide on what basis to charge for usage. Services vary according to whether they are subscription-based or consumption-based. In the case of the former, users pay a fixed fee, while for the latter they are billed according to the number of users, volume of data, transactions, etc, and there is an implied requirement to measure these indicators and allocate charges correctly.

MONETIZATION

Next comes the challenge of settling the transaction. Credit card payments are the easiest place to start for consumer and small businesses. Larger organizations may require centralized billing, which could also be handled with a credit card; however, it is more common for corporations to prefer to use the banking system to make their payments. In this case, a separate invoicing and collection system may be necessary, which can, of course, also be consumed as a service.

Chapter 22

Marketing

Every service should be designed for profitability. This doesn't necessarily mean it generates a positive cash flow. It may represent a net investment into the business. However, it needs to generate at least enough value to cover its costs. Consequently, there is a need to accurately measure the service in order to distribute its proceeds and allocate its costs fairly.

The first step in monetizing a service is to promote its use. For it to maximize its value, potential customers must be aware of its existence and be able to easily subscribe to, or consume, the services.

Some of the techniques to broadcast visibility of the service include:

- Advertising
- Search engine optimization
- Social media marketing
- Leveraging online marketplaces

Online advertising is perhaps the most intuitive marketing channel for publicizing services. However, it isn't necessarily cheap as you might infer from the fact that Google has built its fortune from it. Search-engine optimization has also become very popular since it presents a means of increasing visibility without paying for placement. A recent new means of achieving and managing online recognition and reputation is through social media marketing. Finally, online marketplaces provide a friction-reduced way for buyers and sellers to match needs and offers.

MONETIZATION

Advertising

Product and service promotion traditionally rely on integrated marketing communications that include trade promotions, consumer promotions, personal selling, public relations, and direct marketing. The simplest, and most conventional, approach to advertising is to pay for placement. This could be through tradition-al media, but online services usually allocate the bulk of the advertising budget to web-based advertising. Online advertising is a form of promotion that uses the Internet to deliver marketing messages to attract customers.

Web-based services, such as Google AdWords are the most prevalent. They in-clude contextual ads on search engine results pages (SERPs) and banner ads. But there are also other channels for online publicity, such as social networking, which we will look at in the next section.

E-mail marketing is worth a brief mention. The advantage of electronic mail is that each campaign reaches its users almost instantaneously. It can also scale to the size of the email address database. However, its ease has led to its overuse, so that the vast majority of electronic messages on the Internet today are consi-dered unsolicited and unwanted.

Anyone considering the use of an e-mail marketing program should make sure that the campaign does not violate international spam laws and/or ISP policies that often prohibit the use of email addresses for marketing purposes without explicit consent of the recipients. Two important regulations to consider for any global campaigns are:

- United States: Controlling the Assault of Non-Solicited Pornography and Marketing Act (CAN-SPAM),

- European Union: Directive on Privacy and Electronic Communications Regulations (2003) Article 13

The most acceptable solution to address these requirements is an opt-in regime whereby the recipient agrees (for example by checking a box on a form or send-ing an email) to receive information, news and advertising. In addition to com-plying with regulations, such an approach will generally also lead to higher user satisfaction: recipients will anticipate the messages and perceive them to be rele-vant to their needs and interests.

MONETIZATION

Web-based Banners

As alluded to above, web-based advertising is a booming business. In the next chapter, we'll look into how you can cash in on the business yourself but for now we are interested in how you can leverage it to increase your visibility.

The earliest type of web-based advertisement was a banner. The advertiser paid participating web sites a fee for displaying a graphic banner on specific pages of the site. The cost was initially calculated based on the number of visitors or hits (HTTP requests) claimed by the web site, but quickly aligned to a common me-tric based on impressions (page views).

Cost per mille (CPM) (in Latin, 'mille' means thousand) is a standard measurement in traditional advertising (Radio, television, newspaper) designating the cost of presenting an ad to one thousand listeners, viewers or readers. In online advertising the metric refers to page views. Thus, a website selling ads for a $10 CPM charges $10 for including it on 1000 impressions.

Another metric, the click-through rate (CTR), measures the relative success of a web-based ad. The CTR is obtained by dividing the number of users who clicked on a banner by the number of times the ad was displayed. If five people click on an advertisement that was presented one thousand times then the CTR is 0.5%.

A final ratio, the conversion rate, is perhaps the most important of all. It expresses how many users actually act on the ad. In some cases, the objective might simply be site registration, but the most common purpose of a commercial site is to sell products and services. In this case, the conversion rate measures the percentage of clicks that result in a sale.

Although banner ads started off well, they have become less frequent due to two problems:

Low click-through rates: Years ago, it wasn't difficult to achieve a CTR above five percent. However, users have come to resent random banners since they are often not relevant to them. Current rates of only a fraction of one percent make the cost of each click expensive.

Low conversion rates: The banners were displayed to the wrong people who had no interest or intention to buy. Even if they did click, it was either unintentional or backed by little more than curiosity and rarely led to a sale.

Pay Per Click

A newer mechanism that partially addresses the above problems is called Pay-Per-Click (PPC). As the name implies, the advertiser only pays when a user actually clicks on an ad. However, there is more to the story since the new business model has increased the incentive of the advertising network to improve ad relevance. The term 'PPC' represents the current state of the search-based advertising technology and therefore implies some additional practices including refined targeting and competitive bidding.

MONETIZATION

Refined targeting is most commonly based on location or keywords. Location is a simple concept that is usually deduced from the user's IP address. You can specify the geographical region (e.g. city or country) whose users you want to reach.

You can also decide which search keyword, or keywords, may trigger the ad. You can tailor the behavior by specifying how the keywords should behave. For example, you can constrain the criteria to exact matches or you may wish to include negative keywords (for example you may not want your ad to display when someone is looking for "free" products or services).

A bidding system means that the actual cost-per click (CPC) is not fixed. It stands in contrast to a flat-rate model where the advertiser and publisher agree to a static amount for each click. Instead each user-initiated search query launches a real-time auction for advertising space on a search engine results page (SERP). The advertisers submit in advance the highest amount they are willing to pay for a specific spot. This price may range from a few cents to tens of dollars. When a search is executed, the engine compares the offers and displays the highest bidders on the page.

In a nutshell the process works like this:

1. An *advertiser* joins *search engine*'s PPC program and submits a credit card for billing.

2. The *advertiser* creates a small ad (text with or without images).

    a. The advertiser specifies associated keywords.

    b. The advertiser specifies maximum click cost.

3. A *user* enters one of the keywords or keyword phrases in the *search engine*.

4. The *search engine* finds the matching ads and places them on the *user*'s results page.

5. If the *user* clicks the ad:

    a. The *user* is taken to the *advertiser*'s Web site.

    b. The *search engine* charges the *advertiser* for the click.

The financial terms of the advertising network may vary. Some may require an upfront payment while others do not. The billing periods and thresholds are also areas to look at. For illustration, at the time of writing there was no upfront payment with AdWords and the first charge is levied after 30 days, or at $50, whichever comes first.

The benefits of PPC over banner ads follow from the above. First of all, the advertiser only pays when someone clicks on the ad so you are less likely to be wasting a large budget on users completely uninterested in your service.

You also have the ability to specifically target your audience so that the impressions of your ad are likely to appear only to people who have some interest in your topic. This is particularly important with respect to users who do not click on your ad. In contrast to a banner that generates stigma and contributes to connotations of spam, a targeted ad is much less annoying and serves to increase positive name recognition.

Finally, the leading search engines take considerable pain in ensuring that the ads are not only relevant but honest and helpful to their users. They verify, and subsequently prioritize, selection according to quality scores determined from a combination of measures including long-term click-through rates, ad-text relevance and a subjective assessment of the landing page considering content quality, ease of navigation and the nature of the business. While banner ads are often irritating, search advertising is designed to be useful.

Search Engines

Google is the uncontested leader of PPC. Google AdWords (Figure 22-1) is its main source of revenue, credited with USD$28 billion in 2010[1]. The program includes local, national, and international distribution. Google's text advertisements are short, consisting of one headline and two additional text lines. Image ads can be one of several different Interactive Advertising Bureau (IAB) standard sizes.

AdWords offers demographic site selection for the ads so that campaigns can target user segments based on traits, such as age, gender and income. The data comes from comScore Media Metrix, an Internet audience measurement provider, and is limited to campaigns that target users in the United States.

---

[1] investor.google.com/financial/tables.html

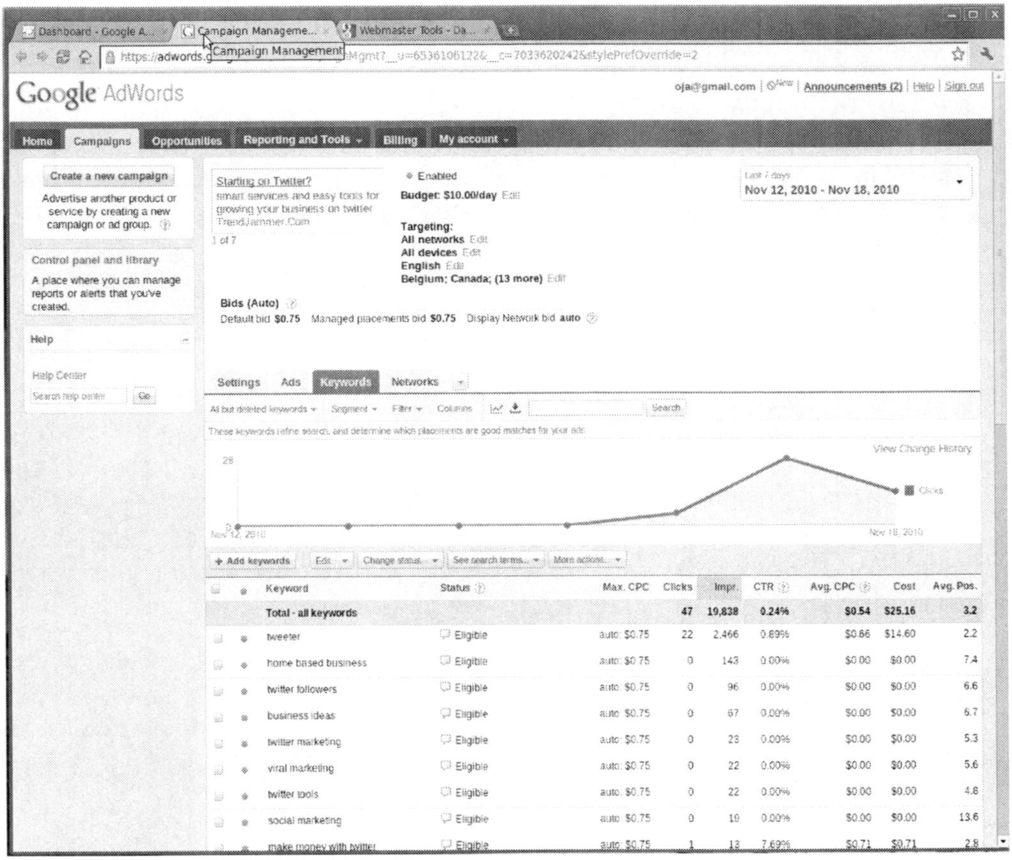

Figure 22-1 : Google AdWords

However, just because Google is biggest doesn't always mean that they are best for you. You may find them expensive and, depending on your products and campaigns, you may have trouble adhering to their rules.

The two most obvious alternatives are Bing (MSN AdCenter) and Yahoo! Search Marketing. They have lower bid prices and can be easier to work with than Google, particularly for small accounts. You may also encounter better conversion rates. Google and Bing reach different audiences and you can use AdCenter to target specific MSN properties in order to reach markets, based for example on age group and gender.

Note that Google and Yahoo! use different campaign formats which make it difficult to transfer advertisements between systems. Bing, on the other hand, has based its standards on Google's ad formats, match types and minimum prices, making it easier to transfer Google AdWords campaigns into Bing without manual editing.

While there may be some significant advantages or disadvantages currently associated with one of the search engines, consider that they will all change over time. With that in mind, you may want to diversify your campaign across systems just to be on the safe side.

Beyond Search

The search engines have created and shaped the PPC market since that is their lifeline. However, they are not the only ones to participate in it. Take eBay, for example. They selected the adMarketplace as their exclusive PPC management platform but have opened it up to other PPC publishers and advertisers. They offer all the regular PPC features including categories and keywords, geo-targeting and day-parting (the ability to restrict campaigns to certain times of the day).

Facebook currently doesn't offer day-parting but they can facilitate extremely refined targeting (age, birthday, hobbies, interests, locations, education, relationship status, language, etc.) to a vast audience. By being able to specify anything from favorite books and films to college major and graduation year, they can produce more hits and better conversion rates.

Second Tier Advertising

There are also a host of second-tier systems, which are often cheaper, especially for expensive keywords. They also provide a means to diversify a campaign even further and increase its coverage, which can be useful when you want as many clicks as you can get. Some of the systems are listed in Table 22-1.

adBrite	Clicksor	Kontera	Miva
AdOn Network	ePilot	LookSmart	PocketCents
Bidvertiser	Exit Junction	Lycos InSite AdBuyer	Search123
BlowSearch	InfoLinks	Mamma	Snap
Chitika	Kanoodle	Marchex	ValueClick Media

Table 22-1 Advertising Networks

MONETIZATION

There are also many niche systems that you may want to consider when your requirement matches their specialty. However, buyer beware! Unfortunately, not all marketplaces are legitimate. Some make their money from sign-up fees but never deliver useful results. You will want to investigate any fringe players extensively before you invest in them.

Practical Considerations

Regardless of which PPC system you choose, there are a couple of practical tasks that you will need to carry out. You will need to create an ad that is both compelling to consumers and reliably promoted by the search engine or advertising network. Then you need to continuously monitor both the cost and the effectiveness of the campaign to make sure it is generating the value you expect.

A good campaign design ensures the ad is placed in front of the right people, and that they feel drawn to the service through its appearance and description, so that they are then willing to act when they arrive at your site.

The keywords are usually the most important metadata determining your advertising success. In picking the keywords, you want to make sure you select words that are often used in search queries. You might want to look at a tool, such as Wordtracker, that is especially geared to this objective. It tallies the number of searches for specific terms and allows you to see the results. Google Trends is another alternative; it provides graphs of the number of Google search queries. By checking these tools you can assess which synonyms might be most effective keywords.

As you write ads, you want to ensure that you encourage the right people to click your ads. It doesn't take much to figure that out. However, it is equally important to discourage the wrong people. Misguided clicks cost the advertiser money and annoy users, which is detrimental to the advertising network. Frustration also contributes to negative associations with your brand, so the incentive for precise targeting is very compelling.

Narrowing your audience might involve negative keywords such as "free" so that your ad only appears to users who have an interest in purchasing. If your service is regional you will want to use geo-targeting to put your ads in front of people close to your business. You may also want to look into day-parting if you have reason to believe that your conversion rate changes according to the time of day.

The ad itself should attract attention but it's important to ensure that it describes the service honestly and accurately. An unrepresentative ad may draw a few extra clicks but will lead to a poor conversion rate, at best, and to rejection from the advertising network, at worst.

This latter point is not to be taken lightly. Some search engines are very stringent on which ads they will accept. Not only will they not permit many items but they dislike superlatives and unnecessary repetitions. They may also insist on spelling, grammar and even disallow abbreviations. For self-serving reasons, advertising networks also generally prohibit phone numbers on the ad – they could bypass the user click.

A landing page, sometimes also called the target or destination URL, is the page to which people are referred when they click on the ad. It is important for this page to be consistent with the ad and relate as closely as possible to the action being promoted. Simple navigation and usability of the site are not only vital to attracting and keeping customers, but they are also criteria that the advertising networks use in evaluating the ad and ranking it for placement.

Once you have launched the campaign, it is critical that you monitor it diligently. One area of vigilance is click fraud. Some publishers may automate false clicks to increase their advertising income at your expense. Alternatively, a competitor may try to weaken you, or take you out of the market, with artificial clicks that never lead to a conversion. If you notice unusual click patterns, then it is worth investigating the source.

Even when there is no foul play, you want to make sure that you are getting value for your money. This means keeping track of how much you are paying and comparing it to what you are receiving in return. From your conversion rate and the average value of each sale, you can derive the amount each click is worth to you. If you are paying more, then the campaign is losing money.

Some systems, such as Facebook, offer both per-impression and per-click charging models. In spite of the advantages of PPC, you may occasionally find that a banner ad is cheaper than PPC. If so, then it is worth considering, but should be treated with special care due to its risk. If you have a very low click-through rate, you may pay an unpredictable amount for discarded impressions.

Search Engine Optimization

PPC and banner ads, also called Search Engine Marketing (SEM), are an effective means of advertising via search tools but they can be expensive. Search Engine Optimization (SEO) is a technique that attempts to accomplish the same objective (frequent appearance in search results) without paying the search engine for the privilege.

SEO analyzes the criteria that the search engines use to determine page rank and relevance to certain keywords. It then tries to optimize the site to conform to those criteria. The technique is not necessarily limited to text searches. It may include images, video or other rich media as well as special purpose search engines.

SEO carries some negative connotations because it is very often misused. Generally you can say that SEO efforts fall into two categories. "White hat" design emphasizes a good user experience, transparent content and easy navigation when building the web site. At the same time, they also make an attempt to align metadata to common searches so that users who are looking for them will be able to find them easily.

MONETIZATION

"Black hat" techniques deliberately attempt to trick the search engines and therefore also the users. They purport to provide products and services that may very well align to user interests but are not representative of the site content. While many users will be frustrated if they visit the site, the black-hat operators bank on the few who are lured into an action that can be monetized.

Search engines depend on high user satisfaction. They are happy to permit, or even encourage, white-hat SEO. But they view black-hat re-engineering in a very dim light.

Black Hat SEO

As (we hope!) you would expect, we take the same standpoint as the search engines. You should be aware of how black-hat SEO operates if for no other reason than to make sure you don't inadvertently cross the major search engines. However, you will be better off in the long term if you focus on creating a great site and let it speak for itself, rather than trick users to visit you.

A favorite black-hat technique is to include invisible text. These are words that will be picked up by the search engines but will not be seen by the users since the text has the same color as the background or is positioned so that it will not be seen. Domain cloaking goes even further by attempting to present different pages to humans and search engines.

To improve their search rankings, some web designers load their pages with an inordinate number of keywords, a technique known as keyword stuffing. You may also come across link exchanges or offers to artificially generate inbound links from unrelated sites.

The rule of thumb is that if anything seems dishonest, especially if it is likely to irritate users, then the search engines are likely to penalize the site and possible exclude it from their indexes. Black-hat methods tend to rely on subtle loopholes in the search engine ranking systems. They are susceptible to algorithm changes and therefore can hope to be effective only for a very short time.

MONETIZATION

White Hat SEO

White hats focus on the long term. They create content for users, not for search engines, and then ensure that content is easily accessible to the crawlers (Figure 22-2). This approach really pays off as search engine designers tend to make updates based on the behavior of searchers. Some obvious advice that benefits both search engines and end users includes verifying that the site doesn't have any broken links, hidden pages or invalid HTML.

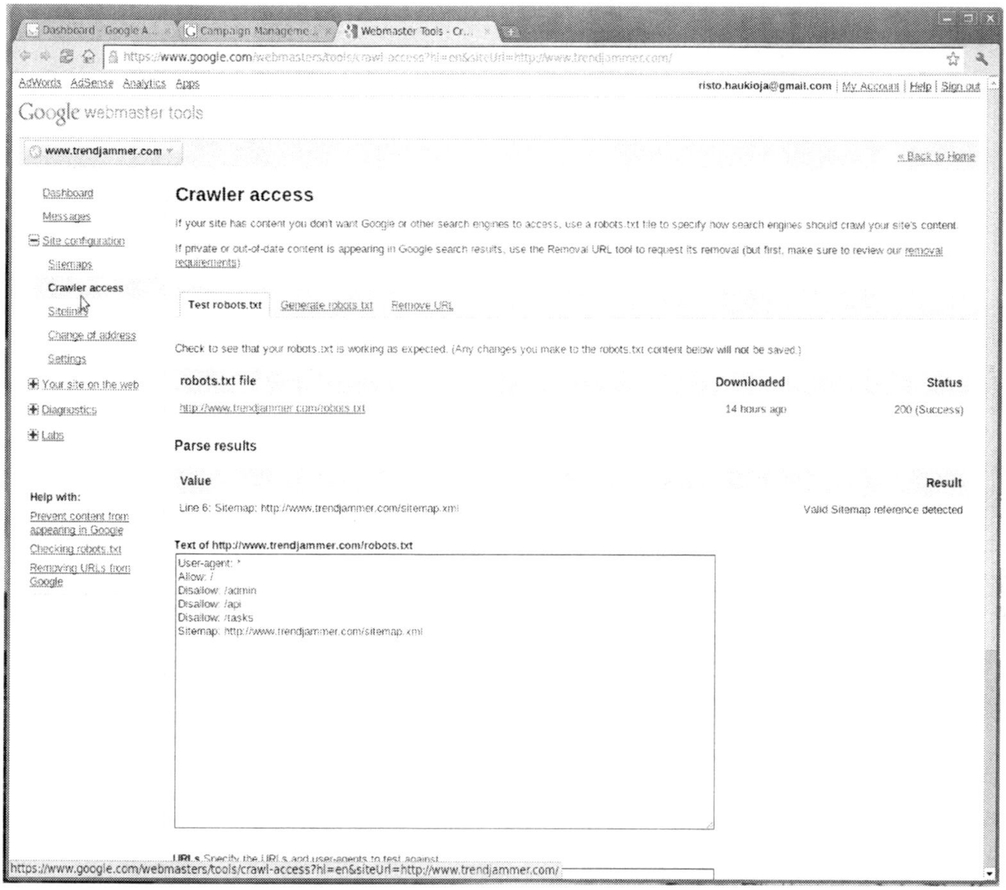

Figure 22-2 : Google Crawler Access

Remember that this is Search Engine Optimization and not Search Engine Maximization! The objective isn't to draw in as many random users as possible, but to attract interested users. This means creating a product/service that customers want and then ensuring page text and metadata convey the value in a way both the user and the search engine will understand. For example, it is helpful to use effective page titles, provide unique content and keep the navigation simple.

Once you have optimized the user experience, you can look at some options that cater specifically to the search engines. Make sure you don't block search engine crawlers (e.g. with interaction that prevents cookies from being accepted). Normalize URLs so that different versions of the URL all count towards the page's link popularity. Include cross-linking between pages on your own site to increase visibility of the most important pages.

It is legitimate to write content that includes frequently searched phrases as long as they are relevant to the page. Similarly, add appropriate keywords to the metadata and any anchor text. Also, feel free to include bidirectional links between your site and others as long as those links are transparent and useful.

Social Media Marketing

Another means of generating publicity that is also largely free is through social media or social networking. One great advantage of this channel is that it not only provides a means of outbound marketing (publicity and advertising) but also can provide great insight for inbound marketing (market research and analysis).

Social media is a huge and growing area. It would exceed the scope of our book to do it justice. Several books have been dedicated to the topic, so you can easily find more depth if you like. But just to put us on the same page, when we talk about social media we include a variety of Web 2.0 services, such as:

Social Networking: LinkedIn, Plaxo, Friendster, Xing, Facebook, MySpace, Orkut, Foursquare

Social news/bookmarking: Digg, Delicious, Reddit

Personal Media sharing: YouTube

Virtual Reality: Second Life

Blogging: WordPress

Microblogging: Twitter

The classification of sites isn't as clear-cut as it may seem above since many services provide several social media functions. Nonetheless, they all tend to have their roots in narrower areas where they continue to demonstrate the most innovation.

Research

MONETIZATION

Before you initiate any advertising, particularly social media advertising, it is worthwhile to use social media to understand the market and industry, both in terms of your customers and your competition. It never hurts to understand your potential audience's complaints about existing products, their feature wish-list and what they like about your competitors.

If you are already doing business, you will want to get as much information as you can on your image as well as what people think of your products and services. It's important to find out what is being said, but you will also want to keep track of where it is being said (which social media resources), so that you can focus any future campaigns where they are likely to be most effective.

A quick start is to search for your name, business name, and product names through a search engine and in the respective social media tools. One of the most distinct characteristics of social media is that it is not static, but can change dramatically over a short period of time. To keep track of what is going on, you need to actively monitor review sites and discussion forums that are related to your products and industry.

If you are short of time, you can subscribe to Google Alerts to receive an email whenever a new result appears in the search listing for certain keywords. You can also subscribe to the search results via RSS so that you don't need to execute the searches repetitively. You may also want to use a social media monitoring tool, such as Alterian or Social Mention.

The social media stream that is leading the pack is Twitter. It is difficult to monitor given the sheer volume of tweets that occur in real time. You can search for keywords and popular hashtags on the Twitter.com site, but you may be overwhelmed by the results (Figure 22-3).

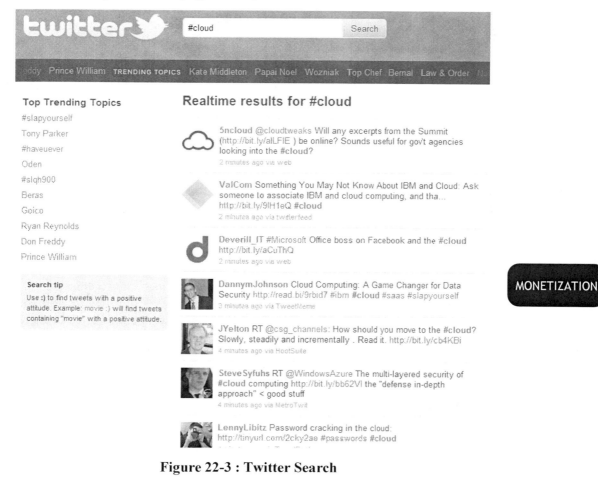

Figure 22-3 : Twitter Search

Figure 22-4 : TrendJammer Trend Manager

To help you cope with large volumes of Twitter data, there are many different related services that you could use. One that we have been involved in creating is called TrendJammer. The TrendJammer Trend Manager is a web-based visual tool that helps you track and analyze relevant trends on Twitter (Figure 22-4). It allows you to monitor keywords and phrases including brand names, Twitter usernames, hashtags, and signature keywords that have significance for your organization or industry. The TrendJammer Engagement Manager, a related service, tracks your performance over time in the three key social dimensions of participation, attention and engaged action, and gives you insight into the most influential people in your Twitter community.

Advertising

Social-media optimization is fundamentally different from search engine optimization. As we saw above, SEO looks at how to generate inbound links by deciding what are the most effective metadata and keyword values. Social network advertising focuses instead on generating enticing content, establishing relationships with influential people and creating effective bookmarks and tags.

Content is the core of social-media marketing. Unique, regularly updated content will draw visitors who are looking for current and relevant information. It's important to position yourself as a valuable user resource even if the benefits are not immediately visible. As your reputation grows, you will be able to capitalize on it.

Some activities include blogs, comments on other blogs, participation in online forums and microblogging (including status updates on social networking profiles). You may also be able to add social media features such as RSS feeds, social bookmarking buttons, user discussions and ratings.

In order to convert visitors to customers, or at least contacts, you may want to require readers to fill out a short form before downloading useful and valued items, such as white papers or webinar recordings.

Relationships drive the activity in social networks. The key to success is to identify the active participants in your community and engage them to further your objectives. One technique is to reward helpful and valuable users. Public recognition and praise is often an effective motivator for people with high social networking potential. You might also link to their sites or find another way to promote something they consider important.

Hyperlinks are the essence of the Internet. Broaden your exposure to your visitors. If you have a YouTube channel, a Twitter account, a Facebook fan page and some blogs, make sure they include cross-references and encourage users to subscribe to each other.

The next step is to increase your linkability by adding and updating content regularly so that social networkers will have plenty of opportunity to broadcast tweets and status updates that reference you. If you reward inbound links, this will be even more effective. The opportunity for a reciprocal link to a blog or personal web site can sweeten the incentive to link to your site.

MONETIZATION

Viral marketing allows your content to spread very cost-effectively, but it depends on proactive support from your customers and users. It is a self-replicating process that leverages social networks as a broadcast medium.

Unfortunately, there is no easy formula for creating viral content. However, there are some prerequisites. It must have broad popular appeal. Additionally, the content needs to be easily distributable, either in a self-packaged format (e.g. media file or PDF) or it must be reachable with a persistent link. Make it as easy as possible to tag and bookmark your site. Users shouldn't struggle to add your blog to their content feed. If you provide a function that generates the necessary URL or code, visitors are more likely to tag your site.

Monitoring

The primary goal of public relations is to ensure that they maximize good coverage and minimize, or mitigate, bad coverage. Criticism can be a threat but can translate into benefits when concerns are addressed. Mention of your company or products can generally take three forms:

Negative feedback: Criticism and problem reports are perhaps the most important. If you do not address them, they have the potential to spread virally. This doesn't mean that you should try to discredit them. It's important to look at the substance of the claim to see if it is accurate. In some cases, there may be a need to correct a product or service and even to pay for damages. Reacting quickly in times like these can help to transform a disaster into an opportunity for demonstrating integrity and agility.

Positive feedback: Favorable reports and reviews speak for themselves. They don't actually require any intervention. However, they can often present an opportunity. You can link to the postings to increase positive exposure and you can identify champions of your products, who you might be able to enlist for additional publicity.

Questions: Many users don't have a particularly positive or negative view of your company or product or service. Instead, they just have a practical problem with it, or a question about it. Social media is a great additional channel for customer support since you can leverage the community for a significant amount of first-level responses and thereby reduce your workload while improving customer satisfaction through a quick response time.

Monitoring social media is an ongoing and multifaceted process. On the one hand, updates occur in real-time and need to be scrutinized quickly. On the other hand, there are many different channels with more appearing every day, often in unexpected places.

Practical Recommendations

MONETIZATION

An obvious prerequisite to success is that your service must be used. Internet search, social networks and other cloud-related technologies can go a long way in increasing your public visibility. As you weigh the options, consider some suggestions:

- Whether internal or external, make sure your audience is aware of your service and what it does!
- Target the search engines, possibly with some paid placement, but always with at least some white-hat SEO!
- Evaluate the advertising networks carefully! Some are scams while others are not aligned with your needs.

- Be wary of CPM-based charges! They expose you to a high risk of un-profitable advertising.
- If you have the resources, focus your attention on social media! They require more effort on your part but the return can also be much higher.

MONETIZATION

Chapter 23

Payments

There are three primary means of monetizing a service. The two most common approaches are a direct-charge model and advertising. The former involves charging the user for the service while the latter gains revenue through sponsored ads on the web site. A third option is to offer a basic service for free, but charge for extended functionality or ancillary consulting and support services.

As your usage model starts to crystallize, you will often find yourself drifting toward one or the other of the revenue options. For example, for:

- Large-volume, small-value transactions – advertising may lend itself well

- Small-volume, large-value transaction – users may be more willing to authorize payments

- Small, but frequently recurring transactions – it may be effective to consolidate multiple transactions with a user balance or move to a subscription model.

Although typically one of these techniques will be dominant, they are not mutually exclusive. A comprehensive strategy may well include elements of all three. In this chapter, we will also look at marketplaces that can serve to facilitate any of the three business models.

MONETIZATION

Valuation Model

Regardless of how you monetize your service, you need to begin by determining what it is worth. Basic economics tells us that there are two perspectives on valuation. You need to look at both the market value and the cost basis.

The first assessment estimates what the service is worth to its users. If your users are businesses, then this may be relatively straightforward. They are primarily motivated by the bottom line. If you can quantify by how much your service generates additional revenue or reduces existing costs, then you have a good basis on which to make your calculations. However, very often services generate value through intangible benefits such as increased productivity or improved customer and employee satisfaction.

If you are dealing with consumers, then the drivers rely on abstract factors such as prestige, comfort and entertainment value. The only effective ways to gauge the monetary worth of these benefits are to ask the users directly or to observe what they are paying for similar services in the market already.

The second perspective of the valuation is related to the costs that are necessary to provide the service. We will look at more specifics when we examine direct charges. However, regardless of your monetization strategy, you need to have a solid understanding of your fixed and variable cost structure. The variable costs tend to be more straightforward as long as you can predict the resource usage pattern for a growing volume of activity.

Calculating the fixed costs may be challenging as you will need to make some assumption about the volume of users and their consumption rate. Cloud-based services are generally very lean on fixed costs since they allocate resources as needed, but they shouldn't be ignored. There is always a significant effort with getting a service up and running, starting from development and the initial burst in advertising and support. You need to ensure that these will be compensated by the incoming cash flows one way or another.

Graded Services

You don't necessarily need to offer the same service to everyone or use the same business model for each customer. You might have several "Editions" of your services that range from free to very exclusive.

The term 'Freemium' refers to limited free services that may be supplemented with additional fee-based functionality or ancillary consulting and support services. It is a popular business model that underpins services such as YouSendIt, LinkedIn, Flickr and Skype. Some of the common restrictions in free versions are limited features and capacity, time-bombed trials, and differentiation according to the type of user (personal versus commercial use).

Note that even the free edition of your service may generate benefit to you. Free users create network effects as they recommend the service to their friends, so your ramp-up of users is likely to be much faster if a version is available for free. After they have signed up and verified the value of your service, you can encourage them to upgrade and receive its full benefits.

MONETIZATION

Direct charges

Let's look at the direct-charge model first since it is more closely related to traditional forms of doing business. If you break down the model, then you really face two different challenges. The first is to determine how much to charge the user; and the second is to actually collect the money.

Pricing

The simplest forms of pricing involve one-time fees or flat subscription rates. These are easy to work with since they don't involve collecting and monitoring resource usage and are less likely to lead to a dispute with the customer. However, they are not always practical since one customer may impose very high costs on you while another only needs a minimal service. Subscriptions also transfer a fixed, rather than a variable, cost to the customer and thereby reduce one of the perceived benefits of cloud computing.

Utility-based services can be priced according to various factors including the number of users, transactions or support calls. Profitable monetization relies on effective alignment of internal costs to external pricing and fine-grained metering to substantiate the charges.

A good starting point is a cost model that identifies the cost drivers and calculates the magnitude and shape of the associated cost curve. The most common internal components will be hardware-related and include computational resources (CPU cores), storage (memory and persistent stores), network bandwidth and infrastructure. Unless you rely exclusively on open-source (or in-house) software, licensing can also be a major cost driver. Most importantly, you need to factor in personnel costs for development (probably the biggest in the beginning, leveling off as your service matures), administration and support.

As you dig down into each of these you may be able to break down the costs even more precisely. For example, if writing data is significantly more expensive than reading it, both in terms of the directly attributable costs and indirect costs such as performance, then you will want to maintain that distinction. As you look at computation, you may also find that some transactions lend themselves to horizontal distribution better than others. If you can execute the software on low-cost instances, the cost per CPU cycle may be lower.

MONETIZATION

You may also need to factor in external costs based on hardware, software and services that you do not own but leverage from other providers. For example, if you are building on a platform service you begin paying for your own usage from a fairly low level of consumption (after exhausting your free quota).

Initial scalability tests are vital as you start predicting your growing infrastructure costs. If you've already designed your application to run on PaaS from the start, it should scale without any huge surprises. Thoughtful planning mitigates the risk of a moment where you desperately need to re-architect your whole service because your database server is running out of capacity.

A best practice in billing is to attempt to align charges as closely as possible to your own costs. In other words, if you expect that most of your cost will come from storage, then you might base the customer-charged price on data volume or storage volume. On the other hand, if you anticipate a high computational load then it might be more sensible to base the price on the number of transactions. If support will be a big burden, you might charge extra for helpline calls. If customer acquisition cost is going to be significant (expensive campaigns or AdWords), you'll have to build that into the model.

As you select your billable units, you need to sum all the variable resource costs that are attributable to each unit. However, it is unlikely that you will be able match up your costs and incoming charges perfectly. So you also need to make sure you include a contribution margin that covers all the fixed costs to be allocated in order for you to reach overall profitability.

This becomes even more challenging if you bill according to multiple criteria or implement a differentiated pricing scheme. There is no magic formula as to how to distribute your fixed costs. As long as you ensure that your total costs are covered, it is up to you and your determination of what the market will bear.

Metering

After identifying the units, you need to determine how to meter the usage. Obviously, you need to start with a solid authentication system, which we have already covered in earlier chapters. Typically this also involves careful logging of all essential transactions, along with the resources that they involve, so that you can later reconstruct the consumption and bill accordingly.

Note that if you charge based on the number of users, or the volume of data, it shouldn't be difficult to get the information you need in order to bill. However, even these numbers are not likely to remain static over the billing period. Whether you are charging for the maximum, the average, or some other formula, you need to be able to establish the history of the account.

Rather than implementing all the instrumentation yourself, you may want to consider a third-party tool. For potential SaaS vendors, OpSource offers a Customer Lifecycle Management (CLM) solution, which automates customer onboarding and then manages the customer purchases with facilities to measure usage and invoice the end customer. CLM automates the process of preparing statements, payments and collections of consolidated invoices based on the rules defined by the vendor. The self-service feature allows customers to add more users and storage or to upgrade to a different plan.

The OpSource Services Bus exposes an API that allows applications running on the OpSource On-Demand platform to tap into web services such as business analytics, on-boarding and billing. It facilitates reporting and visualization of key performance indicators (KPIs) based on data such as: Unit Metrics, Application Events, User Logins, Application Uptime, Bandwidth Utilization, Application Response Time, Monitoring Alerts and Billing Statistics.

The absence of internal billing is often cited as one of the primary differences between public and private cloud implementations. However, this distinction may be misleading since it is not absolutely necessary. In fact, this is one area where cloud technologies can provide an opportunity for better accounting and transparency and thereby add more value to a private cloud than simple virtualization brings to the table. Regardless of whether there is a monetary cross-charge involved, it is always useful to show value and ROI on services. The better they can be quantified, the easier it is to justify. It is therefore just as important to meter and report on transactions and usage in an internal environment.

Settlement

After determining the amount each of your clients owes you, comes the often unpleasant task of getting them to pay. If you are offering internal cloud services, this usually means creating some interfaces to the Enterprise Resource Planning (ERP) system to cross-charge the amount from one cost-center to another, potentially involving some workflow for approvals.

The equivalent for automated external billing would be to create Electronic Data Interchange (EDI) relationships based on standards such as X12, EDIFACT or XML/EDI. These work great once they are in place; however, it takes significant effort to set them up. As a result they are not common for cloud-related billing and are likely to only be of interest to very large organizations that consume and centrally bill customized services.

Direct Credit Card Billing

For consumers, small and medium businesses, and even for departmental applications of large enterprises, it is much more common to use credit-card billing, which has become the de facto payment mechanism of the Internet, contributing directly to the eCommerce boom in recent years.

While it may be possible for you to build your own credit card processing system and establish relationships with the major credit cards, it would come with significant effort and risk. In particular, consider that if you store credit card details then you are likely to be a prime target for hacker and are obligated to demonstrate compliance with Payment Card Industry (PCI) standards. You are also potentially liable for any data leakage and certainly vulnerable to unfavorable publicity if there are any problems.

To fill this need, particularly for smaller merchants, there are a number of credit card processing systems and payment gateway services such as: Chargify, Flagship Merchant Services, Merchant Warehouse, goEmerchant Merchant Accounts, Chase Paymentech, Merchant One and First Data. They verify a customer's credit card information, judge the authenticity of the transaction, then either decline or process the credit card payment, crediting the merchant account with the payment. Many also offer additional services such as a Shopping Cart, Recurring Billing and Fraud detection (e.g. address verification, card verification value).

PayPal

There are also a few offerings, such as PayPal, that make themselves available as trusted intermediaries for smaller merchants, who do not yet have the scale and visibility to establish public trust. PayPal is an account-based system that lets anyone use their credit card, or bank account, to securely send and receive online payments. It is the most popular way to electronically pay for eBay auctions and is also becoming a cheap way for merchants to accept credit cards on their online storefronts instead of using a traditional payment gateway. Users can also use PayPal to wire money to other people without requiring them to get a paid account.

PayPal supplies a set of standard buttons that nontechnical customers can add to their sites without any development expertise. It is augmented with an extensive set of HTML resources available to permit a custom shopping experience. For more sophisticated needs, PayPal exposes its services through an API called Adaptive Payments, which enables developers to build more complex applications that handle payments, preapprovals for payments and refunds. The payments can be ad hoc or pre-approved and can range from simple (sender makes a single payment to a single receiver) to parallel (sender makes a single payment to multiple receivers), as well as chained (sender makes a single payment to a primary receiver; who keeps part of the payment and pays the remainder to the secondary receivers).

While PayPal's target market may be smaller merchants, the service also has appeal for international business. It operates in over 190 countries and supports 20 major currencies. In addition to its mediation of payments, it also calculates overseas shipping, international taxes and facilitates currency conversions.

Amazon Flexible Payments Service

Amazon Flexible Payments Service (FPS) is a similar service, but it is considered by many to be easier than PayPal and allows more flexibility than PayPal's original Payments API. Amazon created FPS for developers, allowing them to integrate with Amazon's retail billing system. The customers can use the same identities, shipping details and payment information that they would for ordering directly with Amazon.

The metering and billing includes dynamic usage tracking and reports as well as an extensive array of payment options including one-time payments, periodic charges, delayed payments and aggregation of micropayments. These can all be set and changed through the API.

Google Checkout

Google Checkout is Google's equivalent to FPS. Once users have signed up and entered their credit or debit card details, they can shop conveniently whenever they log into Google. The financial details and e-mail addresses are not shared with the merchant who simply receives confirmation of the payment. Customers have access to a history feature to track shipping information for all purchases.

On the merchant side, setting up the site involves adding some Google supplied code to let visitors shop via Checkout. As you would expect, Google takes a commission on the sales. Google Checkout is similar to Amazon FPS, and differs from PayPal, in that they do not operate a separate payment service; but rather they use the existing credit card infrastructure to enable payments and online transactions.

Advertising

In the previous chapter, we described outbound advertising using, for example, the main search engines to place paid ads in order to increase publicity for your site. These search engines obviously put ads on their own search engine results pages (SERPs) as a means of generating revenue. But their reach extends much further since they federate their advertising program to a large network of advertisers.

These ads are selected according to the context in which they are being placed. In other words, they are matched up with the content of the displaying web sites. So, you often hear these ads being described as "contextual" or "content-matching".

If you receive a lot of traffic and don't mind including some advertising on your site, advertising can be a viable option for monetizing your service. Typically, this involves signing up for an account with the advertising network and then adding some JavaScript and HTML to your web-page that will obtain the proposed ad whenever your page is displayed.

Note that even though you aren't directly billing your customers based on usage, it is still very helpful to instrument the cloud platform so that it can measure service utilization and resource consumption. On the one hand, you will appreciate being able to validate that the ad-based revenue is calculated correctly by the payer. You may also want to use web analytics to identify how your revenue breaks down according to pages and what usage patterns you are able to find. Fine granularity in your understanding of the advertising stream allows you to maximize page hits (SEO), ensure relevance and place the advertisements effectively.

Google AdSense is the current leader in contextual advertising. Even though Google is dominant, they don't fit everyone's needs. Their terms and conditions are very strict, so many web publishers are not able to use AdSense adverts on their sites. They are either denied from joining the program or soon find their Adsense accounts disabled.

As we saw in the previous chapter, the other two big search engines offer similar functionality. Yahoo Publisher Network and Microsoft pubCenter are not as large as Google but they are still big players in this space.

adMarketPlace and Quigo offer similar functionality. adMarketPlace manages eBay's keywords system, but also includes a network of sites where advertisers can place PPC ads. Quigo is a well-established independent site with broad reach including sites such as Cars.com, USAToday.com, Discovery.com, Newsday.com, HomeStore.com.

Most of the other alternatives to the large search engines are of limited use. Some (such as doubleclick) target only large volume customers and are not suitable for small sites. Others simply lack the volume to make them attractive or may push inappropriate ads to your users. Nonetheless, depending on the content of your web sites, you may find some that match your requirements. A few networks to get you started include: Infolinks, AdBrite, Bidvertiser, Chitika, Clicksor. You can look at them and make up your own mind.

Professional Services

MONETIZATION

In addition to direct charging and advertising, a third revenue stream is services, which usually focus on consulting, integration and support. Since there is some confusion over the disparate meanings of the word 'service', it is important to distinguish between a professional service, usually provided by a human being, and an automated service that is typically delivered through software. Most of this book focuses on the latter, but in this section we want to describe the former.

It's possible to combine human services with either of the other two business models, or indeed to create any combination of the revenue streams. However, services have a special place in the initial phases of launching a cloud service.

The current trend in the cloud is to provide at least basic functionality for free when a web service is first made available. The rationale for this approach lies in generating sufficient network effects to ramp up the user base quickly. As we described in the freemium section above, it may be possible to convert some of the free users to premium subscriptions once they have come to appreciate the value that is on offer.

As the same time, some organizations may want to leverage the innovation that you offer, but will generally have very specific feature and support requirements that are not fulfilled in the initial service. If you can find customers who are interested in piloting and shaping the newest technologies, it is often easiest to offer one-off pilot, implementation and customization projects that satisfy their needs.

Over time, the offer will mature and it may be possible to refine the professional services into off-the-shelf packages when customer requirements are relatively similar. On the other hand, if your cloud service is challenging to implement and integrate in a complex enterprise environment, then expert intervention may be a prerequisite to your success, which you can see as either an obstacle or an opportunity.

Marketplaces

Online marketplaces are really a form of marketing since they increase the visibility of products and services. They provide a friction-reduced way for buyers and sellers to match their respective needs and offers. A number of popular websites, such as Download.com, Softonic and SourceForge (for open-source software) provide a simple mechanism for software developers to register their application and enjoy the opportunity to reach millions of users.

However, there are also a number of sites that also take care of collecting payment and passing it on to the merchant. This has several advantages for developers and small software producers. Firstly, they don't need to concern themselves with the mechanics and risks of charging customers. Secondly, the customers don't need to set up an account with the merchant. They only entrust their payment details to the marketplace administrator.

Some of the most popular marketplaces are more closely related to device platforms than to cloud computing. The Apple iPhone and Google Android, for example, are thriving. If your cloud application targets mobile users, inclusively or exclusively, you may want to look at these marketplaces as part of your business model.

MONETIZATION

But the most important marketplaces for cloud services relate to the platforms on which the services are built. These will extend to all client devices. Some of the main players include Google Apps, Microsoft Azure, Salesforce.com and Intuit, which are worth a brief mention

Figure 23-1 : Google App Marketplace

The Google Apps Marketplace offers products and services that target users with Google accounts and often integrate with Google Apps, using single sign-on, Google's universal navigation (Figure 23-1).

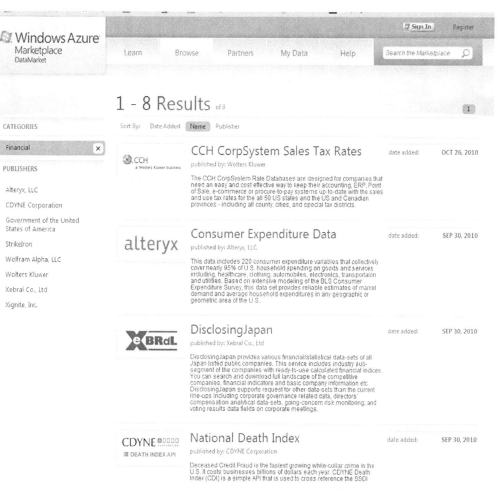

Figure 23-2 : Windows Azure Marketplace

The Windows Azure Marketplace allows developers to share building block components and full end-to-end services built on the Windows Azure platform (Figure 23-2).

The DataMarket section of Windows Azure Marketplace includes data, imagery, and real-time web services from commercial data providers and public data sources. Customers can access datasets such as demographic, environmental, financial, retail, weather and sports. To facilitate further insight, DataMarket also includes visualizations and analytics.

The Applications section of the Windows Azure Marketplace lists components, finished services/applications as well as training and services. In addition to building blocks to be incorporated by other developers into their Windows Azure platform applications, the marketplace includes developer and administrative tools, components, plug-ins, and service templates.

MONETIZATION

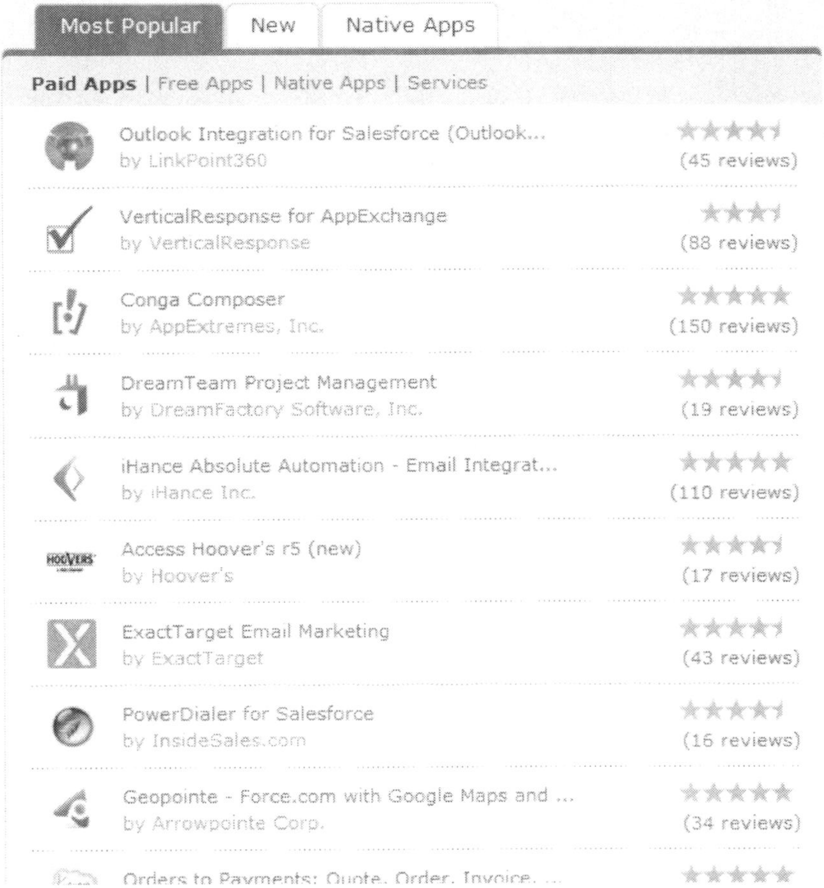

Most Popular	New	Native Apps

Paid Apps | Free Apps | Native Apps | Services

	Outlook Integration for Salesforce (Outlook... by LinkPoint360	★★★★	(45 reviews)
	VerticalResponse for AppExchange by VerticalResponse	★★★★	(88 reviews)
	Conga Composer by AppExtremes, Inc.	★★★★★	(150 reviews)
	DreamTeam Project Management by DreamFactory Software, Inc.	★★★★★	(19 reviews)
	iHance Absolute Automation - Email Integrat... by iHance Inc.	★★★★★	(110 reviews)
	Access Hoover's r5 (new) by Hoover's	★★★★★	(17 reviews)
	ExactTarget Email Marketing by ExactTarget	★★★★★	(43 reviews)
	PowerDialer for Salesforce by InsideSales.com	★★★★	(16 reviews)
	Geopointe - Force.com with Google Maps and ... by Arrowpointe Corp.	★★★★★	(34 reviews)
	Orders to Payments: Quote, Order, Invoice, ...	★★★★★	

Figure 23-3 : Salesforce.com AppExchange

Force.com also provides a marketplace, called AppExchange (Figure 23-3), for buying and selling SaaS services. Once developers have completed and tested their applications they can request publication on AppExchange providing a description of the services along with the details of the pricing and support model. The process entails a security review by Force.com to check for exploits, such as cross-site request forgeries.

Customers can therefore avoid reinventing any functionality that has already been created. They can filter the application list by popularity, price or other criteria. And they have limited financial risk since they can sign up for a free trial before purchasing the service.

Last but not least, the Intuit Partner Platform (Figure 23-4) also features a Marketplace with functionality that caters to their platform.

Figure 23-4: Intuit Partner Platform Marketplace

If you are building your solution on these platforms, you may want to look at the marketplaces in more detail. The objective of this section is merely to familiarize you with the concept. These marketplaces usually allow you to search by business needs, industry or keywords and often provide additional functionality such as demos, video presentations and user reviews/ratings. They may validate the software to ensure it contains no malware and is of genuine use to its customers thereby providing an element of trust to the online sale.

In the end, the success of these websites depends on the number of buyers and sellers. If a high percentage of the market uses them, they become a valuable resource. As long as they offer a full set of functionality at a reasonable price, they are an extremely efficient means of transacting business.

Etelos SaaS Marketplace Platform

The discussion above assumed that you are architecting a new application and have the luxury to design all the instrumentation and any bill collection into the service. In some cases, however, you will want to take existing software and move it to the cloud with as little intervention as possible.

The Etelos Application Platform could help you meet this need by moving a legacy application into its marketplace. It provides a plug-and-play graphical user interface and offers fast time-to-market, application cataloging and syndication capabilities so you can resell partner software with or without value added services.

The Etelos Platform Suite is divided into four different platforms to address different requirements:

> The *SaaS Application Platform* manages the process for packaging the application in the targeted development environment. The solution then moves to a step of enabling automated provisioning, billing, marketing and first-level support. End-users can then try and buy the application through a web interface to the Etelos-hosted service.

> The *SaaS Marketplace Platform* goes one step further in supporting the extension and integration of existing technologies by leveraging the Etelos API which can extend data properties in the application to the account framework.

> The *SaaS Distribution Platform* facilitates private labeling of a marketplace. This involves selecting applications and packaging, installing, supporting and distributing them through a web-based marketplace. The platform caters to distributors of suites of applications which can be provisioned and customized to include value-added service solutions around the core application.

> The *SaaS Syndication Platform* packages SaaS applications and distributes them through a network of web-based storefronts and marketplaces. The approach caters to SaaS providers who wish to significantly grow the number of channels they can use to sell their application.

The benefit of an approach like that of Etelos is that it can provide billing and licensing based on a variety of metrics (CPU, disk space, memory, users, accounts), purchasing mechanisms (credit cards, promotions) as well as bundling and upselling options. This allows you, as the application provider, to focus on the actual functionality rather than the mechanics of online sales.

Practical Recommendations

Utility billing is one characteristic attribute of cloud computing. However, it isn't the only payment modality that is possible. And when it is implemented, there are several indicators that can be used to measure usage. As you investigate the instrumentation and charging options, consider some suggestions:

- Define a business model that will lead to profit! If it shows a loss on paper, then it will not lead to a gain in practice.
- Avoid dealing with credit cards unless you are sure you have the expertise! Instead investigate PayPal, Amazon FPS and Google Checkout.
- For high-volume, low-value services (e.g. information), consider ad-based revenue!
- For low-volume, high-value offerings, consider customized professional services engagements!

MONETIZATION

Deployment

Applications typically run through a lifecycle that includes development, testing, staging and eventually deployment into production. The initial stages of this process constitute a great opportunity for cloud platforms since each project requires temporary resources with volatile loads. Development usually begins with very limited infrastructural demands that gradually increase through unit testing to high volume beta testing and then terminate abruptly when the service is launched in production.

The cost savings through utility pricing of resources and lower fixed costs are quite intuitive. Beyond these, there is also potential for cloud computing to impact the process itself. By minimizing the associated costs, you can afford to engage in more frequent and higher load testing. You can also consider the possibility of multiple simultaneous deployments since it is easier and faster to switch between instances.

Even though there are many benefits in shortening the release cycle and introducing more experimental innovation into your services, you also need to examine some of the challenges of the new model. If alternate instances rely on their own data then it may not be trivial to reconcile changes. On the other hand, if they share the same storage facilities the opportunity to update the data structures is limited. Furthermore, you need to make provisions for rolling back versions when a deployment doesn't work as expected. This can be difficult as it may impact the user experience and requires an accurate change log and testing process to ensure application integrity.

DEPLOYMENT

Chapter 24

Development

Cloud computing has accelerated the existing momentum in the direction of agile development. While the high level lifecycle in a cloud environment does not differ much from a typical software development lifecycle there are differences in practice. When no hardware or middleware platform has to be installed before the actual development work can proceed from Proof of Concept to Production the agile development can happen in a completely different time scale compared to traditional environments.

While this technically shortens the time and reduces some of the effort related to going through the stages in Software Development Lifecycle it does not remove the requirement of having separate environments for the activities in different lifecycle stages. This section can highlight some of the specific activities specifically in cloud computing across the SDLC stages.

A typical software development life cycle involves four primary stages that may be further broken down for large projects. Development is the first phase of the development lifecycle, followed by Testing, Staging and eventually deployment into Production (Figure 24-1). It typically focuses on the activities that programmers carry out independently based on the modules assigned to them.

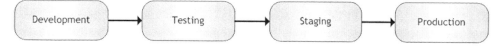

Figure 24-1: Development Lifecycle

The whole lifecycle is usually preceded by a requirements analysis, which leads to a functional specification. This specification is then broken down into a design specification that documents the proposed implementation of each module. It is then the responsibility of each developer to write and test the code needed to implement the design.

DEPLOYMENT

In the 1980s, it was common for software developers to write code using a text editor, manually compile and link the modules and debug them based on compiler messages and observed run-time behavior. This is still possible today, but fortunately programmers also have access to suites of tools that make the job much easier and allow them to become more productive.

A typical development environment for cloud computing supports both writing and testing software. Part of the execution environment may be hosted with a provider, but, even platforms that are offered "as a service", are not always fully cloud-based. Usually a significant amount of the design-time and code-time functionality is run locally on a developer machine with a simple SDK. It would be conceivable to host the SDK in an infrastructure platform but that isn't common as it is usually not cost-effective and puts a dependency on the network without delivering additional value. Over time, as the cost and network elements change and the value of Internet-based collaboration increases, we may see a change.

With this background in mind, let's look at the two main development stage activities, coding and running unit tests.

Coding

The programmer will be most efficient if the environment provides syntax checking, code completion and easy access to documentation on both the programming language and any libaries being used. This usually means taking advantage of an Integrated Development Environment (IDE), such as Visual Studio, Eclipse or NetBeans. However, it is also quite possible to use any text editor, optionally customizing it to provide some language-sensitive features.

In selecting the IDE, the foremost consideration is that it must support a programming language available in the target environment. Additionally, it is worth verifying the extent to which it is able to access cloud services and test, debug and deploy the code in the target environment.

Furthermore, there will be a need to maintain source code that may be shared between several developers. Ideally, the repository will offer versioning and some kind of reservation or check-out system to avoid conflicts. This is an opportunity for cloud-based collaboration. By putting the repository into the Internet, it makes it easily accessible from multiple locations.

DEPLOYMENT

There are two primary repository models: centralized and distributed. In a centralized model, such as CVS and Subversion use, a master repository is stored on a server that developers can access via a client. Users hold a working copy of their project on their local machines, which they must commit to the master repository before any changes are propagated to other users.

In a distributed model, the store is replicated to all peers, so that users can have a full local repository with code, version history and meta-information. Distributed version control systems, such as Git, Mercurial, Bazaar and Monotone, allow programmers to work on features on their own branches, and merge when all the features are ready. Instead of just pushing their code upstream, developers can merge from each other without causing a conflict.

The choice of the system is largely a matter of personal preference and experience. Distributed systems tend to increase network load and make it more difficult to preserve intellectual property. Nonetheless, they are becoming more popular due to their natural resilience and support in offline development. Git, originally developed by Linus Torvald and made available as open source, is the most popular distributed tool. However, the others have their benefits too. For example, Mercurial has better Windows compatibility than Git and is considered easier to learn.

Souce-code Management Platform	Version Control Service
GitHub	Git
Gitorious	Git
CodebaseHQ	Git, Mercurial, Subversion
Bitbucket	Mercurial, Subversion
Google Code	Mercurial, Subversion

Table 24-1 : Source-code Management Platforms

By adding hosting to version control services, sites such as GitHub, CodebaseHQ, Gitorious, Bitbucket and Google Code have created platforms that significantly ease source-code management (Table 24-1).

DEPLOYMENT

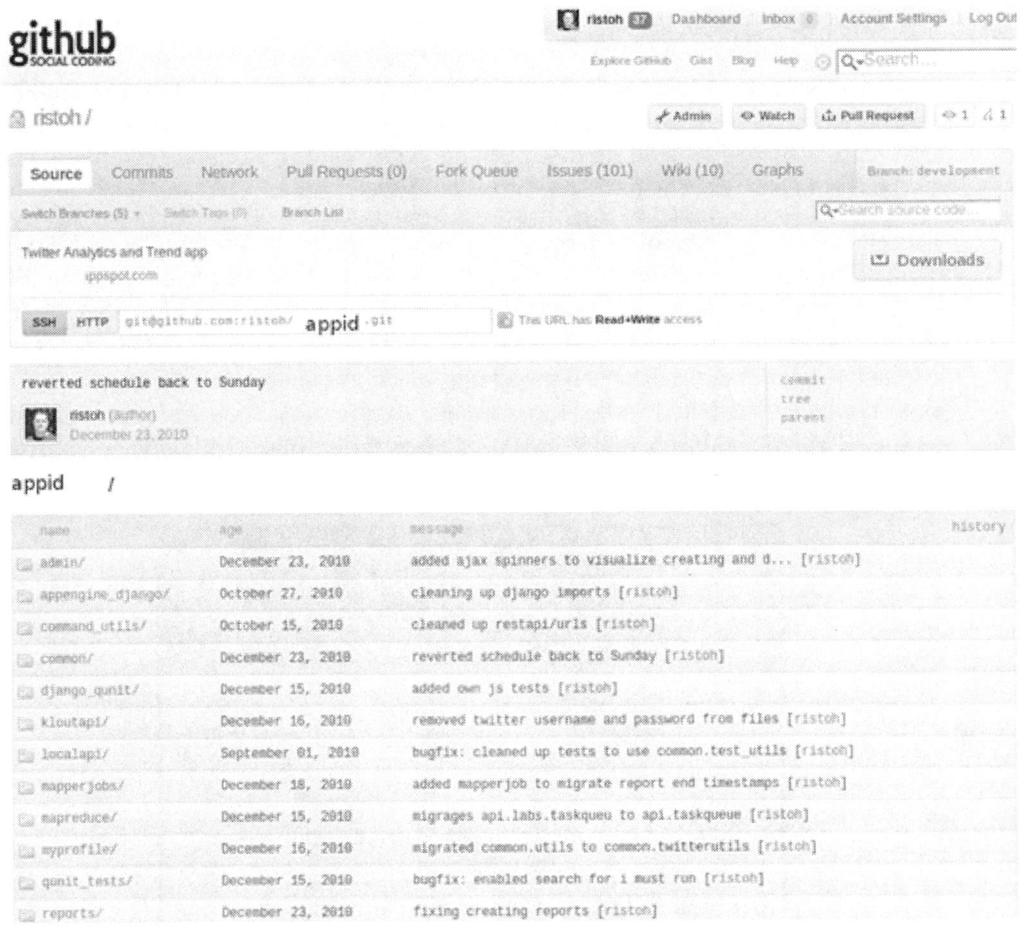

Figure 24-2 : GitHub Project Hosting

Probably the most popular of these is GitHub (Figure 24-2), a web-based hosting service that supports projects using Git. Most benefits come with a price. Distributed source code control is a new work paradigm. As such, it operates according to a different workflow from the traditional (centralized master repository) model. There is a dependency on network connectivity. Work can proceed locally, even when GitHub is down. As each developer's machine hosts the full version history of the project, the probability of losing code is minimized. However, someone still needs to own branches, manage integration and resolve conflicts.

Source code control is fundamental to managing the application versions and deployments. With most cloud services, whether they are based on infrastructure, platform or software services there is a 'write only' capability for deployments. The only way to revert back to a previous version of the application code

DEPLOYMENT

is to check out a known working version from source code control and re-deploy it into production.

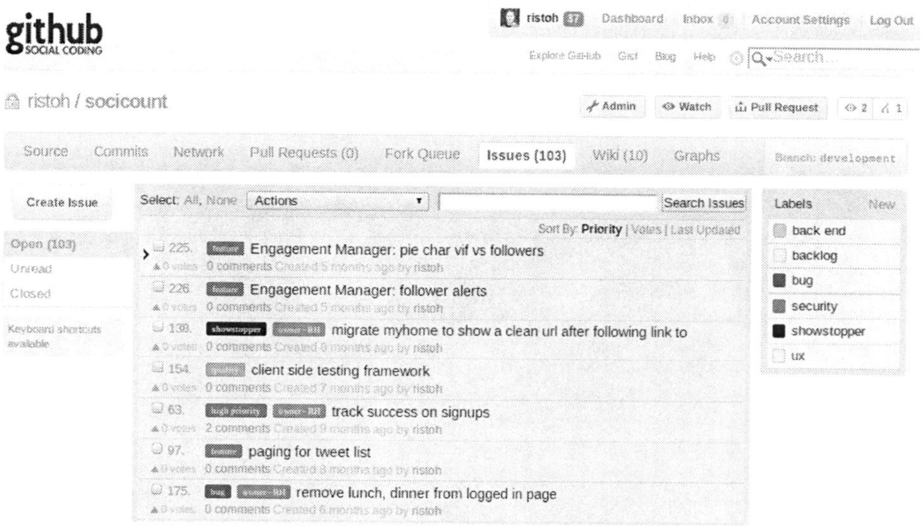

Figure 24-3 : GitHub Issues Tracking

While source code control is one area of potential collaboration during development, there are other ways to also leverage cloud services ranging from hosted issue tracking to discussion forums and wikis. In addition to a source-code browser, GitHub includes in-line editing, ticketing (Figure 24-3) and wikis. The service also offers some social networking with feeds, follower support and a network graph (Figure 24-4) that displays a timeline with the commits of all collaborating developers.

Figure 24-4: GitHub Network Graph

Testing

Developers generally test their code locally within their development environment using unit tests. Once the developer is satisfied that the application is ready, the application moves to a staging server in the cloud provider's environment. At this point it becomes much more difficult to debug the code since many services are running remotely. It is therefore vital to unit test the modules very carefully while they are still under full developer control.

Programmers work largely in isolation in the initial stages. They do not require a full production environment, however it is useful to be able to simulate those parts of the full system that interface with the modules being developed. This means creating and maintaining a set of local data that mimics the production behavior. Having a small amount of production-like data available in the development environment is critical for the success of the development.

Azure

DEPLOYMENT

The Windows Azure SDK includes a version of Azure's cloud server and cloud storage to run in the development environment. The Development Fabric simulates the Azure services while the Development Storage provides interface compatibility to blob, table and queuing services that are implemented on a local SQL Server instance.

Cloud Drive is another useful debugging tool packaged as a sample for Windows Azure. It allows the developer to manipulate and query blog and queue storage using PowerShell file system commands.

App Engine

The Google App Engine SDKs for both Java and Python include a local runtime environment, which is a fairly full featured replica of the production environment. It includes a runtime, datastore that mimics how key/value data is stored in production as well as a set of services, such as taskqueue for offline processing.

App Engine also offers a tool called BulkLoader for importing data from the production environment to a local SDK environment. Additional tools depend on the target environment. JUnit and JMeter are well established for Java applications. Python users will typically use a combination of unittest module, doctest module, and something similar to the jango test suite or nosetests.

In order to ensure comprehensive testing, it is vital to run all the tests under a single test suite and make sure it is part of the release cycle. For the sake of simplicity, a single command should run through all the tests (Listing 24-1).

```
test@user@mysystem:~/app_directory$ python manage.py test
...................................................

.


------------------------------------------------------------
-----------
Ran 25 tests in 0.371s

OK
```

Listing 24-1: Example Command-Line Test

Additional tests include coverage tests and doc tests.

Doctest: The idea of a doctest is not to test that the code is correct, but rather to check that the documentation reflects the code. Doctests lend themselves well for creating an introduction to a library by demonstrating how the API is used. This is especially important if you are considering opening up the API to the public as part of an effort to foster a broad ecosystem.

Based on the output of Python's interactive interpreter, the doctest can mix text with calls that exercise the library, and display the results. The underlying concept is that code, testing and documentation are intrinsically related and need to evolve together. Programs can be comprised of all three allowing for easier verification of consistency.

Coverage test: The purpose of a coverage test is to identify how much of the code is being tested by the test suite. If it returns low values this would be a warning that potential errors could go unnoticed so it may be worth extending the set of test cases. In practice, coverage tests use a test assessment tool, such as coverage.py[1] (Listing 24-2).

```
test@user@mysystem:~/app_directory$ python manage.py test
my_app
.....
-----------------------------------------------------------
-----------
Ran 5 tests in 0.371s

OK

-----------------------------------------------------------
-----------
Unit Test Code Coverage Results
-----------------------------------------------------------
-----------
Name                    Stmts    Exec   Cover    Missing
-----------------------------------------------------------
my_app.models      38      33     86%    13-14, 37, 40, 75
my_app.views       48      41     85%    74, 76-81
-----------------------------------------------------------
TOTAL                       86      74     86%
```

Listing 24-2: Example Coverage Test

Amazon Web Services

Infrastructure services may represent a significant component, or even the core platform of some cloud-based applications. In some ways the testing of these elements is easier than for applications built on platform services. There is not necessarily a significant discrepancy in the environment between a virtual machine executing locally and one running on EC2. Even if the service consumes other cloud services (e.g. Amazon S3 or RDS), there is no functional difference in calling them from a private data center rather than from EC2.

DEPLOYMENT

Nonetheless, especially for large engineering projects, it may be worthwhile to replicate the infrastructural environment at least partially. In the case of AWS, this is made much easier through the availability of Eucalyptus, which maintains interface compatibility with EC2.

---

[1] from Ned Batchelder's site: nedbatchelder.com/code/coverage/

Practical Recommendations

Cloud computing will have a profound impact on developers not only due to the new platforms they entail. New SDKs and testing environments may bring some challenges but they also give programmers more options. As you assess the implications, consider a few suggestions:

- Use a distributed source-code repository!
- Try to make unit tests mimic the production environment!
- Create documentation automatically (e.g. with doctest)!
- Ensure tests are complete! Implement a coverage test.

DEPLOYMENT

Chapter 25

Testing

Testing involves integrating several modules and performing regression tests to ensure that they interoperate and deliver the required functionality. This phase is also known as alpha or integration testing. In contrast to unit testing, which is conducted by the developer using white-box techniques, integration testing should be conducted by another testing team and generally employs black-box or gray-box techniques.

The process is for the team to install the code that comes out of the build. If the build does not work, then the release manager knows there is a problem. Most companies have a code curfew, until when the developers submit any code to be included in the next build. The build is automatically run every night using the code cut from the curfew time.

If the installation completes successfully, a regression test is run. If it passes, then the code is released to the test team, on one or more test servers. The testers then run their test scripts against the test plan and test schedule, which is driven by the requirements and change control documents.

Continuous Integration

In software engineering, continuous integration (CI) implements a continuous process of applying quality control, whereby small pieces of effort are applied frequently. Continuous integration aims to improve the quality of software, and to reduce the time taken to deliver it, by replacing the traditional practice of applying quality control after completing all development.

DEPLOYMENT

In a traditional environment, a developer takes a copy of the current code base on which to work. As other developers submit changed code to the code repository, the working copy gradually ceases to reflect the repository code. When developers submit code to the repository they must first update their own code to reflect the changes made to the repository since they took their copy. The more changes the repository contains, the more work developers must do before submitting their own changes.

Eventually, the repository may become so different from the developers' base-lines that the time it takes to integrate the new code exceeds the time it took to make the original changes. In a worst-case scenario, developers may have to discard their changes and completely redo the work.

Continuous integration involves integrating early and often to reduce timely re-work and thus reduce cost and time. Some projects require committing all changes to the mainline at least once a day (once per feature built). By committing regularly, every committer can reduce the number of conflicting changes. Furthermore, frequent minor conflicts encourage team members to communicate about the changes they are making and collaborate in resolving them.

A regular (nightly) build is not difficult to implement if it is automated. A single command should have the capability of building the system. Many build-tools, such as 'make', have existed for many years. Other more recent tools, like Ant, Maven, MSBuild or IBM Rational Build Forge are frequently used in continuous integration environments. Automation of the build should include deployment into a production-like environment.

In many cases, the build script not only compiles binaries, but also generates documentation, website pages, statistics and distribution media (such as Windows MSI files, RPM or DEB files). Ideally, the build is also at least partially self-testing: once the code is built, all tests should run to confirm that it behaves as the developers expect.

Tools

Figure 25-1: CruiseControl

Popular tools for continuous integration, testing and release make it easier for developers to integrate changes to the project, and for users to obtain a fresh build. They include CruiseControl (Figure 25-1) and Hudson as well as commercial tools such as Rational Team Concert and Team Foundation Server.

CruiseControl is a Java-based framework for a continuous build process. It is often considered the de facto standard for continuous integration. There are variants for the Microsoft .NET platform (CruiseControl.NET) and Ruby (CruiseControl.rb).

Hudson is also written in Java and runs in a servlet container, supporting CVS, Subversion, Mercurial, Git, StarTeam, Clearcase, Ant, NAnt, Maven, shell scripts and other modules.

Rational Team Concert is a commercial software development collaboration platform with a built-in build engine by IBM including Rational Build Forge.

Team Foundation Server is Microsoft's commercial continuous integration server and source code repository. It is a logical choice for .NET projects or Azure services.

Regardless of the tool, an automated, continuous build increases the productivity of all involved.

Cloud Integration Testing

While the individual modules will have been unit tested in the development phase, it is important to also validate that the build has worked successfully and that the modules interact with each other as expected.

Fundamentally, there are three options for testing applications:

- Running the tests locally

- Running the tests in a parallel environment with the same provider

- Running the tests in a distinct cloud environment

Especially for complicated applications, running all of the tests locally can become a tedious and time-consuming task. Deploying the application and testing it in the cloud can save significant time and local development resources. As the testing increases in scope, the differences between the SDK and the actual cloud computing environment provided by a PaaS vendor become more apparent. Especially if an application has a complicated workflow, local testing can only cover a fraction of the actual workflow and data.

DEPLOYMENT

There is therefore a compelling case for running complex tests in the cloud. However, this doesn't mean that all tests need to run in an environment that is identical to production. The full barrage of stress and performance tests will occur during staging.

The purpose of the integration tests is to validate the code, which may be possible in a simpler environment. There is some merit to considering an infrastructure service with all the virtual machines running the SDK and effectively providing an on-demand test-ground.

Effective testing requires software to be tested with representative samples of data that mimic production. This need becomes more critical as the lifecycle advances. However, the basic challenge of creating or importing the data into the test environment is similar to what it was in the development phase.

Tools

One of the most popular tools for testing web-based applications is Selenium (Figure 25-2). The Selenium IDE, previously known as Selenium Recorder, is implemented as a Firefox extension, and allows recording, editing, and debugging tests. Scripts may be automatically recorded and edited manually providing auto-completion support and the ability to move commands around quickly. Some of the features include *record* and *playback*, *debug* and set *breakpoints* and a *trace* option that asserts the title of every page.

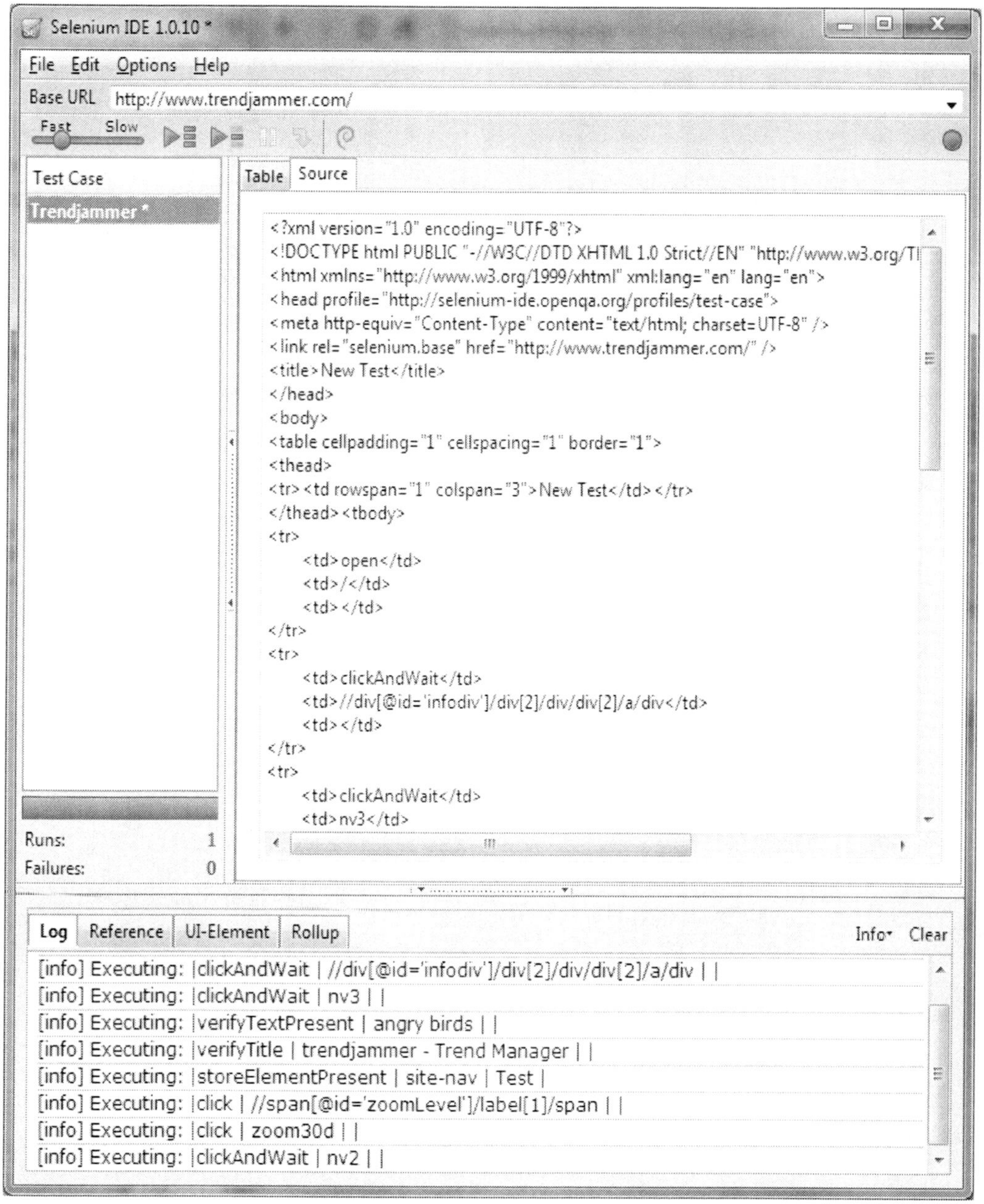

Figure 25-2: SeleniumIDE

Another option is Watir (Web Application Testing in Ruby) which has also inspired WatiN – (Web Application Testing In .Net) and Watij (Web Application Testing in Java). Beyond these, there are a variety of lesser known alternatives such as Sahi, WebUI Test Studio, Windmill, FIT and FITnesse.

DEPLOYMENT

Practical Recommendations

Testing is an area that stands to benefit from cloud computing since the physical environment is abstracted and can be recreated at will. It is therefore possible to ensure greater consistency and efficiency than was common before. As you put together a test plan, consider some suggestions:

- Integrate often! The more frequently you integrate components, the earlier you will become aware of any problems or inconsistencies that often lead to discarded work.
- Consider using the cloud to mount test environments! In addition to benefits of cost, a packaged environment will guarantee consistency between tests.

DEPLOYMENT

Chapter 26

Staging

Testing is loosely connected to the alpha phase of software development, which ends with a feature freeze, indicating that no more functionality will be added to the software. At this time, the software is said to be 'feature complete'. After it has been tested by the development team, the code is moved onto the staging server where the businesses and end users test the code and sign off that it is fit for production. This is also called the "Beta" testing phase, which focuses on reducing impact to users, and often incorporates usability testing.

In a highly integrated continuous deployment environment with shortened development cycles, a feature or a fix can go through all the steps in the development lifecycle in less than a day. Consequently it is possible to deploy new production releases quickly and frequently – even multiple times a day.

The users of a beta version are called beta testers. They are usually customers, or prospective customers, of the organization that develops the software, willing to test the software for free, or for a reduced price.

Testing related to cloud computing typically includes the following activities:

- Testing scalability including production data quantities and usage volumes

- Testing performance and usability under realistic conditions

- Testing for cloud provider idiosyncrasies (such as scheduled downtime on App Engine)

DEPLOYMENT

Test Environment

Staging is a more advanced phase of testing. It usually runs in an environment that closely reflects production. It not only deals with testing all the functionality, but also load testing and may be made accessible to customers to obtain their approval prior to final production release.

Unit and integration testing can be completed in a virtual environment. You should, however, conduct your performance testing in an environment with hardware and software that is identical to the production environment. The staging server should be a mirror copy of the production server. Its primary purpose is to test the completed application to ensure that the application doesn't break the existing production server applications. No actual code development should ever take place on a staging server—only minor tweaking of OS parameters or application settings.

There are two main components to testing at the Staging phase, User Acceptance Testing and Operational Acceptance Testing.

User Acceptance Testing (UAT)

User Acceptance Testing involves functional testing by a select group of users in addition to the automated regression tests that were conducted during the integration phase. UAT helps to uncover obvious software errors that have missed the automated tests. It also provides feedback about the usability of the system and the extent to which the service fulfills user requirements.

Beta version software is likely to be useful for internal demonstrations and previews to select customers. Some developers refer to this stage as a preview, a prototype, a technical preview (TP) or as an early access. Since many technophile users are eager to see new functionality as soon as possible, beta testing can be a benefit for all involved.

Operational Acceptance Testing (OAT)

Operational Acceptance Testing validates that all the non-functional attributes of a system, which are tested to ensure that the system is within the specified parameters. The original requirements of the project are examined to verify compliance.

OAT concentrates on such areas as maintainability, supportability, reliability, recoverability, installability, compatibility and conformance.

One of the biggest tasks for high-volume applications is load and performance testing, which assesses the ability of the system to operate at the desired levels of users with the resources that have been allocated. This is necessary even in an elastic environment since resources are only accessible once they have been provisioned. If there will be a need for them, the system must either request them automatically or they must be planned in advance.

DEPLOYMENT

The ability of the system to perform reliably and to recover from problems is also tested. Backup recovery and data integration tests are performed to test that system data is recovered properly. The contingency plan for disaster recovery is tested and implemented to test that the system can recover effectively. Also within the remit of Operational Acceptance Testing are security assessments such as Denial-of-Service and Penetration Tests.

Staging Levels

When the application grows more complex it often makes sense to introduce multiple levels of staging/testing. Some mission critical environments have as many as 7 different environments along the path from development to production. Each one represents a step closer to what the production environment is like.

Cloud computing has the potential to dramatically accelerate this trend. Since you can fire up instances on demand, there is little cost associated with having a number of different variants to test multiple options in parallel. They can also be very useful if the need presents itself to rollback a live system to a previous version.

Cloud Staging

Staging in the cloud includes running the application code in a production-like environment and going through all the production activities with a representative dataset. The actual technique for staging the application will depend very much on the platform used.

In the case of a custom platform built on an infrastructure service, such as EC2, Rackspace or GoGrid, the whole staging operation is determined by the developer. It could be as easy as using a duplicate instance of the production environment and running it with a different domain name.

In an environment like that of App Engine, this would include running the application as a different version under the main production application ID. The workflow would process the data sets that reside in the production data store. Thus, it is necessary to identify and resolve any potential data store schema issues related to different reprentations of data between the old production and the new staging version of the application.

On Azure, there is a separate staging environment for applications. The Azure service management portal provides two slots, one for production and one for staging. They are identical except for the URL that is used to call them. You can therefore fully test the staging environment until you are comfortable that it is ready for production without impacting the production slot.

Local Data

The cloud testing environment needs to be as separate from production as practically feasible. App Engine offers an interesting, but limited set of capabilities for testing in the cloud. The approach with App Engine is that a single application can have several versions of the application code, but all of them generally operate on the same back-end data.

App Engine recently (September 2010) released a namespace capability to their datastore, which enabled allocating data to specific segments in the application. While the primary use case for this is to separate one customer's data from another, the namespace could also be used to separate test data from production data.

When testing schema migration, data segmentation is a very sensitive issue. It is easy to contaminate the application data by running through a set of integration tests with a new set of application code that differs from the production version. A best practice would include running two different applications with different application IDs and a completely separate code and data set in order to completely isolate test and production datasets.

A typical testing activity on App Engine would include running the application on a separate application ID for a few days, working through the potential cron jobs that need to run, and identifying data store indexes that need to be created in production before the application can run.

Having a representative sample of production data in this testing environment is essential for successful testing. This is one of the more complicated issues when using a PaaS Service, such as App Engine. As of the time of writing, Google does not offer direct tools for migrating data between the primary production environment and other cloud environments. The bulkloader, which was mentioned in the previous section, only works between a local SDK environment and the production cloud. In order to migrate or copy data from the production (App Engine) cloud environment, one has to spend significant time developing the data migration code.

In other infrastructure-based cloud environments, such as Amazon EC2, the migration data stored in an SQL based relational database is far easier. The customer simply dumps the SQL data, moves the data file over to new the test environment and builds a new database instance from the dump.

Load Testing Tools

A major advantage of cloud computing is the elasticity that it provides to the testing infrastructure. This is particularly important for load and performance testing, which can require significant resources, albeit only typically for very short periods of time.

As you might expect, a variety of tools available have emerged to cover this need. Some of them, such as SOASTA and LoadStorm specifically target cloud testing. Others, such as HP LoadRunner and IBM Rational Performance Tester have been around for some time, but have also recently added cloud-specific capabilities.

SOASTA

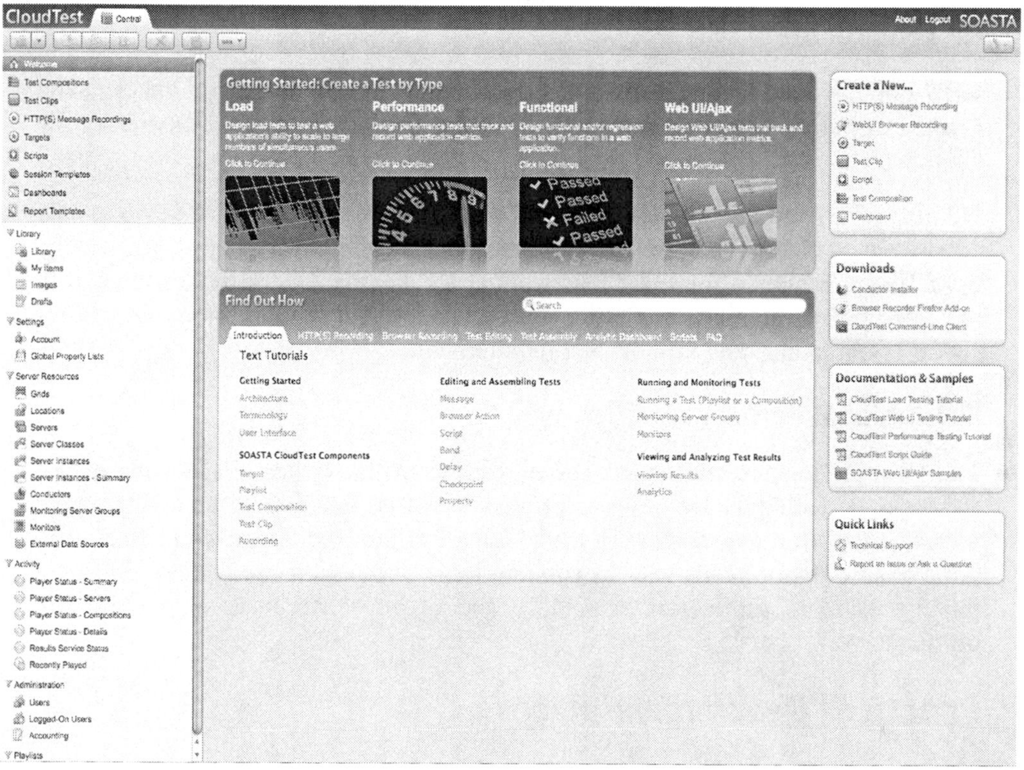

Figure 26-1: SOASTA CloudTest

SOASTA CloudTest (Figure 26-1) integrates test design, monitoring, and reporting to test and deliver Web applications. It is available both as an on-demand service in the cloud or as a (physical or virtual) appliance. It offers functional/regression, load and performance testing and works with Internet Explorer, Firefox or Safari with support for common web-based standards such as SOAP, REST, Ajax and JSON.

LoadStorm

DEPLOYMENT

LoadStorm is a performance testing tool built on the Amazon EC2 cloud computing infrastructure with both subscription and usage-based pricing. The tool is very visual with graphs showing various metrics, such as how many requests per second are being generated compared to the kilobytes per second of throughput moving between the browsers and servers.

It can display response times or percentage of errors occurring. Other reports show you the slowest pages, images, stylesheets, and Javascript responses. Error reporting lists every resource request that failed and the status code provided by the server.

HP LoadRunner

HP's popular load testing software, LoadRunner, is now available via Amazon Elastic Compute Cloud (Amazon EC2) under the name of LoadRunner in the Cloud.

HP also offers testing services delivered via Software as a Service (SaaS) to take advantage of cloud elasticity to quickly expand testing capacity cost-effectively. Specifically designed for spike load testing, HP Elastic Test provides the ability to scale up to large loads in a utility-based fashion and thereby more quickly respond to unplanned and ad-hoc test requirements.

IBM Rational Performance Tester

The IBM Rational Performance Tester workbench facilitates load testing on the IBM cloud (technical preview) to provision virtual test agents and to generate virtual users on a pay-as-you-go basis. IBM Rational performance testing solutions enable performance tests to emulate large population user transactions and thereby validate application scalability and diagnose application performance bottlenecks.

Practical Recommendations

The staging phase of the development lifecycle is particularly important for cloud services, which need to achieve a large scale and are exposed to stringent security demands while relying on many externally managed components. At the same time, there are cloud services that can assist in many areas, such as load and penetration testing. As you develop the staging options, consider a few suggestions:

- Make sure you test all non-functional areas, including security and performance!
- Use load testing tools to simulate Internet scale!
- Isolate your information so that you don't contaminate production data during staging!

DEPLOYMENT

Chapter 27

Production

Production is the final phase of the lifecycle. It must scale to meet the demands of the entire user base and should be largely error-free since support can be very costly. The execution platform will usually include a set of run-time environments (such as a JVM, Python or PHP) and programming languages. It may also provide a set of library functions, data storage facilities and integration mechanisms (such as a queueing system) for communication with other modules, internal and external.

The terms RTM ("release to manufacturing" or "release to marketing"), GA (General Availability or General Acceptance) and FCS (First Customer Shipment) are often used in retail mass-production software contexts to indicate that the software has reached a point that it is ready for the general market and will be delivered or provided to the customer through physical media. A similar maturity level is also needed for cloud services when they are released into production.

This is the last phase of a software release cycle and immediately follows the staging process. As a quality assurance mechanism, a final approval process follows staging to make sure that all interested parties sign off before the application goes into production. However, in many modern web environments, the approval process has been automated and integrated into the continuous integration process, sometimes referred to as continuous deployment.

Whether manual or automated, when the application has approval, it moves to production. If the deployment is successful, the application becomes part of the production service.

DEPLOYMENT

Release

Release refers to the activity of deploying application code into into one of the above mentioned environments. The two main factors to consider are that the deployment completes successfully and that service is disrupted as little as possible during the transition.

The first point is obviously extremely important. Assuming that the software was tested extensively during the staging phase, the main objective is to ensure that the deployment process itself maintains the integrity of the service. It is therefore vital to test the process of copying software and making it available with non-critical services before deploying the main user-visible services.

The second issue concerns the downtime of the application during the go-live. In some cloud environments like Google App Engine or Microsoft Azure, it is possible to support deployment with zero downtime and no production disruptions, provided the deployments are well planned. In other cases, deployments should be as small as possible to minimize any chance of interruption in production.

Some of the cloud SDKs offer very nice tools to automate deployments. These have the benefit of diminishing the risk of an incomplete deployment and can also accelerate the process, thereby minimizing the downtime. For example, App Engine has a deployment tool in its SDK that can be used to migrate the application over from SDK to either a Testing environment with a different application ID / version or to staging and production with different versions of the application. With Microsoft Azure it is as simple as requesting an in-place upgrade, or swapping the VIP (Virtual IP Address) of the staging and production slots, using the service console. Similarly, for infrastructure services you would typically just update the DNS entry to point to the newly deployed service once it is ready.

Data Migration

If the application's design ensures a clear separation of data and code, there should ordinarily be relatively little impact on the data during a deployment. However, there are two cases that may require at least some thought.

During the initial deployment you may need to seed the data. Since there is no real risk before the service is live, you can attend to this case carefully and use any bulk migration processes that are necessary to transform and load the data for use.

A much more delicate situation is when you have to change the data structures. If you re-factor the data or utilize alternate data sources then the interfaces may change and there is the potential for a significant number of problems and disruptions.

Needless to say, if you can avoid the problem by refraining from schema changes it will make your life much easier. When you see no other options you can still decouple the migration from the deployment by abstracting the data structures to an intermediate layer. If you use a virtual view of the data and allow it to proxy the actual requests, then you can migrate the data structures independently of the deployment and potentially even over an extended period of time.

Release Cycle

Part of the value proposition of cloud computing, and SaaS in particular, is the notion that the service can be updated frequently, so new functionality reaches the users regularly. This means software bugs are fixed quickly, security vulnerabilities are patched before they are exploited, and new features are added as soon as the developers can code and test them.

As already alluded to above, every single deployment exposes the service to a risk of failure as well as potential downtime during the transition. The only way to manage this risk effectively within a regular or continuous deployment process is to comprehensively automate the deployment and test it very carefully. Some of the tools used heavily for deployment in cloud-like environments include Cfengine, Puppet and Chef. We will look at them in more detail in the next section.

Rollback

No matter how careful you are in deploying new versions, there is always the chance that you won't discover that there is a critical problem until it is already in production. Unless, you have a rollback position, you could end up with production down for hours.

In practice this means that you need to retain the most recent production releases in a ready state for quick redeployment. They might be instances at your cloud provider's site that can be easily switched with a namespace change. Or they may simply be code that is retained in your repository. In the latter case, you must validate that you can package and deploy them with minimal delay in the case of an emergency.

You might also look at compartmentalizing the application. In addition to the general benefits that SOA promises for loosely coupled applications, there are also advantages to a fine-grained deployment model. This would not only reduce the rollback impact but minimize the effort to deploy small fixes.

DEPLOYMENT

Practical Recommendations

In a cloud-based scenario, deployment often just means flipping a switch so that the staging environment goes live. It is easier to roll out new functionality, so there is an argument to be made that it should be done more frequently. However, there are still risks that need to be considered so it is critical to have a thorough migration plan. As you design the final steps in the deployment process, consider a few suggestions:

- Don't underestimate the challenges of migrating data! If you want to deploy new versions of an application, it will not be possible to swap staging and production environment. You will also need to reconfigure the release to point to the correct information.
- Always ensure that you have a rollback position! If a deployment fails, it must be possible to minimize the damage.
- Automate the deployment! It is the only way to minimize the downtime and visible impact on the user.

DEPLOYMENT

Operation

After an application has been launched, the challenge becomes operational: it is necessary to configure, administer, monitor and support it. As more providers enter into the mix, the administration has the potential to become excessively complex. To minimize confusion, there is a clear need to integrate processes with well-defined policy-based service management. At the same time, there is also the opportunity to avail of cloud-based services for monitoring, service desk, and other management tasks.

All of these facilities need to be planned at the design stage in order to reach the highest level of automation. While standardization and abstraction of components will facilitate this process, constructive collaboration between development and operations is necessary to ensure that the requirements of both groups are fully addressed.

OPERATION

Chapter 28

Configuration

The automation of infrastructure configuration is central to cloud computing. In order to support rapid scale out and failover, it is necessary to capture and maintain infrastructure and application configuration data. It enables companies to automate the provisioning of managed components, which is critical to minimize the operations surrounding support of large user bases and regular deployment of applications.

What does configuration mean? It is a set of functional and physical parameters of an item that impact a system's performance and functionality. A configuration item is a hardware or software product with an end-user purpose. These attributes are recorded in configuration documentation, baselined and integrated into formal configuration change control processes.

Some of the configuration items defined by ITIL include Applications, Images, Operating Systems, Clusters, Storage Allocations, and even User Instructions and Documentation. Examples of configuration information include:

- Version of (3rd party) operating systems and software running on different stages of the lifecycle

- Configuration of in-house software / applications under source control

- Configuration of in-house software outside source code control

- Deployment and rollback of configuration and software versions

- Managed certificates

A configuration management system helps to track these parameters in order to ensure the integrity of the system and isolate problems when a service does not function as expected. The main components include:

- Configuration description language to define dependencies and inheritance

OPERATION

- Repository usually structured as a hierarchical file-system

- Distribution protocol to securely retrieve and transmit files

In the simplest cases, configuration management can be as easy as keeping the versions of the code/application in a pre-defined folder structure and deploying them to a hosting/cloud computing provider. In a more complex case, there's a dedicated configuration management database that tracks all the related items, instances running in production, operating system versions in use, software version and all of their relationships to each other.

CMDB

A configuration management database (CMDB) is one or more integrated repositories detailing all of the organization's IT infrastructure components and other assets that are instrumental in delivering IT services. The concept is not new but has increased in popularity recently since ITIL made it a cornerstone of their Configuration Management process. The CMDB defines the authorized configuration of all significant components in the IT environment. It helps an organization understand the relationships between these components and to track changes in their configuration.

BMC, CA, HP and IBM, sometimes called the Big Four of IT management have developed sophisticated solutions around their CMDBs. Auto-discovery is a central function that helps with the initial population of the database as well as the ongoing validation of the Change Management process.

Its techniques include passive network polling, port scanning, packet inspection, active queries to well known services and heuristics based on names and directories. There are obvious limitations around querying disconnected devices, assessing financial costs, or determining precise physical location. Nonetheless, a CMDB provides valuable insight into the infrastructure and facilitates policy-based management.

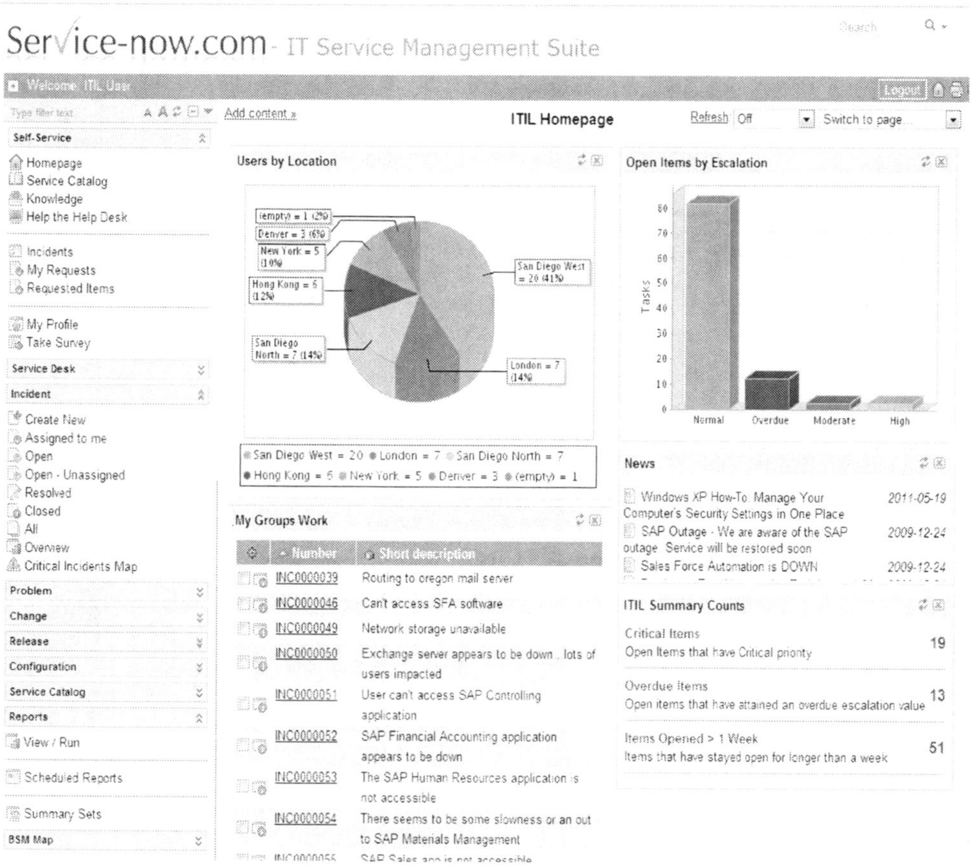

Figure 28-1: Service-now.com IT Service Management Suite

An interesting CMDB-based service management solution that is available on demand comes from Service-now.com (Figure 28-1). They provide a full cloud-based suite of ITIL capabilities including Service Desk, Service Catalogue, and management of Problems, Incidents, Changes, Releases and Service Levels. A Business Service Catalogue displays the list of IT services along with their scope, service level and costs. Once the businesses have subscribed to a particular set of services, they can check their status with a dashboard showing the health, as defined by the SLA. They can also drill down into the applications to view their historical status and service composition. Additional features include visibility into cost and expense lines and project management tools.

CMDB can provide significant value, particularly to large organizations. At a minimum, cloud applications that cater to enterprises need to be aware of a possible CMDB and facilitate the integration as seamlessly as possible by exposing all configuration information and settings.

OPERATION

DevOps

In spite of the benefits of a CMDB, some would argue that it perpetuates an excessively infrastructure-oriented view of an enterprise architecture (Urquhart, 2010). A CMDB provides the facility to define applications as configuration items but, in doing so, relegates them to the same status as operating systems and storage.

Cloud computing, on the other hand, is very service-centric. Services are much more dynamic, complex and customizable than most infrastructural components. As a result there is a stronger need to facilitate a diverse set of operational needs that can rarely be achieved through a set of static configuration values and instead requires active involvement of the operations team.

These requirements represent a break from the past, where operations took a passive role in software execution, manually installing standard software according to guidelines handed to them. Instead, there is a need for increased collaboration between the development and operations teams to optimize and automate application deployments. This new approach is often called DevOps.

While a CMDB is still needed for infrastructure configuration and is important for federation of multiple configuration management systems, there is a tendency to include locale awareness into the applications. By avoiding isolated decisions it makes it much easier to re-locate applications between environments, such as a public and private cloud.

The simplest way to encapsulate configuration instructions with an application is to package a shell script with it. The problem with this approach is that while scripts contain a list of actions to achieve their goal they normally lack any way of checking if the system is in the correct initial state and whether the desired outcome has been achieved.

A declarative configuration-management system, on the other hand, allows the user to specify the desired system state and then takes the necessary action to push the system into this state. It can probe the current state of the system, and deploy changes when the state needs to be corrected. If a system already is in the desired state, it may or may not redeploy the changes. The tools can also regularly examine the target systems and detect when they have diverged from the desired state.

Several open-source systems have gained recent popularity with just-in-time configuration that ensures mobility at the architectural or topological layer. The two best known are Puppet and Chef, both Ruby-based although they can manage a wide variety of applications. Twitter uses Puppet while EngineYard uses Chef, for instance.

Puppet

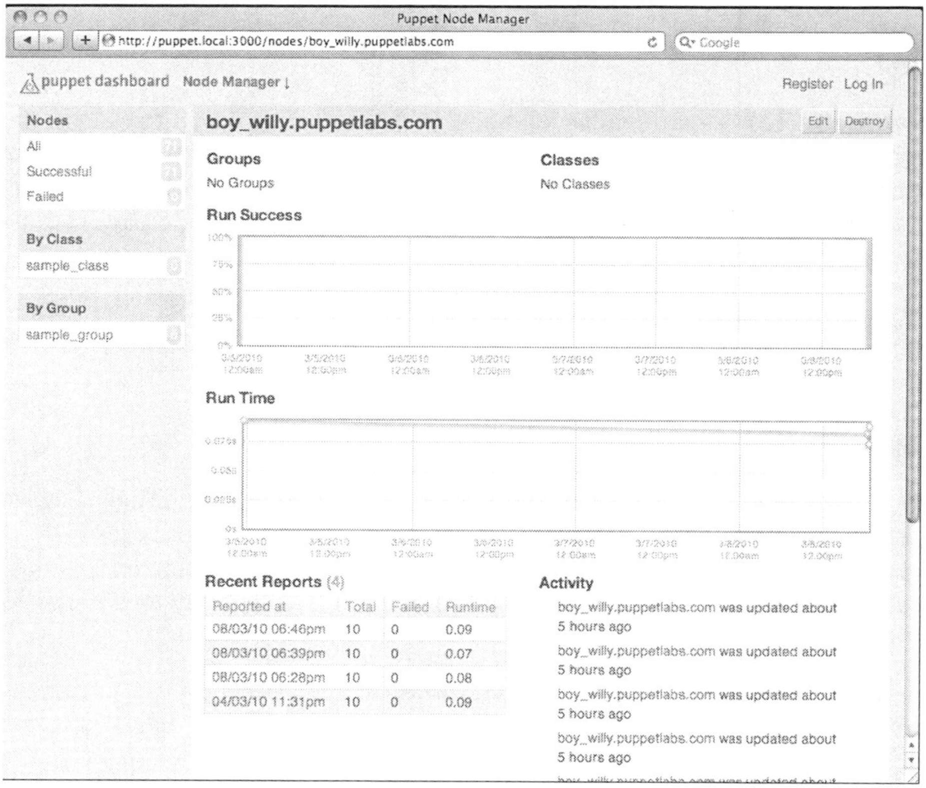

Figure 28-2: Puppet

Puppet is the most widely adopted open source data center automation and configuration management framework today (Figure 28-2). In that sense, it is the reference that others measure against. It provides system administrators with a platform that allows consistent, transparent, and flexible systems management.

Some of the key elements of Puppet include:

Puppetmaster: centrally manage the configuration for thousands of nodes

Dashboard: visualize, explore and command puppet infrastructure

Secure infrastructure: built-in SSL-based public key infrastructure

Puppet Modules: break down puppet configuration into reusable units including some free community-developed modules

A declarative language describes the system configuration, so that administrators can reproduce any configuration on other systems. The framework can help enforce configuration policies and automatically correct systems that drift from

OPERATION

their baseline. Puppet also provides an audit trail of all systems, which can be kept in version control for compliance purposes.

Chef

Opscode's Chef is very similar to Puppet in its objectives but is a newer system and therefore not as widely known or used. Although both are written in Ruby, Puppet's domain-specific language hides it more than Chef, which expects users to be familiar with Ruby. Depending on your skill level with Ruby, you may consider this a benefit or a drawback.

Opscode also offers a hosted version of the Chef open-source configuration management software, which is interesting if you want to minimize your in-house footprint.

Capistrano

While Puppet and Chef are receiving significant attention, due to their high degree of scalability and full automation capabilities, they are not necessarily the best for every set of circumstances. Capistrano and Fabric are simpler approaches that provide the users a greater degree of control and visibility over the operation.

Capistrano is another Ruby-based tool for automating tasks on one or more remote servers. For example, it automates tasks that previously required a login and suite of custom shell scripts. It executes commands in parallel on all targeted machines, and provides a mechanism for rolling back changes across multiple machines.

Fabric

Fabric is a Python library and command-line tool to copy files and execute remote SSH commands for application deployment or systems administration tasks. It provides a basic suite of operations for executing local or remote shell commands and uploading/downloading files, as well as auxiliary functionality, such as prompting the running user for input, or aborting execution. Typical use involves creating a Python module containing one or more functions, then executing them via the fab command-line tool.

Selection Criteria

In assessing these and numerous other packages that provide similar functionality, including Cfengine, Bcfg and LCFG, there are several criteria to consider such as size of the customer base and developer base, commercial track record, documentation, range of use cases and platform support.

You may want to look at the configuration languages both in terms of how familiar your developers are with them and how well they handle your requirements. There is a significant difference between a domain-specific language, like Puppet uses, and straight Ruby from Chef, or Python from Fabric.

There are also philosophical differences around dependency management. Puppet, for instance declares these explicitly, while with Chef they are implied through the order of the commands.

Provisioning Automation

There are also provisioning automation vendors that leverage tools like Puppet, Chef and Cfengine to facilitate enterprise-class release automation across physical, virtual and cloud environments. A good example of this approach is rPath. Its services are included in two integrated products: rBuilder and rPath Lifecycle Management Platform. Some of its capabilities include system version control, automated dependency discovery, policy-based system construction and automated update of deployed systems (Figure 28-3).

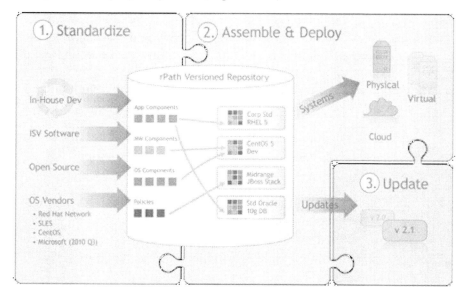

Figure 28-3: rPath deployment process

rBuilder provides automated, policy-based system creation, deep compliance features, and the ability to generate multiple output formats from a single system definition

The rPath Lifecycle Management Platform ensures complete management and control of deployed applications with capabilities including:

OPERATION

- Automated administration of patches and updates

- Complete system reproduction and rollback capabilities

- Application and systems audit and reporting for compliance management

- A centralized management console for start-up and shutdown across targets

The entire system together with all of its components and dependencies are stored and managed in a version control repository which provides consistent control over the lifecycle of the deployed system.

Both rBuilder and the rPath Lifecycle Management Platform offer a set of APIs for programmatic access.

There are numerous other commercial cloud management services, such as Rightscale and enStratus. Generally, they have either built their own DevOps scripting languages, or adopted others.

Practical Recommendations

As enterprise architecture refocuses on applications as the primary element of configuration, there are many opportunities to optimize the operations of cloud computing services. To achieve an optimal level of efficiency, it makes sense to automate all processes as much as possible. As you specify your configuration management systems, consider a few suggestions:

- Promote collaboration between your developers and operations personnel! They need to have joint responsibility for provisioning.
- Consider service management from the cloud! Depending on your needs, it may be cheaper and easier to set up.

Chapter 29

Administration

As IT administration evolves in sophistication, system managers are spending less time on day-to-day repetitive tasks and instead must focus more on the strategic requirements and plans for IT. An increasing number of monitoring and diagnostic tools can automate some basic operational procedures.

Self-service portals are becoming common for end-user functions such as password reset, account unlock and employee updates. These reduce the IT burden while at the same time improving security and reducing user frustration at raising a ticket and waiting on hold for a call center to take and process support requests.

At the same time, there is still a need for IT technical support as well as service managers to have full visibility and traceability of all processes and transactions. They must be able to identify root causes of problems and to ensure that the system is functioning as anticipated. There may also be additional requirements for obtaining logging and accounting information in bulk, and mining this data for improved planning of functionality and capacity.

Administration Portal

Since cloud computing is primarily web-based, the logical interface for administering it is a portal. Ideally all management tasks will be accessible through a single console, which might contain functions such as:

- Adjust and aggregate billing
- Report analytics
- Create, Update, Delete users and roles
- Define and monitor services
- Install and update packages
- Define and inspect configuration
- Start/Stop service instances

OPERATION

- Tracing problems and incidents
- Provide performance metrics for capacity planning

Most cloud providers offer a portal to manage their services. Amazon has an AWS portal, Microsoft has an Azure Portal and Google provides an App Engine management console. A challenge arises when several different cloud providers offer disparate portals. As long as administrators are specialized to given services, they will not see this as a problem. However, it becomes tedious for an overall administrator to obtain a synoptic view when the information is dispersed across many different pages.

If the capabilities all have public interfaces and are accessible, for example through RESTful web services or SOAP requests, then it may be possible to aggregate the most important functions and indicators into a dashboard, which can serve as an entry point that directs the user to the appropriate service portal for further action. This is an approach that is facilitated by cloud management solutions such as RightScale and enStratus.

IT Service Management as a Service

While this chapter is primarily about running Service Management *for* the cloud, it is interesting to note that there are also SaaS-based offerings, such as Servicenow (Figure 28-1, mentioned in last chapter), that facilitate running Service Management *in* the cloud. They are a logical choice for organizations that have no in-house service management platform and wish to minimize any further on-premise installations.

IT Operations Management

Part of the incentive of moving to a public cloud is to reduce the amount of internal operational activity. However, there may still be some need for internal involvement, particularly when the services involve hybrid configurations that also run on internal systems.

In any case, much of the internal infrastructure is local such as the printers, scanners and local network equipment. End-user desktops and mobile devices are also closer to on-site operations personnel. So there is an absolute requirement for some ongoing local operations, which must also be connected with the operational management groups of the service providers.

Backup

OPERATION

One area that is of particular concern to business continuity is backup. We looked at this area from a developer perspective in the discussion of resilience. But you also need to consider the operational dimension. Operations personnel are under increasing pressure to meet aggressive backup requirements. Users demand the ability to store more data but yet expect more frequent backups and faster restores. Legal regulations mandate long-term readability. At the same time, virtualization has all but eliminated any scheduled downtime while outsourcing and multi-tenancy have increased the requirement for media encryption.

Backups are required for a variety of reasons including:

- End user access to data that has been removed

- End user access to historical data

- Audits, Troubleshooting, IP retention

- Legal requirements for eDiscovery

As already mentioned, these requirements are often most effectively satisfied with an archiving platform that can de-duplicate and classify the data to address these functions and can also provide enterprise search. Offloading these responsibilities onto an archiving platform also relieves the backup function from many of its long-term requirements so that it can focus on offering fast and reliable disaster recovery.

Regardless of which backup and archiving techniques are used, they are an important part of the business continuity plan and therefore must form part of the software architecture for any cloud-based solution, either as dedicated external services, or the equivalent functionality built into the application.

Service Request Fulfillment

Most cases of user-based service requests are very simple. They might include password assistance, software installation and configuration, or provisioning access to services for themselves and others.

In some cases, these requests will be the outcome of a call, or ticket, that the user has logged with the helpdesk. In other cases, the user will be able to trigger the request through a web-based portal. In order for the process to work in a scalable fashion, there must be some agreement on standard services. They should be published as part of a service catalogue so that users can easily understand the request process and eligibility.

For requests that carry significant risk or financial consequences, an authorization and approval process may also be required, which should be included in the functionality of the service desk. What is important from a cloud perspective is to ensure that the workflow can be validated by the organization fulfilling the request.

OPERATION

If the service desks of the cloud providers do not have visibility into the organizational structure of the customer, then it is difficult for them to verify and ensure managerial approval. This implies a need for Identity Management federation, or at least replication of organizational attributes, as part of a directory-synchronization with the provider.

A request that is likely to become much more common in the future is the deployment of new services. In the past this would hardly be considered a user request, as it would have entailed procuring additional hardware and software and would be need a series of approvals. However, in a utility computing model, you need to assess this question as part of the application and service design. It is now possible to dispatch new services at very low risk and cost. It therefore becomes possible to reduce the overhead needed to manage the request.

Nonetheless there are still some risks and concerns that need to be addressed before dispatching additional services, including reservations, scheduling and compliance checking. If these, and the necessary authorization, can be accommodated in a workflow it can be possible to automate the entire provisioning with a self-service portal that allows a user to choose a virtual machine, configure it and launch it as needed.

Change Management

The area between user-based service requests and more extensive change management is not always obvious and depends to a large extent on the organization involved. However, in all companies there are likely to be services that are too critical for automated change requests.

It isn't a question of the type of operation on the service. These can include adding and removing server instances, changing system and networking configuration settings, deploying or removing software, deploying patches and upgrading versions, or changing memory and storage allocation. The issue is much more related to the criticality of the service and the impact that any changes can have on it.

If a service is important to the business then it is necessary to have a process in place to record, assess, authorize and monitor the change. In order to analyze the potential impact, ITIL offers a set of nine questions (called the 9 Rs) that should be addressed for any of these changes:

- Who Raised the change?

- What is the Reason for the change?

- What is the Return required for the change?

- What are the Risks involved in the change?

- What resources are Required for the change?

- Who is Responsible for the change?

- What is the Relationship between this change and other changes?

If the cloud solution assists in evaluating these questions, and recording the responses, it is much easier to identify potential impact as soon as possible. Furthermore, an initial assessment facilitates problem analysis and correction.

Change management can become very complex when many parties are involved. As the number of service providers increases, the combinations of potential intersections grow exponentially. It is therefore vital to receive as much information as possible in a structured manner.

The processes for requesting and approving changes also need to be coordinated with internal mechanisms regulating network connectivity, directory and remote access.

New Release Management

One major recurring change is the need to perform upgrades to increase functionality, solve problems and sometimes improve performance. As we discussed in the Deployment section, new versions can disrupt services because they may drop functions, implement them differently or contain undiscovered bugs.

There is some flexibility in the granularity of release units. Due to the complexity of interfaces in a service-oriented architecture there may be a case for infrequent major releases that are rolled out in bundles in order to minimize the total testing effort. On the other hand, an automated testing process may be able to handle frequent minor releases, which will provide user benefits more quickly. The question is ultimately a business decision that pits the value of accelerated functionality against the incremental costs of additional testing.

Monitoring

While a great deal of the service delivery may be outsourced in a cloud solution, this doesn't completely remove the continuous responsibility of checking and reporting on service health. The due diligence required in defining key performance indicators and service levels prior to signing the contract is critical.

Nevertheless, someone also needs to take ownership for the stability of the system after it is operational. This involves both proactive planning to ensure business/service continuity as well as reactive processes for coping with any problems that occur. This chapter focuses on the former while the next will address the latter.

OPERATION

Note that these systems don't necessarily need to be designed from scratch. Established enterprise management frameworks are gradually adding capability to cope with cloud-based services. Some, such as Hyperic, offer plug-ins for Google Apps, Amazon Web Services and other cloud providers. HP Cloud Assure projects future cloud services availability by diagnosing and reporting on potential performance and security issues before they impact the business.

Amazon CloudWatch is a web service that provides monitoring for AWS cloud resources, starting with Amazon EC2. It provides customers with visibility into resource utilization, operational performance, and overall demand patterns including metrics such as CPU utilization, disk reads and writes, and network traffic.

Pingdom is another network monitoring tool that tracks uptime, reachability, responsiveness and performance. It also has a means of sending SMS or email alerts when there are problems. When Pingdom does detect an error, it automatically performs additional tests to assist in troubleshooting.

Ganglia is a performance monitoring framework for distributed systems. It collects metrics on individual machines and forwards them to an aggregator that presents the global state of a cluster. This is of particular interest when using Hadoop since the Hadoop performance monitoring framework can use Ganglia as its backend.

While Ganglia will monitor Hadoop-specific metrics, general information about the health of the cluster should be monitored with an additional tool. Nagios is a machine and service monitoring system designed for large clusters. It provides useful diagnostic information for tuning the cluster, including network, disk, and CPU utilization across machines.

Capacity Management

Long-term capacity management is less critical for on-demand services. Elasticity of resources means that enterprises can scale up and down as demand dictates without the need for extensive planning. You can even employ reactive monitoring tools, such as RightScale, to automate the requests for more resources.

Nonetheless, there is some value in proactively estimating requirements. Even though the costs of increasing demand may be absorbed by corresponding additional revenues, this doesn't mean that your financial benefactors don't want to see an estimate and budget for how these costs may develop. In addition to ensuring profitability, they also need to plan for cash flow, taxes and capital budgeting, which may be impacted by these numbers.

OPERATION

You may uncover idle capacity that is limited due to unforeseen resource bottlenecks when you have scaled too much in one direction and not enough in another. For example, you may be adding network bandwidth to solve a problem that is actually based on contention for disk I/O or even server utilization.

It's a good idea to verify that your service provider will be in a position to deliver all the resource requirements that you anticipate. If you will be requiring more vertically scaled capacity for single-threaded processes and your provider has specialized in low-clock-speed multi-core chipsets, then you may need to look at other alternatives that match your requirements for that service.

There are several aspects of capacity planning that need to be evaluated in parallel. You can monitor existing performance and extrapolate future patterns based on anticipated demand. You can model current and future applications based on specified performance parameters. You may also have the possibility to influence the demand and usage in terms of timing and volume so that you can optimize your resource reservations for the best value.

Availability Management

Just like capacity management, availability planning is not a one-time action. In addition to reactive management such as monitoring, measuring and analyzing incidents, you also need to proactively plan and design availability improvements.

There are many dimensions to availability. If there have been outages, it is important to identify frequency, duration and timing (night, week-end, peak time). A deeper look at the components of the incident response (detection, diagnosis, repair, recovery) is also helpful since each phase has different implications in terms of the amount of information the helpdesk can communicate to users about expected uptime.

Other metrics that may be relevant are:

- Mean time between failures
- Mean time to restore service
- Mean time between system incidents

The service-level calculation implies an in-depth understanding of user requirements, which are monitored against SLAs. The question is not only whether the service-levels are being met, but whether they adequately reflect business requirements or whether they need further refinement. In other words, are current performance levels, events, alarms and escalation paths sufficient?

The final criterion should be the impact on business processes. If there are any business processes that have sustained unacceptable impact, the logical question is whether you should change provider. Are there alternate providers of the same service? If not, you may also want to perform an extensive analysis into the fail-

OPERATION

ure points of outages (network, virtual infrastructure, application) to assess what kind of redundancy can help to address and mitigate the failures.

It is vital to monitor and compare these availability levels not only with the SLA but also with benchmarks and reports from other cloud providers. If your provider is meeting its contractual obligations, but these do not reflect the service levels of its competitors, then you have leverage to renegotiate more favorable terms in the contract.

Access Management

The Identity section described the challenge of identity management in a multi-provider world. Its impact on service management comes in several forms. On the one hand, federation must be negotiated and managed. For example if there are schema changes, or if attribute semantics change in the corporate directory, then these need to be coordinated with service providers leveraging the identity store.

Changes in access policies and procedures also need to be synchronized. A given transaction may have required only first level approval during the initial implementation, but now requires a second signature. The access requirements of the service provider to enterprise resources may also change as a result of service requests. For example, the service provider may require increased integration with the enterprise service desk. The question for the service manager is first: who authorizes these and how are they approved? Once the procedural aspect is worked out, the changes also need to be implemented on a technical level, which may require support from the networking and security departments in order to implement the necessary proxy and firewall configurations.

Practical Recommendations

Administration of a heterogeneous system is more difficult than that of a homogenous system. The challenges in multi-sourced cloud environment are significant. Nonetheless, a rigorous design can minimize the disadvantages. As you ensure that you have all the bases covered, consider a few suggestions:

- Create an overview dashboard! Your administrators need to be able to see all relevant information at a glance. Even if it means mashing up other services, the benefit is compelling. It reduces the risk of oversight and simplifies the management burden.
- Coordinate and integrate service management between all vendors across all areas! This is easier said than done, and yet it is vital to a well-run operation.

OPERATION

Chapter 30

Troubleshooting

The objective of a mature operational model is to ensure that nothing goes wrong. Unfortunately, this ambitious goal is rarely attained for any length of time. Problems continually surface in the hardware, software and even the operational processes themselves. When these do occur, it is important to document, identify and resolve the issues. It is also necessary to take care of the users who not only fight with the technical problems of the system, but often introduce additional human errors into the equation. We will look at each of these areas in turn.

Incident Management

While Operations Management takes a proactive role to maintain system health, Incident Management caters to the reactive side by addressing issues that have already occurred. It revolves around an incident model that describes:

- Steps to handle incidents
- Chronological order of steps, dependencies and co-processing
- Roles and responsibilities
- Timescales and thresholds
- Escalation procedures (contacts)
- Evidence-preservation activities

A standard incident management process involves:

- Incident logging
- Incident categorization
- Incident prioritization
- Initial diagnosis
- Functional and hierarchical incident escalation
- Investigation and diagnosis or root cause and impact

OPERATION

- Resolution and recovery
- Incident assessment and closure

The key consideration in a cloud-computing scenario is how to expand this model to include multiple providers. There must be agreement on activities and thresholds that trigger incidents. Furthermore, it is necessary to enable integration of the incident response systems across firewalls.

While incident management is a vital component for any service, there is a trend for it to diminish in relative importance in many cloud-based solutions. Recovery-oriented computing takes the standpoint that a virtualized infrastructure makes it easier and faster to stop and restart instances than to attempt to solve spurious problems. This facility allows diagnostic resources to be reallocated to fundamental and recurring system problems.

Problem Management

Problem Management refers to tracking and resolving unknown causes of incidents. It is closely related to Incident Management but focuses on solving root causes for a set of incidents rather than applying what may be a temporary fix to an incident.

It follows a similar sequence as was required for incidents. As such, in addition to cloud-specific challenges, they also share some commonality including cross-organizational collaboration. It is vital to define roles and responsibilities contractually and to ensure full co-operation in diagnosing and resolving problems even when it is not obvious in which realm the root cause may lie.

Event Management

Event Management tracks discernible occurrences with significance on the management of IT infrastructure or the delivery of IT services. It thereby facilitates early detection of incidents and provides both clues for problem solving and input for capacity planning.

It typically involves both active monitoring/polling tools, which generate alerts when they encounter exception conditions, and passive tools that detect and correlate alerts.

Some of the most common events to be observed include (ITIL, 2007, p. 94):

- Configurations items
- Environmental conditions (fire, smoke)
- Software license monitoring (compliance and optimal utilization)
- Security (e.g. intrusions)
- Auditing use, tracking performance

One set of concerns in the public cloud is the contractual challenge already described above. It is necessary to come to an agreement on the events and thresholds that trigger alerts and on the mechanisms for relaying the information to the destination.

A multi-tenant environment also presents some potential complications. Co-tenants may create disruptions, akin to environmental conditions, that need to be signaled. If the multi-tenancy involves the sharing of physical resources, then it will complicate performance monitoring and projections since performance may be affected by competition for resources.

Support

One of the biggest challenges of operating a service is the interface to all the humans who are involved in the process. Technical integration can be fully automated but users tend to have requirements that are not as easy to specify. At the same time, they are the most critical elements of the system. It is vital to support them as efficiently as possible so that they can proceed with their business processes.

Every technology requires a support model. This is not new with cloud computing. However, the heterogeneous, multi-vendor composition of services can complicate support models that had previously been simple and streamlined. On the positive side, the technologies can introduce increased infrastructural stability. Nonetheless, it is very difficult to troubleshoot problems that span organizational boundaries, where each player has an incentive to cast the blame on other parties.

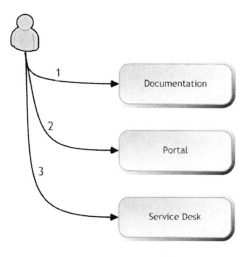

Figure 30-1: End-user Support Path

End-user support should progress in tiers that successively address more difficult and less common problems (Figure 30-1). It begins with simple documentation and on-line help to orient the user and clarify any obvious points of confusion. A self-service portal can then help to trigger an automatic process to fulfill common requests.

These first two levels have the advantage that they don't require any costly human intervention other than that of the affected user. The rest of the support process is then collectively considered the service desk, which may range from desk-side support for common problems to requesting code changes from the developers.

A key pre-requisite to the end-user support process is to test the functionality extensively. This can involve professional testers who typically focus on errors in the code. They may also report unintuitive and complex areas of the interface so that, where it isn't possible to change the software, at least it is possible to prepare the users.

On top of technical testing, it is also vital to obtain some input from typical business users. Selecting a random sample of employees with diverse backgrounds and roles can help to give an advance glimpse of the types of problems and challenges other users will encounter.

Documentation

Documentation is notorious for being ignored. There is little point in giving users volumes of technical information that they are unlikely to use. Instead it is more efficient to focus on the most important questions and concerns and address them clearly.

This might be in the form of an electronic mail message. It might be a printed brochure that is distributed to the users. It can also be an on-line tutorial that is triggered when the user logs on to the application. Ideally, the documentation will not rely on any single communications channel but will include a combination of several mechanisms.

In order to focus the users and avoid overwhelming them, it is necessary to study what actually changes for the user and what the user needs to do differently with the new system. If the system involves new functionality, or the user is new to the application, then there should also be some form of Getting Started guide, which walks the user through the initial setup and common processes.

While the information that is thrust on the user should be kept to a minimum, this doesn't mean that there cannot be a more complete system of on-line help and documentation available. The user then only needs to receive a pointer to the repository and can subsequently choose to investigate some problems on their own.

Portal

A self-service portal can help to automate request fulfillment. Common tasks like provisioning an account or resetting a password may be processed without any call center interaction. This yields a benefit in reduced support costs and may also improve user productivity since there are no delays associated with logging a call and waiting for a response.

However, for the portal to work effectively, it must be obvious to the users where to go and what to do once they get there. This means that the portal location must be widely communicated and ideally linked to other portals that the users visit regularly, including the application itself.

The portal also needs to cover the right tasks. It may be worth investigating what the most common requests are that the user cannot accomplish in the base applications. These often include subscriptions, unsubscriptions and requests for additional resources.

The business logic of the portal functions depends on the nature of the request. If the functions are universally available, the authorization is simple. For example, it may be the case that any user can subscribe to a service or request a password reset with simple authentication. On the other hand, requests that involve additional costs to the organization and department may require multiple levels of approvals.

Where a cloud service provider is operating the portal, there can be connectivity and security ramifications. The portal needs to be able to authenticate the users and the approvers, which may imply federated identity management in order to validate user credentials stored on a corporate directory server. In some cases, the requests may also have cost implications that need to be registered with the enterprise resource planning (ERP) system (for internal charges) or the billing system (for externally provided services).

Service Desk

Regardless of the level of infrastructure and automation that is put into place to offload the central IT department, there will always be cases where unanticipated problems arise and the user needs expert resolution. Service desks are the organizational units which are in place to handle these cases.

The term "service desk" often also refers to the actual tool that is used to track tickets, such as questions, problem reports and requests. It is interesting to observe that, like many other management components, there are also SaaS-based ticket-tracking systems, such as ZenDesk (Figure 30-2), for companies that want to minimize on-premise equipment.

OPERATION

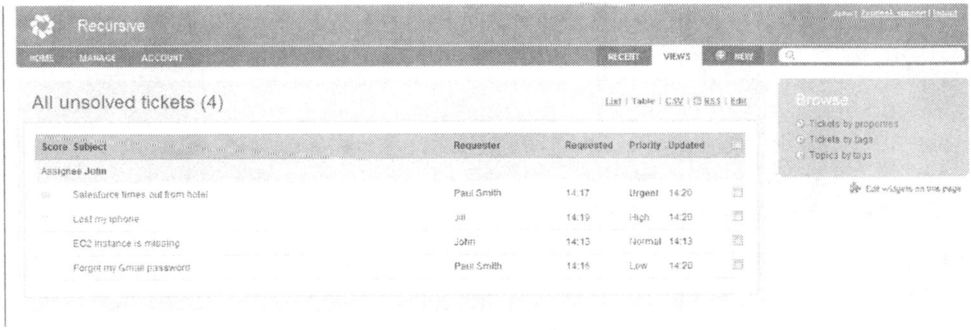

Chapter 30: Troubleshooting

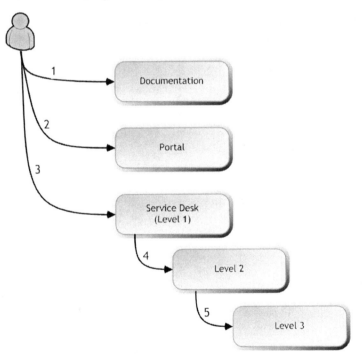

Figure 30-2: ZenDesk Ticket Tracking

Support Tiers

A call center is typically organized in a hierarchy of several tiers with 3 levels being the most common (Figure 30-3).

Figure 30-3: Call center escalation path

Level 1: The first level of support is responsible for triage and can address simple recurring problems with a scripted response.

Responsibilities typically include:

- Log incident and service request details

- Provide first-line investigation and diagnosis
- Escalate incidents not resolved in time threshold
- Inform users of progress
- Close resolved incidents and requests
- Perform user-satisfaction callbacks and surveys
- Update the Configuration Management System

There may also be an interface with small teams of desk-side support, particularly for larger locations. Where there is no desk-side support, the support requirements increase since it is much more difficult to diagnose many problems remotely particularly where hardware failures come into play.

Level 2: Second-level support is usually much more specialized to certain applications and services. The specialists may not be familiar with the internal design of the products, but they will know how to use advanced features and be aware of the most common product bugs. They will also undertake some research of the internal knowledge management systems to see if they can identify a known problem before escalating it further.

Level 3: If the problem is particularly difficult, or has never been encountered before, then internal knowledge of the products may be required. Third level support should ultimately be able to solve any critical, reproducible problems with debugging tools. If they are not able to find the root cause themselves, then they will often have access to the development teams who can step through the code to isolate the problem.

In order to troubleshoot production issues at all levels, there needs to be a clearly identified process for replicating production issues in a staging environment and, if required, also in the testing environments. Even so, reproducing problems in a separate context will always be difficult. To compensate, it is important for the application to provide a mechanism for detailed logging and tracing.

This need is even more acute when working on a platform service where there is no access to the operating system that typically includes extensive resource logging. The burden therefore falls on the application for instrumentation with the appropriate logging that will expose underlying reasons for issues.

When relying on public services, whether they be at the infrastructure, platform or software level, it is critical to have an identified support channel to the provider. Depending on the terms of service this channel may be held to strict service levels or it may not. It is wise to ensure that the application does not promise service quality to its users that it cannot obtain from its provider.

Amazon, for example, provides only minimal support for AWS by default. However, AWS Premium Support is available for a fee. The pricing is on a monthly basis and currently promises to support an unlimited number of support cases ranging from operational issues to technical questions during development, test or integration.

Service Knowledge Management System

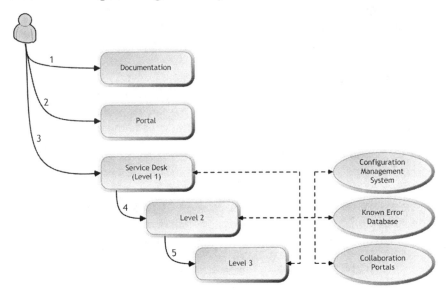

Figure 30-4: Knowledge Management System

A critical factor in keeping support costs down is to expedite problem resolution by leveraging previous solutions and all information that is known about the components related to the problem (Figure 30-4). In order to facilitate these operations, call center personnel (particularly levels two and three) will have access to a variety of tools including:

Configuration Management Database: a listing of the attributes of all configurable entities in the system being supported

Known Error Database: list of common error symptoms along with the root cause analyses and procedures to correct or work around the problem

Collaboration portals: additional information assembled by the call center that provides background on the technology and products that are being supported

Practical Recommendations

Troubleshooting a multivendor operation can be a nightmare. The tendency for each service owner to shift blame seems to be universal. However, clear instrumentation as well as well-defined performance indicators and service levels will help to minimize the impact. As you develop the process, consider a few suggestions:

- Create a self-service portal for common requests! It can be more efficient for users and reduced the load on the service desk.
- Ensure there is a well-defined escalation path that is coordinated and agreed between all vendors!
- Shift the focus from incident management to problem management! In accordance with the premise of recovery oriented computing, it is often easier to restart a service than to troubleshoot a rare and spurious problem.

Chapter 31

Refinement

Cloud computing introduces a new model of IT procurement and planning. Once a service has been commissioned, there should be no more need for proactive planning. There may be no new equipment to buy and no capital expenditures to include in the budget. The provider will automatically update the platform with the incremental functionality that is in highest demand.

There is the danger that the new approach will lead to purely reactive decision making. The developer only needs to respond to exceptions. When service levels are unsatisfactory, or the service provider suffers an outage, then there will be a need to take an active position. Until then, it is possible to refrain from interference in the service.

A reactive approach may sound appealing since it reduces your overall service management cost by minimizing involvement. There are, however, two disadvantages to consider:

- The lack of vision and planning may blindside you where a vigilant approach would give you much more advance notice of any problems looming on the horizon.

- It neglects the opportunity cost. Even if the service is running satisfactorily there may be better options on the market, which you don't leverage. This omission can put you at a disadvantage compared to competitors who are more proactive.

There are three aspects of a proactive approach that are worth considering separately. There should be a continuous analysis of the corporate strategy execution to determine whether it is successful in accomplishing its objectives. In addition, you need to also look at two aspects of the external environment for an assessment of a cloud strategy. On the one hand, the business environment may be changing, which can have a significant impact on your strategy. It is also very likely that the underlying technologies will be in flux and should be reassessed as you reconsider strategic and technical choices.

OPERATION

Improvement Process

A major part of a systematic improvement process is to perform a continuous gap analysis that tracks execution progress against the objectives. The idea is to begin by analyzing the vision to determine mission and objectives. The next step is to assess the current status and then to compare it to the desired and expected position. You then take the gap between these two points and consider how to bridge it. After implementing corrective actions, you need to determine if they were successful and then repeat the whole process for the next cycle of refinement.

A gap analysis is largely a technology-agnostic process. However, there are ramifications from cloud computing that may make the task both easier and harder. The key challenge in identifying a gap is to quantify both the objectives and actual performance. The estimation of direct costs may be made simpler through increased financial visibility and simplified cost allocation. On the other hand, intangible benefits or drawbacks in the areas of productivity, security and risk may be very difficult to measure.

Business Landscape

Astute business leaders constantly monitor the external environment for threats and opportunities. There are two levels to consider. At a high level, you should continuously reassess your business strategy to ensure that you are optimizing your competitive advantage, investing in the right products and targeting the right market segments. If you change your corporate strategy, then it is likely to affect the level of investment that you allocate to IT and the results that you expect from it. These are implications that are not specifically related to cloud computing, although they may trickle down from the IT budget and objectives.

It is also possible to undertake a more specific analysis. You might assess changes in demand and factor inputs, as well as the competitive landscape, with an eye on the technical alignment of each. For example, if you foresee a reduction in demand of a core product, you can investigate the technical connections that its production and distribution imply.

This data, aggregated over a series of trends, can collectively serve to analyze the entire business portfolio, and model the technical implications of alternate strategies. Given the interdependence of services that may be involved in creating and selling multiple product lines, it would be misleading to assess each in isolation. A portfolio approach has the advantage of providing a composite view.

Technology Evolution

It's not hard to find a set of forecasts of the hottest technologies for the coming years. Brainstorming through a set of potential technical scenarios can be a useful exercise, taking care to analyze their effect on your service. Regardless of whether those particular changes take place, there is bound to be an evolution of many of the technologies involved in the Internet-based services you use.

The recurring questions that need to be addressed for each development are how it impacts the existing processes and whether it is possible to leverage the changes to your advantage. For example, new SaaS offerings (such as unified communications) might become available or increase in attractiveness. You may be able to convert some of your IaaS services to PaaS, or convert PaaS services to SaaS and increase your efficiency and cost-effectiveness.

There may be improvements and changes in underlying technologies that you can harness. Increased standardization may enhance your options and reduce the risks associated with services that were previously only marginally attractive. You may also find new or enhanced services on the market that surpass your current selection in risk, cost or quality.

Note that a superior alternative doesn't automatically mean that you should switch as the migration costs and risks may far outweigh the comparative advantage at any point in time. However, it does present a new option that should be highlighted for more careful assessment.

The technologies used by customers, suppliers and partners also require close monitoring. If the processes are to be tightly integrated, then changes in a partner product may have an effect on the interfaces and connectivity that is required. Ideally, the new product will continue to support the same standards as are already in use, but there may be subtle compatibility problems that crop up.

Even more importantly, the fact that the components interoperate doesn't mean that they are optimized. Every new development carries with it the potential for simplification and fine-tuning. It is worthwhile to investigate if it is possible to use the newest externally induced changes for an additional advantage.

Continual Service Improvement

The ITIL Continual Service Improvement illustrates the nature and importance of feedback from all levels to all levels. Service Design will uncover some challenges and opportunities to improve the Service Strategy. When the design is actually put into place, it is likely the Service Transition will reveal further areas for fine-tuning, both at the strategic and design level.

And during on-going operations it is vital to have a process in place to feed back as much as possible into the strategy and design as well as the transition mechanisms, so that future iterations can leverage the experience.

In other words, even if you manage to build a highly successful service, it is vital to reassess every element described in this book on an ongoing basis.

OPERATION

Appendix A

Case Study - TrendJammer

In order to illustrate some of the concepts that are describe in this book, we've included a short overview of the TrendJammer, a social media analysis service that we've designed and implemented.

This appendix gives a summary of what the application does, how it works, and what the main design tradeoffs were. The objective isn't to focus on the algorithms themselves, but to give you an idea of how the principles we have covered apply to an actual commercial service.

What does the application do?

TrendJammer is a service that targets small, medium and large companies that are working on incorporating social media into their business. It focuses on Twitter and helps with questions like:

- What is good performance using Twitter?

- Who should I follow?

- What should I tweet about?

- What are the industry benchmarks?

- What tactics should I use to get to a Twitter trending topic?

- What is the best way to integrate social media to my website/blog/email newsletter?

Two major components of the service are the Trend Manager and the Engagement Manager.

Appendix A: Case Study - TrendJammer

Trend Manager

Trend Manager is a web-based visual tool that helps you track and analyze relevant trends on Twitter. Trend Manager allows you to monitor keywords and phrases including brand names, Twitter usernames & hashtags, and signature keywords that have significance for your organization or industry. An interactive graphing interface shows you the hour-by-hour activity for each of your selected key phrases, allowing you to understand the *who*, *when*, *what*, *where* and *why* of Twitter trends, for any topic you are interested in.

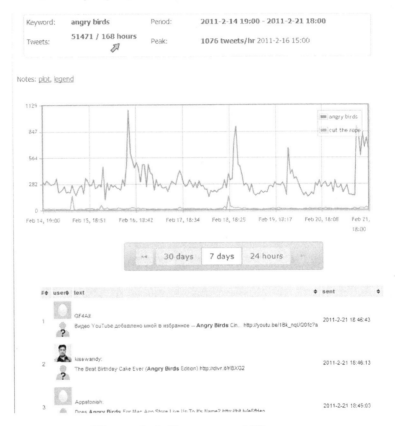

Figure A-1: Engagement Manager

Engagement manager

Engagement Manager targets organizations that want to use social media for inbound and outbound marketing. It is another web-based service (Figure A-1) that helps you understand and improve your engagement and campaign performance on Twitter. Engagement Manager tracks your performance over time in the three key social dimensions of participation, attention and engaged action, and gives you insight into the most influential people in your Twitter community. You also receive a weekly executive dashboard view via email, summarizing your Twitter results against your customized goals (Figure A-2).

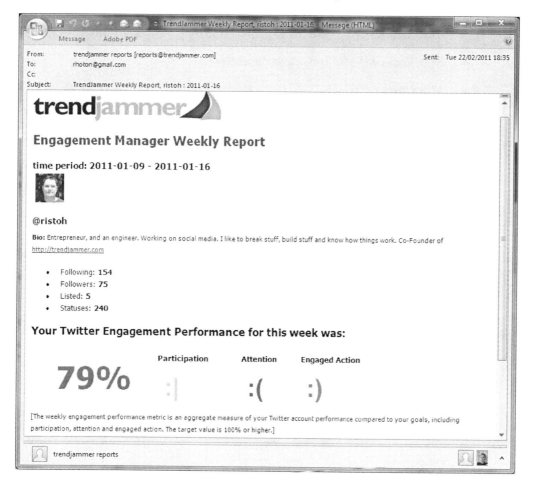

Figure A-2: Weekly Report

Basic structure

TrendJammer is built on App Engine using the Python runtime environment with the Django framework. The code is organized into Django packages, which each have Views and Models, in accordance with the MVC paradigm. These packages include:

- Twitter access (authorization)

- Tasks

- URL shortening (bit.ly wrapper)

- Reports package

- Admin

- Test utilities

- MapReduce to run consistent maintenance tasks

- Main App

- Common (shared models)

  o Users module

  o Tweets module

  o Keywords module

  o Counters module

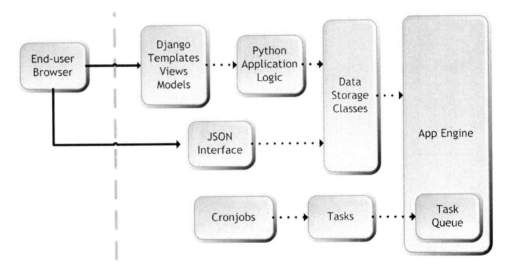

Figure A-3: App Engine Components

As shown in Figure A-3, Google App Engine supplies the run-time environment, including a Data Store layer and Task Queue. The application supplies a set of Python classes (e.g. Tweets, Users, Roles) to modularize all data access with methods for reading, writing, querying and examining relationships., These classes are exposed to an Application Logic layer that is called by Django Templates. The end user's browser communicates directly with the templates for user-visible content. Additionally, a JSON interface exposes some classes allows the browser direct access to the underlying data.

How it works

Most TrendJammer processing occurs in the background. The primary user activity is limited to initially recording accounts, keywords and hashtags, as well as a set of engagement objectives, followed by subsequent visualization of a dashboard that presents the results.

There are three main cron jobs that orchestrate the bulk of the batch processing: Twitter Fetch, Analytics, and Reporting. Each of these launches a set of subordinate tasks that execute the required functionality. These generally operate in two phases. The first extracts and processes all the information. The second then transfers all the information to a persistent store.

Twitter Fetch

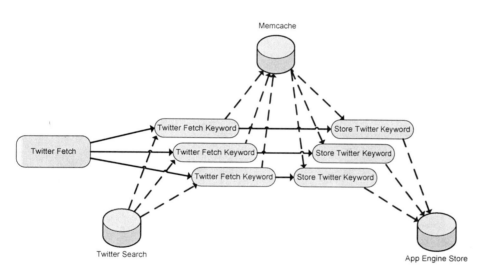

Figure A-4: Twitter Fetch Jobs

As mentioned above, each user registers a set of Twitter accounts and keywords to follow. The resulting volume of information can range into the hundreds of thousands of tweets a day so there is a need to fetch and analyze the data in the background.

A cron job is scheduled on a regular basis (e.g. every 5-60 minutes) to obtain the relevant data from Twitter. Rather than performing the entire processing itself, it queues a set of tasks, with each task dedicated to a single keyword or account (Figure A-4). This first set of tasks queries the Twitter Search API for recent Twitter activity and an active snapshot on status (e.g., number of followers, tweets) of accounts, however it does not persist these to disk, but rather caches them locally and wakes up a corresponding new task to store the data.

The second set of tasks serves to decouple the Twitter queries from the data write. This creates additional resilience. For example, in case of write failures to the data store there is no need to repeat the earlier calls to the Twitter API. The task will only reprocess the write.

Analytics

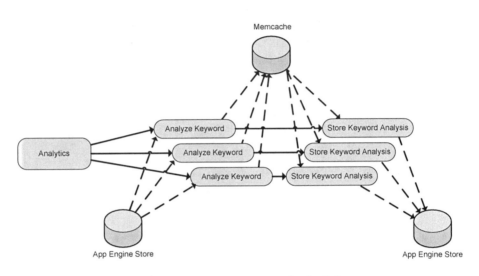

Figure A-5: Twitter Analysis Jobs

A similar set of tasks perform the analysis on the raw Twitter data (Figure A-5). An initial cron job triggers analytics with a suite of tasks based on Twitter accounts and keywords. Once the data has been analyzed, they are cached in Memcache and a set of corresponding tasks write the results to the App Engine Store, where they are visible through a JSON interface.

Reporting

Reporting also follows the same paradigm. An engagement defines a set of goals for each account and keywords. The Reporting cron job (which may be daily or weekly) initiates the process. The tasks are generally assigned on a per-user basis although it is possible to define shared reports.

The process goes through the output of the analytics phase and performs some additional consolidation, and summarization. It stores the results in the App Engine data store, which is also represented through the JSON layer. Upon completion, it also sends an email message to the user, with key-encoded links.

Design decisions

Since the service is still in its infancy, we haven't yet necessarily exploited all the potential that cloud-based applications can tap. Nonetheless, in the course of architecting the solution, we faced many of the design decisions that have been described in this book. We can share some of them with you to give you an idea of what might be involved for similar services.

Model

Since we developed the application from scratch, it was natural to look at a Platform-as-a-Service architectural model. This approach reduces the administrative burden and scales well, while requiring little up-front investment. We continue to consider infrastructure-based services, such as AWS, for analytics and other special-purpose tasks.

However, the initial priority is to keep the architecture as simple as possible. Multiple platforms create additional operational overhead and require more diversified development expertise. As the system grows, the benefits of other services may become increasingly important, but in the short term a single platform is sufficient.

Platform

The specific platform chosen was Google App Engine using Python and the Django framework. Some of the main criteria were already mentioned above. It is relatively easy to get started. There is no need for setting up and supporting an operating system. It scales automatically as the system grows. And it is relatively cheap (although the price of massive queries can be more substantial than might be expected).

The choice of using Python rather than Java stems partially from its inherent advantages as a newer language – it tends to be leaner with less extraneous scaffolding. At the same time, it also enjoys stronger support in App Engine since it has been available longer.

There are several web development frameworks for Python, each with their own set of advantages. We selected Django since it the most widely used and comes with the best documentation.

Presentation

TrendJammer is currently only available through the browser. There is a mobile interface but it only differs from the desktop version in using an alternate cascading stylesheet.

The server uses Memcache rather than disk for both performance and cost considerations. For the analytics use case, no real-time content is necessary; and it isn't currently implemented except for custom engagements. However, the user interface does make AJAX calls, for example to refresh content from Django templates.

Identity

The main user identity mechanism is Gmail, which functions as the base user store. A built-in App Engine Users class recognizes all Gmail users allowing the application to distinguish between identities and also obtain name and email address.

TrendJammer is registered as a Twitter application and uses OAuth to gain authorization read Twitter data and, when needed, define followers.

Personalization is primarily limited to content stored in the App Engine data store. This includes configuration information, such as Twitter accounts, personalized goals, search keywords and hashtags.

Integration

The external integration is limited to Gmail and Twitter, both of these are accessible via synchronous APIs. However, internally the integration is largely asynchronous. Scheduled cron jobs trigger the processes which then create a number of tasks that are orchestrated with the App Engine Task Queue.

The fine-grained modularization of processing units is an attempt to create loose coupling, which relies on Memcache as for caching intermediate data. An alternative means of transferring information between tasks would be to use an HTTP POST.

MapReduce would be a good logical fit for the entire process. Eventually we may be able to replace the complex set of tasks with map and reduce functions. However, at present App Engine MapReduce is not able to limit the scope of the functions in accordance with filter criteria. Since it would run over the entire data set, it would not be an efficient solution for the core processes.

Information

All internal data is stored in the App Engine data store which uses a Key-Value representation and supports a subset of SQL called GQL. The store is highly scalable and therefore meets our requirements and there is no need to supplement it with any additional database for most customers.

Resilience

The granular decomposition of the service into small loosely coupled tasks is the most important factor in achieving reliability. It minimizes the impact of failures and allows local asynchronous recovery that doesn't affect other processing.

Additional logic is also necessary for App Engine specifically in order to deal with failures and scheduled outages. During periods of system maintenance, no Memcache or disk writes are possible. However, real-time activity (Tweets) is still occurring and shouldn't be lost. As a work-around the information is temporarily passed between tasks HTTP POST, which limits the size of the tasks and is therefore less efficient, but preserves the integrity of the system.

The platform is inherently elastic, so the application doesn't need to explicitly take care of scaling. App Engine will horizontally replicate compute instances as needed and the data store is based on Google's BigTable, which is extremely elastic.

Monetization

TrendJammer is available as a subscription-based service. It is usually packaged as part of a larger engagement service that includes a jumpstart to assess the company objectives and map them to appropriate Twitter target elements. Beyond these, advanced consulting and customization facilities are available on request.

Deployment

The code is developed and unit-tested locally with the Google App Engine SDK. Staging occurs on live site as a sub-URL of the main instance. Once the code is stable it can then be moved into production.

GitHub is used for source code management and issue tracking.

Operations

Since the application is largely confined to Google App Engine, many administrative activities are carried out by the platform itself. Additionally, Chartbeat provides real-time site support and maintenance; and Google Analytics is used for tracking site health and usage.

Google MapReduce is also used for maintenance tasks data cleansing, data store schema migrations, backups and comprehensive analytics tasks.

References

Anderson, J. C., Lehnardt, J., & Slater, N. (2010). *CouchDB: The Definitive Guide: Time to Relax.* O'Reilly Media.

AndroLib. (2011, March). *AndroLib Statistics.* Retrieved March 2011, from AndroLib: http://www.androlib.com/appstats.aspx

Berkeley/Stanford. (2008, September). *The Berkeley/Stanford Recovery-Oriented Computing (ROC) Project.* Retrieved March 2011, from http://roc.cs.berkeley.edu/

Berners-Lee, T. (2006, July). *Linked Data.* Retrieved March 2011, from World Wide Web Consortium: http://www.w3.org/DesignIssues/LinkedData

Chang, F., Dean, J., Ghemawat, S., Hsieh, W. C., Wallach, D. A., Burrows, M., et al. (2006, November). *Bigtable: A Distributed Storage System for Structured Data.* Retrieved March 2011, from Google labs: http://labs.google.com/papers/bigtable-osdi06.pdf

Chodorow, K., & Dirolf, M. (2010). *MongoDB: The Definitive Guide.* O'Reilly Media.

Ciurana, E. (2009). *Developing with Google App Engine.* Apress.

Greenberg, J. (n.d.). *JavaScript Optimization.* Retrieved March 2011, from http://home.earthlink.net/~kendrasg/info/js_opt/

Henderson, C. (2006). *Building Scalable Web Sites: Building, Scaling, and Optimizing the Next Generation of Web Applications.* O'Reilly Media.

Hewitt, E. (2010). *Cassandra: The Definitive Guide.* O'Reilly Media.

ITIL. (2007). *The Official Introduction to the ITIL Service Lifecycle.* London: UK Office of Government Commerce: TSO.

James, C., & Stolz, M. (2009). *The True Cost of Latency.* Retrieved March 2011, from http://www.slideshare.net/gemstonesystems/true-cost-of-latency

Kaufmann, R., & Gayliard, B. (2009, January 13). *http://www.ddj.com/go-parallel/article/showArticle.jhtml?articleID=212900103.* Retrieved March 2011, from Dr. Dobb's: http://www.ddj.com/go-parallel/article/showArticle.jhtml?articleID=212900103

Konchady, M. (2008). *Building Search Applications: Lucene, LingPipe, and Gate.* Mustru Publishing.

Lam, C. (2010). *Hadoop in Action.* Manning Publications.

Lin, J., & Dyer, C. (2010). *Data-Intensive Text Processing with MapReduce.* Morgan and Claypool Publishers.

Linthicum, D. S. (2009). *Cloud Computing and SOA Convergence in Your Enterprise.* Addison Wesley.

Loeliger, J. (2009). *Version Control with Git: Powerful Tools and Techniques for Collaborative Software Development .* O'Reilly Media.

Mangino, M. J. (2008). *Developing Facebook Platform Applications with Rails.* Pragmatic Bookshelf.

Mather, T., Kumaraswamy, S., & Latif, S. (2009). *Cloud Security and Privacy.* Sebastopol: O'Reilly.

McCandless, M., Hatcher, E., & Gospodnetic, O. (2010). *Lucene in Action.* Manning Publications.

McCarthy, J. (2010, August). *Hadoop Day in Seattle: Hadoop, Cascading, Hive and Pig.* Retrieved March 2011, from Gumption: http://gumption.typepad.com/blog/2010/08/hadoop-day-in-seattle-hadoop-cascading-hive-and-pig.html

Messmer, E. (2010, May 20). *Novell Identity Manager extended to cloud.* Retrieved March 2011, from Computerworld UK: http://www.computerworlduk.com/news/security/20357/novell-identity-manager-extended-to-cloud/

Moon, B. (2009, October). *4 Emerging Trends of the Real-Time Web.* Retrieved March 2011, from Mashable: http://mashable.com/2009/10/29/real-time-web-trends/

Murty, J. (2008). *Programming Amazon Web Services: S3, EC2, SQS, FPS, and SimpleDB.* O'Reilly Media.

NIST. (2009, October). *The NIST Definition of Cloud Computing.* Retrieved March 2011, from National Institute of Standards and Technology: http://csrc.nist.gov/groups/SNS/cloud-computing/cloud-def-v15.doc

North, K. (2009, August). *Databases in the Cloud: Elysian Fields or Briar Patch?* Retrieved March 2011, from Dr. Dobb's: http://drdobbs.com/database/218900502

O'Reilly, T. (2006, May). *Database War Stories #7: Google File System and BigTable.* Retrieved March 2011, from O'Reilly Radar: http://radar.oreilly.com/archives/2006/05/database-war-stories-7-google.html

Perry, G. (2008, August). *Cloud Computing Terminology.* Retrieved March 2011, from Thinking Out Cloud: http://gevaperry.typepad.com/main/2008/08/new-cloud-compu.html

Pilgrim, M. (2010). *HTML5: Up and Running.* O'Reilly Media.

Ping Identity. (2009, September). *Digital Itentity Basics.* Retrieved March 2011, from Open Source Federated Identity Management: http://www.sourceid.org/content/primer.cfm

Plugge, E., Hawkins, T., & Membrey, P. (2010). *The Definitive Guide to MongoDB: The NoSQL Database for Cloud and Desktop Computing.* Apress.

Reese, G. (2009). *Cloud Application Architectures: Building Applications and Infrastructure in the Cloud.* O'Reilly Media, Inc.

Rittinghouse, J. W., & Ransome, J. F. (2009). *Cloud Computing: Implementation, Management, and Security.* Boca Raton: CRC Press.

Roche, K., & Douglas, J. (2009). *Beginning Java Google App Engine.* Apress.

Ross, J. W., Weill, P., & Robertson, D. C. (2006). *Enterprise Architecture as Strategy.* Harvard Business Press.

Sanderson, D. (2009). *Programming Google App Engine.* O'Reilly Media.

Smiley, D., & Pugh, E. (2009). *Solr 1.4 Enterprise Search Server.* Packt Publishing.

Souders, S. (2009). *Even Faster Web Sites: Performance Best Practices for Web Developers .* O'Reilly Media.

Souders, S. (2007). *High Performance Web Sites: Essential Knowledge for Front-End Engineers.* O'Reilly Media.

TABB Group. (2008, April). *The Value of a Millisecond: Finding the Optimatl Speed of a Trading Infrastructure.* Retrieved March 2011, from TABB Group: http://www.tabbgroup.com/PublicationDetail.aspx?PublicationID=346

Turnbull, J. (2008). *Pulling Strings with Puppet: Configuration Management Made Easy.* Apress.

Urquhart, J. (2010, March). *Understanding the cloud and 'devops'.* Retrieved March 2011, from The Wisdom of Clouds: http://news.cnet.com/8301-19413_3-10470260-240.html

Vaquero, Rodero-Merino, Cáceres, & Lindner. (2009, January). *A Break in the Clouds: Towards a Cloud Definition.* Retrieved March 2011, from http://ccr.sigcomm.org/drupal/files/p50-v39n1l-vaqueroA.pdf

Velte, A. T., Velte, T. J., & Elsenpeter, R. (2009). *Cloud Computing: A Practical Approach.* New York: McGraw Hill.

Venner, J. (2009). *Pro Hadoop.* Apress.

White, T. (2010). *Hadoop: The Definitive Guide.* Yahoo Press.

Index